UNDERSTANDING DIGITAL TRANSMISSION AND RECORDING

IEEE PRESS UNDERSTANDING SCIENCE & TECHNOLOGY SERIES

The IEEE Press Understanding Science & Technology Series treats important topics in science and technology in a simple and easy-to-understand manner. Designed expressly for the nonspecialist engineer, scientist, or technician, as well as the technologically curious—each volume stresses practical information over mathematical theorems and complicated derivations.

Books in the Series

Blyler, J. and Ray, G., *What's Size Got To Do With It? Understanding Computer Rightsizing*

Deutsch, S., *Understanding the Nervous System: An Engineering Perspective*

Evans, B., *Understanding Digital TV: The Route to HDTV*

Gregg, J., *Ones and Zeros: Understanding Boolean Algebra, Digital Circuits, and the Logic of Sets*

Hecht, J., *Understanding Lasers: An Entry-Level Guide,* 2nd Edition

Kamm, L., *Understanding Electro-Mechanical Engineering: An Introduction to Mechatronics*

Kartalopoulos, S. V., *Understanding Neural Networks and Fuzzy Logic: Basic Concepts and Applications*

Lebow, I., *Understanding Digital Transmission and Recording*

Nellist, J. G., *Understanding Telecommunications and Lightwave Systems,* 2nd Edition
Sigfried, S., *Understanding Object-Oriented Software Engineering*

Ideas for future topics and authorship inquiries are welcome. Please write to IEEE PRESS: The Understanding Series.

Other books by Irwin Lebow

Theory and Design of Digital Machines, coauthored with T. C. Bartee and I. S. Reed (McGraw-Hill, 1962)

The Digital Connection: A Layman's Guide to the Information Age (W. H. Freeman / Computer Science Press, 1991)

Information Highways and Byways: From the Telegraph to the 21st Century (IEEE Press, 1995)

UNDERSTANDING DIGITAL TRANSMISSION AND RECORDING

Irwin Lebow

IEEE Press Understanding Science & Technology Series
Dr. Mohamed E. El-Hawary, *Series Editor*

The Institute of Electrical and Electronics Engineers, Inc., New York

IEEE Press
445 Hoes Lane, P.O. Box 1331
Piscataway, NJ 08855-1331

Editorial Board
Roger F. Hoyt, *Editor in Chief*

J. B. Anderson	S. Furui	S. Kartalopoulos
P. M. Anderson	A. H. Haddad	P. Laplante
M. Eden	R. Herrick	W. D. Reeve
M. E. El-Hawary	G. F. Hoffnagle	D. J. Wells

Kenneth Moore, *Director of IEEE Press*
John Griffin, *Senior Acquisitions Editor*
Linda Matarazzo, *Assistant Editor*
Denise Phillip, *Associate Production Editor*

Cover design: William T. Donnelly, *WT Design*

Technical Reviewer

John B. Anderson, *Rensselaer Polytechnic Institute*

This book was typeset in Times Roman by Impressions, Inc.
and printed and bound by Data Reproductions Corporation.

To Grace and Barbara,

coauthors of my next book.

This book may be purchased at a discount from the publisher when ordered in bulk quantities. Contact:

IEEE Press Marketing
Attn: Special Sales
445 Hoes Lane, P.O. Box 1331
Piscataway, NJ 08855-1331
Fax: (732) 981-9334

For more information on the IEEE Press,
visit the IEEE home page: http://www.ieee.org/

Printed in the United States of America

10   9   8   7   6   5   4   3   2   1

ISBN 0-7803-3418-3

IEEE Order Number: PP5387

Library of Congress Cataloging-in-Publication Data

Lebow, Irwin
    Understanding digital transmission and recording / Irwin Lebow.
      p.   cm.— (IEEE Press understanding science & technology
series)
    Includes bibliographical references and index.
    ISBN 0-7803-3418-3
    1. Data transmission systems. 2. Digital modulatin 3. Sound—
Recording and reproducing—Digital techniques. I. Title.
II. Series.
TK5105.L42   1997
004.6—dc21   97-34940
                                                  CIP

CONTENTS

PREFACE

Digital transmission first hit the big time in the early 1980s with the introduction of the compact disc. Although it had been used with increasing frequency in various specialized applications during the thirty years or so prior to the coming of the CD, it remained well behind its analog predecessor as a factor in the commercial market.

The speed by which the digital CD relegated the analog record to a historical curiosity was nothing short of spectacular. But to communications engineers this marketplace success was no more spectacular than the way the CD system became the long-sought blockbuster application of Claude Shannon's information theory. Many of us found it ironic that these first mass-produced embodiments of Shannon's theory were found in our living rooms instead of in more conventional communications environments.

Information theory was also thirty years old when the CD first appeared. Although a flurry of ingenious coding and decoding schemes applying the theory had followed within a few years of Shannon's monumental work, they found little practical application because they were too expensive to implement. Engineers had to wait for integrated circuit technology to catch up with the mathematics before they were able to reduce these coding schemes to practice at affordable prices, and the CD was the application that did it first.

But the triumph of digital transmission was not to be confined to recording applications. By this time, the telephone companies were using digital transmission in their backbones spurred on by their need to increase capacity with optical fibers. The 1980s also saw the rise of the Internet. This network of computer networks, which had started out slowly in the late 1970s under U.S. government auspices, began to grow exponentially in the late 1980s when it was opened up to commercial users. Since most of us access the network through the telephone system, here was the opportunity to apply digital technology and Shannon's theory to increase the transmission speed over telephone lines. The fact that this speed has increased by more than an order of magnitude using equipment that costs around $100 is no less spectacular than the success of the CD.

The telephone-line modem and CD are only the most popular of the digital transmission and recording applications. As digital transmission has become an increasingly important factor in the overall market, new applications have been emerging all the time. The purpose of this book is to explain the fundamentals behind it all.

About the Book

I wrote the book with two kinds of readers in mind: (1) practicing engineers who have been out of school for a number of years and who either never learned the principles of digital signaling or have forgotten much of what they learned and (2) undergraduates studying science and engineering. My objective throughout the book is clarity and intuitiveness. Said in another way, I have tried never to lose the forest for the trees. This stress on an intuitive presentation is one of the distinguishing features of this book and is, in part, a consequence of its heritage.

The book has its origins in another book I published in 1991 entitled, *The Digital Connection*. Its goal was to give readers with little or no technical background some basic understanding of digital technology and its significance. Because *The Digital Connection* was written for laymen, equations were a no-no. I was therefore forced to find explanations for essentially mathematical concepts using pictures instead of mathematics. For example, to explain the nature of digital communication signals, I had to show how the frequency components of a time waveform are related to the time parameters of the waveform, something that is easily done mathematically using the concepts of Fourier analysis. I did this using the model of a tuning fork oscillator pulsed to turn on and off at a particular rate, and simply from pictures showed the relationship of the time and frequency representations. I was faced with the same kind of problem in explaining how to regenerate analog signals from their digital representations without using the mathematics of the sampling theorem. Again pictures came to my rescue.

In writing *Understanding Digital Transmission and Recording* I have tried to let the reader have his cake and eat it too. I retained the intuitive flavor of *The Digital Connection* while, at the same time, supplementing its pictorial approach with mathematics appropriate to the target audience. Thus, the chapter on Fourier analysis retains the notions of pulsing a tuning fork along with the mathematics. It is this highly intuitive approach that distinguishes this book from others covering many of the same topics. And it is this approach that makes this book valuable as an undergraduate text.

Finally, I have taken the opportunity to introduce the new developments that have occurred since the publication of *The Digital Connection*, most notably high-definition television and the higher-capacity version of the CD, known as the digital versatile disc or DVD, that can store substantial amounts of digitized video.

The Contents of the Book

The first four chapters provide the background. Chapters 1 and 2 are at an elementary level covering the relationship of digital communication to computing and introducing some of the concepts of information theory. Chapter 3 reviews the fundamentals of analog transmission and Chapter 4 introduces the mathematics of Fourier analysis applied to digital signaling. It helps if the student has been exposed to Fourier analysis before, but it is not essential.

Chapters 5 through 7 are at the heart of digital transmission. Chapter 5 presents Shannon's coding theorem at an elementary level. It introduces different classes of modulation and the relationship of modulation to coding. Then Chapters 6 and 7 amplify this discussion for power-limited and band-limited channels, respectively. In the latter chapter, the telephone line is used as the example of a band-limited channel, and the chapter begins with some comments on the digitization of the public telephone networks. A reader with limited mathematical background might skip the more mathematical parts of these two chapters the first time around.

In Chapter 8 the discussion shifts to that of converting essentially analog information such as speech and video into digital form and back again. It is here that the sampling theorem is described. This chapter also introduces the ideas of data compression so essential to voice and television transmission and to digital video recording. Among other topics, it includes a description of the elements of the MPEG-2 compression scheme to be used in digital television broadcasting. Finally, Chapter 9 is devoted to CD recording and playback, and includes the DVD. The description of digital recording and playback builds on the discussion of more conventional transmission in the earlier chapters.

Acknowledgments

I am grateful to several people who provided me with information that helped me to make the book as up-to-date as possible. Bill Tompkins, Shaum Mittal, and Richard Clewer were kind enough to provide information on some of the currently used modulation/coding schemes. Jules Cohen, Mark Richer, and Glenn Reitmeier brought me up to date on the latest in the high-definition television saga.

During the preparation of the manuscript for this book I was collaborating with my wife Grace on another book on a radically different topic. As always, I am grateful to Grace for her understanding and patience during this process.

Irwin Lebow

1

DIGITAL COMMUNICATION AND ITS COMPUTER CONNECTION

1.0 Introduction

Communication is the act of sending information from one place to another. Digital communication means that the information is in digital form. The easiest way to understand what this means is to imagine transferring information from one digital computer to another. Since information is stored in a computer as a string of digits, digital communication is the process of sending these digits over some communications medium—radio or wire—to the other computer.

What do the digits stand for? They can represent bank balances, documents, pictures, voice signals, video signals, in short, anything at all. Of course, the processes by which the various forms of information are inserted into the computers vary widely with the source of the data. But ultimately all have to get into some kind of computer in some way. In fact, you can think of dividing the communication problem into two parts: (1) converting the information into digits and later extracting the information from the digits and (2) sending and receiving the digits. But however you slice it, the processes of digital communication are intimately related to the processes of digital computing. And so, it is only natural to begin the discussion about communication with the digital computer.

1.1 Digital Computing

The digital computer is the very symbol of the information age. Yet digital computing is as old as the first man who learned to add and subtract with the aid of the *digits* on his hands and feet. Using the same principles, the modern *digital* computer represents all quantities as digits or whole numbers and performs its calculations by manipulating these digits much as we do in hand calculations.

In contrast, an *analog* computer represents all quantities by proportional physical measurements such as distances or electrical voltages and computes by manipulating these distances or voltages. The venerable slide rule is an example of a simple form of analog computer, which uses distances along a scale to represent the numbers to be manipulated.

An analog computer always has some practical accuracy limits. The slide rule, for example, is accurate to about one part in a thousand, limited by how accurately a person can read the engraved scale. While most electronic analog computers are considerably more accurate than manual slide rules, each improvement in accuracy is successively more difficult to achieve. Digital computers have the fundamental advantage over analog in being able to perform calculations with arbitrarily high accuracy. You know that, in principle, you can multiply twenty-digit numbers as easily as three-digit numbers; it's just more tedious and takes longer. The same thing holds true in a digital computer, only the computer does not mind the tedium.

1.2   The Evolution of the Digital Computer

The basic idea of the digital computer is due to Charles Babbage, an English mathematician who lived in the first part of the nineteenth century. His machines, called the *Analytical Engine* and *Difference Engine*, were mechanical. The most famous early electronic digital machine, widely considered to be the true forerunner of the modern computer, was the *ENIAC*, constructed in 1946 at the Moore School of the University of Pennsylvania by a team led by John Mauchly and J. Presper Eckert, although it is now generally agreed that some of the fundamental ideas underlying the ENIAC were first demonstrated in the work of John V. Atanasoff of Iowa State University between 1937 and 1942. The basic structure of the computer as we know it today stemmed directly from the ENIAC team together with the famous mathematician, John Von Neumann, of the Institute for Advanced Study in Princeton. Almost all modern computers use this structure and are referred to as *Von Neumann machines*. It is interesting to note in passing that Von Neumann was one of an unusually large number of outstanding scientists who came to the United States from Nazi-dominated Hungary just before World War II, far out of proportion to the small population of Hungary. During the 1940s physicists viewed this "Hungarian phenomenon" as akin to a violation of the second law of thermodynamics. While nuclear physics and atomic energy have been the most publicized areas in which these émigré scientists contributed to the United States, Von Neumann's contribution to the embryonic digital computer field was no less significant.

The analog computer was well established by the time of these earliest digital computers. However, it was not long before the digital computer began to supplant the analog computer in many application areas. Of course, one of the reasons was the superior accuracy of the digital machine. But perhaps even more important was the astonishing rate at which advances in electronic component technology increased the power and speed and decreased the cost of digital computing. This technology included the development of first the transistor and later the *integrated circuit*, a small wafer or chip of silicon on which large numbers of transistor circuits are fabricated. The analog computer also benefited from these component advances, but to a much lesser extent.

The first integrated circuits were fabricated in the 1960s. Progress was rapid as the numbers of transistors on a chip increased from tens to hundreds to thousands and now millions. By the 1970s, they were sufficiently advanced to permit a pocket-size calculator to be built at a reasonable cost, followed shortly thereafter by the earliest desktop computers. The art of analog computing was also advanced by the development of integrated circuits, but not nearly to the extent of the digital computing art. The analog computer has all but disappeared. Even the slide rule, long the indispensable tool of the engineer and scientist, had to give way to the pocket calculator, the phenomenon that the Bloom County comic strip dating from the mid 1980s captures so cleverly in Fig. 1-1.

BLOOM COUNTY   **by Berke Breathed**

Figure 1-1   The eclipse of the slide rule (from the Washington Post Writers Group).

1.3   Representing Analog Measurements Digitally

Some kinds of data fit naturally into the digital or whole number representation fundamental to the digital computer. Monetary values are a good example of this category because dollars and cents are measured in discrete units. Prices do not vary over a continuum of values, but in discrete steps.

But how about the kinds of data that do take on a continuum of values, for example, the measurements that we are accustomed to make with a ruler? How can such analog data be represented digitally? Let's look at an example to illustrate how this is done.

Suppose you need to measure the dimensions of your living room for a wall-to-wall carpet installation. With these measurements, you can use a pocket calculator to compute how much carpet is needed and what it will cost. If you have large enough feet, you could walk the length of the room heel to toe and count the number of "feet," making the assumption that your foot is roughly 12 in. long. Another, more accurate technique would be to use a steel tape. In the first case, the accuracy is perhaps plus or minus 3 in. In the second case, the accuracy is about plus or minus $^1/_8$ in., about twenty-five times more accurate than the first. Suppose that the first measurement technique estimated the length as 15 ft. 2 in. or, in decimal notation, 15.16667 ft. The steel tape measurement estimated the length as 14 ft. $11^7/_8$ in. or, in decimal notation, 14.9895833 ft. Any representation of a physical measurement by a number makes a statement about the accuracy with which you know the parameter being measured. Most of the figures to the right of the decimal point in our example measurements are an illusion of accuracy. Since the first measurement was accurate only to within 3 in., any digit beyond the first place to the right of the decimal point is meaningless; we should call the measurement 15.2 ft. In the second case only two decimal places are warranted, giving us 15.00 ft. Since we will ultimately use this number in a digital computer, we would use three decimal digits for the crude measurement and four for the more accurate measurement.

Thus, even though the length of the living room can have a continuum of values, the number of possibilities is limited by the accuracy with which the quantity is measured. The accuracy must be sufficient for whatever computation is to be made.

Representing the length of a room with three decimal digits is equivalent to saying that the length can have one of the one thousand possible values from 00.0 to 99.9 ft. When we use four decimal places, there are ten thousand possible values from 00.00 to 99.99 ft. In this way, data with a continuous range of possible values are represented by a discrete range of numbers. The general rule is this: one decimal digit can specify one of ten things; two digits can specify one of one hundred things; three digits can specify one of one thousand things, and so forth.

For practical reasons, digital computers represent numbers by binary rather than decimal digits. But the same principle holds: one binary digit or bit represents one of two things; two bits, one of four things; three bits, one of eight things, and so forth. For example, digital recordings are made by measuring the amplitude of the analog electrical signal at the output of a microphone to about 16 bits allowing the digitized amplitudes to take on one of 2^{16} or about sixty-five thousand possibilities. As we shall see later, this much accuracy is needed for high-quality sound reproduction.

1.4   Computing and Communications

The genius of the computer structure that became known as the Von Neumann machine was its programmable nature. With this structure it was theoretically possible for the computer to perform *any* computation. Of course, there were practical limitations as to what a computer could do; for one thing, the early computers were severely limited in speed and capacity, making many problems that were theoretically possible quite impractical. In addition, the pioneers vastly underestimated the job of programming. Nevertheless, in the years following the ENIAC, computers were beginning to perform tasks well beyond the scope of the laborious mathematical calculations that motivated the construction of the ENIAC and its early successors. More and more, the tasks were beginning to demand the exchange of data between users who were not collocated with their computers and even from one computer to another. For example, one of the first "blockbuster" applications was the airline reservation system known as SABRE, built for American Airlines by IBM in the early 1960s. SABRE permitted airline employees and travel agents throughout the country (and later the world) to access the entire American Airlines network, to make reservations and seat assignments and all the other things to which we have become accustomed.

SABRE was a private system dedicated to airline reservations. Just a few years later, the Department of Defense began the development of a more general computer network that would permit computers to exchange data for a variety of purposes. This network became known as the ARPANET, named after the Defense Department's Advanced Research Projects Agency, and it went into operation in 1972. By the end of the decade, this network was expanded to embrace other networks and thus was born the network of networks known as the Internet that by the early 1990s became the symbol of all the clichés of the modern information age—the information superhighway and the national and global information infrastructures. From its humble beginnings not too many years after the birth of the computer, computer networking had become a part of our culture.

It is clear to us today that computing and communications are two parts of a single whole. Of course, there are certain things that relate to communication in a very narrow sense: the science and engineering of transporting information reliably and economically. There are also things that relate to computation in a very narrow sense: computational mathematics and the engineering of low-cost, fast, and reliable computing circuits. But once we leave these specific realms, the two merge into a broad, new field. Various names have been suggested for this symbiotic union; *compunications* and *telematics* are examples of names that were suggested in the past. Neither these nor any other catchy phrase has caught on. Most of us are content to use the term *information technology*.

Today's intimate relationship between computing and communications did not come as easy as it might have. This is due mostly to the fact that telecommunications—analog, of course—preceded computing by close to a century. By the time the digital computer came along, telecommunications was a mature field. While it has been evolving slowly from analog to digital, it has always maintained its parental roots.

Computer engineers, seeing the need to network computers, pressed for digital communication capabilities. In some cases, the communications professionals were not as responsive as they might have been, so many computer engineers became communications engineers in their own right. The first computer networks were developed largely by computer engineers, rather than by traditional communicators.

These same cultural divisions were present in academia, where departments of computer science were often established independent of the electrical engineering departments that housed the communicators. But after a time, the divisions began to break down as technical advances in both fields made it clear that this division was not only artificial, but counterproductive. Today, the trend is back toward combining the two in unified electrical engineering and computer science departments. This permits the maximum benefits to be derived from the synergy between the traditional disciplines.

2

ELEMENTARY CONCEPTS
OF COMMUNICATING
INFORMATION

2.0   Short- and Long-Distance Communication

The word *telecommunications* signifies the transfer of information over long distances. At the conceptual level there appears to be no difference between sending information to a location a foot away—say, from one place to another within a computer—and to one 15,000 miles away, for example, between a computer in New York and one in New Delhi.

While there is no difference at the conceptual level, at a practical level there are major differences having to do with speed, cost, and accuracy. When the distances are very short, say within a computer, we tend to think of the process of transferring information from one place to another as virtually trivial. In fact, we do not normally think of it as communications at all. But when the distances are long, the communication is something to think about, if only because an additional outlay of funds is required. Take the case of transferring a large memory file containing millions of bits of data from a computer in San Francisco to one in New York. We want the data transfer to be accurate, and we want it to take place within a short time interval. If the memory file were in the same room as the computer, there would be little concern. But long-distance, highly accurate, high-speed data transfer can be expensive.

On a more personal level, the millions of ordinary people without any technical background who use the Internet to exchange E-mail, participate in newsgroups, buy and sell stocks, or do their banking from home would never tolerate the system if it were excessively expensive, if they had to wait too long for their messages, or, even more important, if the messages they received were filled with errors. It is interesting to note that the theoretical analysis describing telecommunications from the point of view of accuracy and efficiency was formulated in the late 1940s, the time that the first digital computers were developed, well before anyone could have recognized the ultimately close relationship between the two fields.

The accuracy of communication is measured by the faithfulness of the received information to the transmitted information. In any practical telecommunications medium, there are disturbances of various kinds that distort the telecommunications signals. The greater these disturbances, the more difficult it is to achieve some desired degree of accuracy. With analog telecommunications as with analog computing, each increase in accuracy is successively more difficult to achieve. The essential advantage of digital telecommunications and the reason for its increasing use is that any desired degree of accuracy is obtainable no matter how high the distortion. That is why the forms of communication that we do not ordinarily think of as data transfers between computers—voice and video, for example—are moving from analog to digital, and that is why the digital compact disc has replaced the analog LP record as the recording medium of choice. The advantages of going digital are great. That is why developing the technology to realize these advantages has been so important.

This chapter begins the discussion of the basic concepts that make up digital communication presented at an elementary level. Much of the rest of the book is an elaboration on these concepts.

2.1   Data and Information

Since communication is the process of transmitting information from one place to another, it is important to examine the concepts of information. The word has many shades of meaning. We tend to use it interchangeably with the word *data*—dictionaries are imprecise about the distinctions. Nevertheless, even in imprecise, everyday language, the word *data* implies a collection of words or numbers, the meaning of which has yet to be determined. The word *information* implies that the words and numbers have been processed in some way to extract some meaning or significance.

Digital communication is concerned with the transfer of digits from one place to another. When do these digits represent information, and when do they simply represent data? An example drawn from the way computers work will illustrate the point. The heart of a computer is its so-called *central processing unit* or CPU—the numbers 286, 386, 486, and Pentium designate successive generations in the personal computer CPU art. Any CPU contains two main parts: a control unit that sends signals throughout the computer to coordinate all its activities and an arithmetic-logic unit that does all the number manipulation.

Now imagine a computer with a primitive arithmetic-logic unit that can only add and subtract. It decides which to do based upon direction from the control unit. In this primitive computer, the control unit must be able to communicate just one of two things to the arithmetic-logic unit: "add" or "subtract." Based upon this statement, the arithmetic-logic unit takes the appropriate action. The control unit therefore sends information to the arithmetic-logic unit with this command. How much information? Since the transmission commands one of two things, a single binary digit will suffice to carry the information: it might send a 1 to designate *add* and a 0 to designate *subtract.* Thus we say that 1 bit of information has been sent. The word *bit* does double duty: it stands for a binary digit and also for a unit of information.

This might lead you to think that a binary digit always carries 1 bit of information. This is not necessarily so. To see this, imagine that the control unit can send only addition instructions and that the arithmetic-logic unit knows this ahead of time. In this case, no information is transferred when the control unit sends an addition command, because the control unit is telling the arithmetic unit something it already knows. This transmission consisted of a bit of *data* that carried no information and therefore need not have been sent at all.

But that's an extreme case. How about a more realistic intermediate case in which the control unit sends addition instructions three-quarters of the time and subtraction instructions one-quarter of the time? In this case, the binary digit carries a fraction of a bit of information. Equation 2-1 shows how much. Suppose p is the probability that the transmitted digit is a 1 and 1-p, the probability that a 0 is transmitted, then the information transferred, designated by the symbol H, is given by

$$H = [p \log p + (1 - p) \log (1 - p)], \qquad (2\text{-}1)$$

where the logarithms are taken to the base 2. H is plotted against p in Fig. 2-1. At the extreme left end of the curve, the transmitted digit must be a 0, and at the right end, it must be a 1. At these extremes H is zero, and no

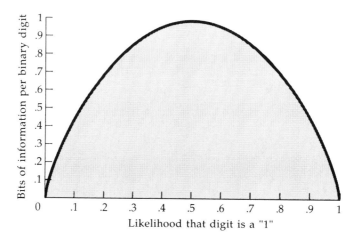

Figure 2-1   The information carried by a binary digit.

information is transferred. In the center, it is equally likely that a 1 or 0 is being sent, and the maximum information of 1 bit is transferred. For the case at hand where p is 0.75, the amount of information sent is approximately 0.8 bit.

2.1.1   Information Means Choice

Now imagine that there are sixty-four possible messages that can be transferred from one place to another. Both the sender and the receiver know the content of the sixty-four messages. The sender labels the messages from 0 to 63—in binary form, 000000 to 111111—and sends one of them using this binary label. It does not matter how simple or complex the messages are, provided that both the sending and receiving ends know their identity. One message might designate the entire Bible; a second, the complete works of Shakespeare; and so forth. The job of the recipient is to distinguish among the sixty-four possible labels to identify the correct one. How much information is transferred? As before, that depends upon how likely it is that the sender will transmit any particular message. If they are all equally likely, then the amount of information being transferred is the full 6 bits. At the other extreme, if one message—say 000000—is always sent (i.e., the probability of sending any of the others is zero), there is no need to send the message at all, and no information is transferred. For any other distribution of message probabilities, the amount of information transferred is between 0 and 6 bits, following Eq. 2-2, a generalization of Eq. 2-1.

$$H = -\sum_{j=1}^{n} p_j \log p_j. \qquad (2\text{-}2)$$

In the equation, p_j is the probability of sending the jth message, and n is the total number of possible messages—sixty-four in our example. If it is equally probable that any message is sent, then the information transferred is log n or 6 bits when $n = 64$.

Now if the *information* transmitted is much less than 6 bits, then transferring 6 bits of *data* is wasteful. What can be done about it? Our intuition tells us that we should use fewer bits for the more probable messages than for the less probable ones. This is the reasoning that Samuel F. B. Morse used when he devised a code to facilitate the transmission of information with his new invention, the telegraph, in the 1830s. His binary digits were long and short bursts—dots and dashes. Morse knew something about the relative frequency with which the different letters are used in ordinary English, and he designated the most frequently used letters with the shortest sequences of dots and dashes and vice versa. Thus, the letter *e* is designated by a single dot and the letter *q* by the relatively long sequence *dash-dash-dot-dash*. Following his example, if we know the relative frequency at which the messages are sent, then we can take our message labels, encode the most likely with short codes and the less likely with longer codes, and reduce the average number of transmitted bits to something close to the actual amount of information being transferred.

The following table gives an example of a set of eight messages with their probabilities and an assignment of sequences of bits to represent each message.

Message Number	Probability	Codeword	Codeword Length
m_1	$1/2$	1	1
m_2	$1/4$	01	2
m_3	$1/16$	0011	4
m_4	$1/16$	0010	4
m_5	$1/32$	00011	5
m_6	$1/32$	00010	5
m_7	$1/32$	00001	5
m_8	$1/32$	00000	5

This example is idealized because the probabilities are all negative powers of 2. Because of this, the length of each codeword can be made exactly equal to the logarithm of the probability of each message with the result that the average number of bits transmitted is exactly equal to information transmitted in accordance with Eq. 2-2 as follows:

$$\frac{1}{2} \times 1 + \frac{1}{4} \times 2 + \frac{1}{16} \times 4 + \frac{1}{16} \times 4 + \frac{1}{32} \times 5 + \frac{1}{32} \times 5 + \frac{1}{32}$$

$$\times 5 + \frac{1}{32} \times 5 = \frac{17}{8} = 2\,\tfrac{1}{8}.$$

This is to be compared to the 3 bits that would have been transmitted if the messages were assumed to be equally likely. If the probability of each message were not precisely a power of 2, then the average length of the message would exceed the information transmitted by some small amount.

It should be noted that the bit representations of the messages have to be chosen carefully to avoid ambiguity, so that a given bit stream can be interpreted in only one way. For example, the bit stream 0001110101 can only be interpreted as coming from the sequence $m_5\, m_1\, m_2\, m_2$.

2.1.2   Huffman Coding

There is a procedure for optimizing the bit assignment for an arbitrary probability assignment that is known as Huffman coding. Figure 2-2 shows how this is accomplished for six messages with the indicated probabilities. The procedure is as follows:

1. List the messages in order of decreasing probability.

2. Label the lowest by 0 and the next lowest by 1. (These will be the least significant digits in the code.)

3. Combine these bottom two entries by adding their probabilities and insert into the list maintaining the order of decreasing probabilities.

4. Repeat step 2 with the new listing. The digits assigned will be next to the least significant.

5. Repeat step 3.

6. Continue to apply steps 2 and 3 until a single entry of probability 1 remains.

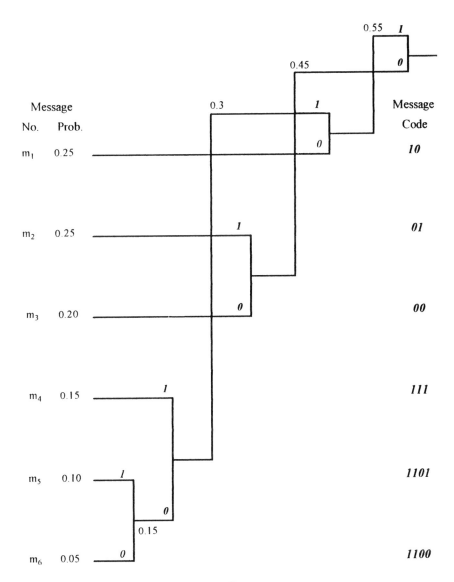

Figure 2-2   An example of Huffman coding.

According to Huffman's algorithm, the first step in Fig. 2-2 is to designate m_5 by a 1 and m_6 by a 0 and then combine them on a single branch with their combined probability 0.15. This new branch is then combined with the m_4 branch to form a new branch with probability 0.3 that leaps above m_1 with probability 0.25. This process continues until only a single branch remains with probability 1, yielding the transmission codes listed at the right. The average number of *bits* transferred with this code is 2.45, only about 11% larger than the *information* transferred—2.21—computed from Eq. 2-2. If the message probabilities are ignored, then 3 bits are needed to transfer the information, about 36% larger than the information transferred.

We have, in effect, defined information transfer in terms of the amount of *choice* being transferred. In a choice between one of two equally likely messages, a single bit of information is transferred. In a choice between one of ten equally likely messages (one decimal digit), between 3 and 4 bits of information are transferred.

Note that this definition of information has nothing to do with the inherent information content of the data referred to by the labels. Thus, only 1 bit is needed to distinguish between the transmission of Hamlet and MacBeth, assuming that the receiver has perfect copies of each and needs only the information relative to the choice between the two. However, if one computer wants to send a copy of Hamlet to the other, the situation is completely different. In this case, all the text of the play would have to be converted to a sequence of binary digits. If this conversion were performed without regard to the letter or word frequency in the text, then 0s and 1s would occur with equal frequency, and the communicated information *rate* as defined above would be far in excess of the actual information *content* of the text. Taking into account some of the properties of the alphabet and the language would enable us to reduce the data rate toward something closer to the true information content. Taking into account the semantic content of the language would reduce the information rate still more. If we knew how to gain insight into this inherent information content, we could, in principle, encode the data so that many fewer digits would be required for the transmission, something closer yet to the true information content of the text.

This information-oriented approach points out a difference between short-and long-distance communication. If the distances are very short—say, within the computer itself—then the chance of a signal being identified incorrectly at the receiving end is extremely low. But if the distance is long enough to require, say, a telephone circuit, there is a chance that the message being transmitted will be corrupted enough to make the receiver misidentify the message. This corruption of the message introduces ambiguity in the receiver's decision process, which is equivalent to reducing the information transferred by the data. In other words, if 6 bits of information were transmitted by the sender, something less than 6 bits would be received by the recipient. Suppose that 1 bit is lost in its entirety so that 5 rather than 6 bits are received. Then every received message can be one of two things, depending upon the identity of the missing bit. In other words, since 5 bits represent a choice of one of thirty-two things instead of one of sixty-four, the result is a confusion factor of one in two messages. Since confusion of this sort is intolerable if it occurs too often, the communicator must either reduce the information transmission rate of the source or improve the communications medium to ensure that less information is lost.

2.2   Goals of Communications

The primary goal of telecommunications is to preserve the information content of the transmission to the extent necessary for the application at hand, or, in other words, to transmit the data representing the information with an *accuracy* commensurate with the application. The essential virtue of digital communication is that its accuracy can be controlled with ease. The same goal exists for analog communication, although its accuracy is harder to quantify and control.

A second goal is *efficiency*. While its dictionary definition is *the production of a desired effect without waste*, it has various definitions depending upon context. Thus, the more efficient your automobile engine, the more miles your car gets from a gallon of gas. But efficient does not necessarily imply cheap. If a highly efficient automobile engine costs a great deal more than a less efficient one, then the net cost to the customer may be greater despite the fuel savings. The solution to a problem may be both cheap *and* efficient, but not necessarily.

A scientist seeks to understand nature for its own sake, whereas a technologist or an engineer is one who applies scientific knowledge to practical ends. To state that the goal of telecommunications is to achieve accuracy and efficiency in the communication of information is to give you a scientist's perspective. The telecommunications engineer's goal is to use this scientific knowledge to develop or produce telecommunications components and systems that do an acceptable job at an affordable cost. Telecommunications scientists have developed a whole body of analytical techniques that improve the accuracy and efficiency of information transmission in the face of the distortions and noise that corrupt the telecommunications signals. Which of these techniques turn out to be of practical use is determined by an engineer in some specific context.

An example from the telecommunications world is illustrated in Fig. 2-3. Suppose that a company must send large data files from a computer in San Francisco to one in New York using telephone lines. From the size of the data file and the time sensitivity of the data, the data-processing director determined that the data had to be sent at the rate of at least 56 kbps (kilobits per second). Furthermore, this transmission must be very accurate—so accurate that, on the average, no more than one in ten million bits transmitted can be received incorrectly. The telecommu-

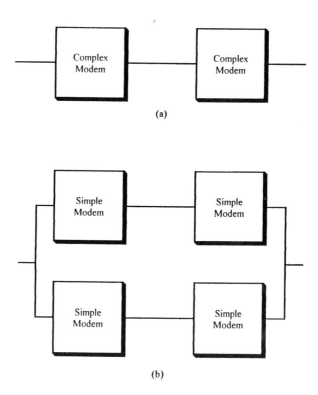

(a)

(b)

Figure 2-3   Two ways to achieve high-rates. (a) A single phone line with complex modems. (b) Two phone lines with simple modems.

nications manager could do the job in one of the two ways shown in the picture.

In Fig. 2-3(a), the modems are sophisticated enough to support a rate of 56 kbps using an ordinary phone line, while maintaining the desired transmission accuracy. In Fig. 2-3(b), the modems are simpler and cheaper but can only meet the accuracy requirement at half the rate. Therefore, to meet the rate requirement, two phone lines are needed. The first case uses the phone line twice as efficiently as the second case. But since the telecommunications manager is interested only in cost, not in efficiency, he or she will choose the efficient solution only if the cost of the efficient modems is less than the cost of the less-efficient modems plus the cost of the additional phone line.

It is interesting to note that the modem state of the art has improved enormously as a result of new theoretical insights coupled with advances in integrated circuit technology. (Chapter 7 discusses the technical details.) When computer communication began in the 1950s, 1200 bps was the standard and 2400 bps was at the cutting edge. In the mid 1990s, any computer user can buy a 28.8 kbps modem for scarcely over $100. But achieving twice that rate on a telephone line without tailoring the line would require a much more sophisticated modem.

2.3 Information Theory

The fundamental science underlying telecommunications, addressing and explaining in an elegant way the fundamental issues of efficiency and accuracy, is called *information theory*. Its foundations were laid in 1948 with the publication of two papers by Claude Shannon, then at the Bell Laboratories and later a member of the MIT faculty. In the years since this great work, many others have developed the mathematical techniques that have permitted practical application of his results, capitalizing upon the advances in component technology as in the foregoing example.

Shannon was the first to formulate the notion of information as choice. He called it *entropy* because of its remarkable resemblance to the thermodynamic quantity of that name. Entropy is a macroscopic variable along with such other thermodynamic variables as energy, temperature, and heat. In the latter part of the nineteenth century, physicists were able to derive these thermodynamic variables from a statistical picture of the atoms and molecules of the underlying material. At the heart of the description of, say, a volume of gas is a model in which the gas molecules are distributed among elementary cells designated by position and velocity. If p_j is the probability that a molecule is in the jth such cell, Eq. 2-2 gives the entropy of the system, and the summation is over all the possible combinations of position and velocity. At equilibrium the entropy is maximized, and Eq. 2-1 tells us that this occurs when the particles are as close to uniformly distributed as possible among the cells. It is not that information and thermodynamics are related, per se. Rather, it is the fact that both depend upon a fundamental quantity in the same mathematical form.

Others had recognized the relationship between information and entropy as well, but only Shannon was able to put everything together in such a coherent fashion. Jeremy Campbell, an English science writer, notes in his book, *Grammatical Man*, that a year before Shannon's publications, Norbert Wiener, a mathematician well known not only for his intellectual accomplishments but also for his eccentricities, was observed by Robert Fano, a younger colleague, to mutter "Information is entropy" between puffs on his cigar while walking the halls of MIT.

Shannon's ideas, while developed solely for communications engineering, have been very influential in other fields. To quote Campbell, "Essentially [Shannon's] papers consisted of a set of theorems dealing with the problem of sending messages from one place to another quickly, economically and efficiently. But the wider and more exciting implications of Shannon's work lay in the fact that he had been able to make the concept of information so logical and precise that it could be placed in a formal framework of ideas." And indeed, *Grammatical Man* addresses itself to the insights provided by information theory and the thermodynamic concept of entropy to such fields as linguistics, genetics, and cognitive processing.

Not everyone agrees with such a broad interpretation. Even Shannon, a very self-effacing, introverted man who published seemingly only under duress throughout his career, suggested in an article in 1956 that "information theory has perhaps ballooned to an importance beyond its actual accomplishments." Speculations on the ultimate importance of information theory are beyond my purpose. Rather it is Shannon's seminal contribution to communications in the narrow sense that is my concern, both because of its intellectual stimulation and for the foundation it provides for the practical business of telecommunications.

2.4   Signals and Noise

Transmission efficiency is defined as the transmitted information rate as compared to the maximum sustainable in a communications channel. It is now appropriate to ask what properties of a communications channel determine this maximum data rate. Let's look at an analogous problem: What factors determine how much water can be transported through a pipe from a pumping station? Two things seem evident: The greater the water pressure developed at the pumping station and the larger the diameter of the pipe, the greater the rate of flow should be. There also is the effect of the condition of the inner surface of the pipe. If this surface is rough and uneven, the water will flow turbulently rather than smoothly, and this will inhibit the rate of flow of the water.

In communications, the amount of energy in the signals is analogous to the water pressure, and the *noise* level is analogous to the roughness of the pipe. Intuitively, the greater the signal energy and the less the noise, the greater the information rate that can be supported. The analog of the pipe size is the *bandwidth* of the communications channel. We will concentrate on signal energy and noise energy in the rest of this chapter and will return to bandwidth later. The effects of signal strength and noise are universal. The channel may be acoustic, electrical, or optical; it may be analog or digital. The important parameter in determining the communication characteristics is the ratio of the signal strength to the noise, rather than the absolute value of either one. The following story provides an illustration of why this is so.

Jack and Jill meet one day for lunch in a picnic area in the center of a large park. The only sound intruding on their conversation is the barely audible traffic noise coming from the heavily traveled public roads bordering the park. His lunch break nearly over, Jack starts walking away, leaving Jill behind. After a few moments, Jack remembers something that he had meant to say and turns around to tell her. He is now a few yards away, and he has to raise his voice a bit so that Jill can hear him over the now more audible road noise. Once again, Jack turns around and continues walking. After another 20 yd or so, he has another thought and turns around to catch Jill's attention. Now he must shout in order to make his voice heard over the traffic noise. In fact, Jill misses a few words and has to shout back to ask him to repeat his sentence. He does so, and Jill shouts her agreement. Jack rushes along. Again he turns around to say something else. But now he is about 100 yd away, and he has to shout as loudly as he can just to attract her attention. Even so, she can barely hear him. The automobile noise that seemed so faint when the two were together is now loud enough to mask the reduced intensity of Jack's voice.

The example demonstrates the qualitative effect of signal energy and noise on the transmission and reception of sound. When Jack and Jill were at a normal conversational distance, Jack's voice level was high enough to be understood perfectly. The noise level relative to the intensity of his voice was negligible. When they were a few yards apart, Jack was able to raise his voice enough that Jill was able to hear and understand him well enough, although the traffic noise was now discernible. When separated by a greater distance, Jill had all she could do to make out Jack's words. She even missed a few. But when they were separated by the length of a football field, Jack could not shout loud enough to overcome even the low level of the traffic noise.

We can make an important observation from this example. As Jack moved away from Jill, his voice energy reaching Jill was reduced by the square of the distance separating them. In contrast, the noise level remained the same. It just appeared to increase because of the reduced voice energy. This illustrates the earlier point that what is important is not the signal or noise energies themselves, but their ratio.

Another observation from this example is that acoustic communications have a very limited range. If Jack had had a megaphone he might have increased his conversational range a little, but ultimately distance would have defeated him. He would have been forced to walk back to within earshot of Jill or to wait until both were at their offices so he could call her on the telephone to complete the conversation.

To send information over long distances, it is essential to be able to boost the energy level of the communication signals enough to overcome the background noise. Practically speaking, this means using a medium that transports the signals electrically or optically rather than acoustically. The reason for this is that it is easy to amplify electrical signals and difficult to amplify acoustic ones.

It is significant that there is no purely mechanical equivalent to the process of amplification. For example, the first phonographs were all acoustic. Singers had to shout into the equivalent of a megaphone to produce enough energy to drive the stylus used to cut the record. The music was played back again with a megaphone-like horn. A great leap forward in music reproduction occurred in the 1920s with the use of the first electrical systems. The music to be recorded was first converted from acoustical to electrical form using a microphone, was amplified electronically, and then was reconverted to mechanical form to cut the record. For playback, the weak acoustic signals were converted to electrical form, amplified electronically, and then reconverted to acoustic form in a loudspeaker. The multiple conversions (transductions) from acoustical to electrical form and back again do take their toll in musical fidelity. But this is a small price to pay for the revolution in sound quality brought about by the use of electrical techniques.

2.4.1   Communication Requires Energy

Just as it takes a certain amount of energy to generate light, to heat water, or to propel an automobile, so it takes a certain amount of energy to communicate information. Since the ratio of signal energy to noise energy is the factor that determines the quality of the sound reception, the number of joules of signal energy depends upon the number of joules of noise energy present. In the earlier example, Jack's voice signals had to be strong enough to counteract the distant auto noise. In a hypothetical situation in which there is no noise at all, there is a threshold value of signal energy required for the receiver to perceive that a signal is present. If you were in a perfectly noiseless room, you could hear even the faintest whisper, provided its energy exceeded that minimum level necessary to trigger the fundamental physiological processes of hearing. But we can safely ignore this hypothetical case. In all practical cases, noise of one kind or another is always present, and the signal energy usually must be at least a few times as large as the noise energy for satisfactory reception. One of Shannon's most quoted results that we discuss more fully in chapters 5 through 7 is the existence of an ultimate theoretical limit, not achievable in practice, in which the signal energy can be just under 70% of the noise energy while, at the same time, the transmission is perfectly accurate.

2.4.2   Noise

Noise is a foreign signal of any origin that competes with the communications signal that you want to hear. The optical signaling scheme used to inform Paul Revere of the route of the British in 1775 might not have succeeded had there been enough stray light from other sources to mask the lantern signals from Boston's Old North Church. The traffic noise that disturbed Jack and Jill is an example of acoustic noise. Another example of acoustic noise is the boisterous conversation from a nearby restaurant table that interferes with your business lunch. Noise can also be electrical, and it can come from many sources. You may hear it when using the telephone. When listening to the radio, you sometimes hear interference from *static*, the name commonly given to atmospheric noise caused by electrical storms. You may see "snow" on your television set, particularly if you live in a fringe area far enough from the broadcasting station that the signal level is diminished. If you replace your rabbit-ears antenna with a more powerful rooftop antenna, you are increasing the amount of broadcast signal energy that enters your TV. The snow will diminish because the signal level has been increased relative to the noise level. Signals can also interfere with themselves. The "ghosts" on your television screen are the result of multiple reflections from objects in the path of the television signal. Each of these reflections is delayed by a small amount relative to one another, resulting in multiple copies of the same signal entering the antenna at slightly different times.

Some noise sources are easy to identify, for example, a lightning bolt or a loud talker. But some are more difficult because they are the combined effect of a large number of noise sources. For example, the traffic noise intruding on Jack and Jill was produced by a large number of automobiles. Similarly, the needle scratch from an old record is the result of a very large number of fluctuations caused by abrasions of the record, and the soft background hiss that you hear on the telephone or radio is the result of a very large number of interfering signals. Whenever the number of interfering signals is large, the most useful way to describe their effects is to address their aggregate behavior. Noise of this kind is called *thermal noise*.

2.4.2.1 *Thermal Noise.*

Electrons in all materials are continually in motion, often colliding with one another and with the atomic nuclei. In each of these collisions, energy is transferred from one particle to another. If you play pool, you have probably observed another example of this effect: when one ball hits another head on, the first ball stops and the second moves with almost the speed of the first ball before the collision. In other words, aside from a small amount of frictional loss, all the kinetic energy of the first ball is transferred to the second in the collision.

If we were to plot the velocity of an individual electron as a function of time, we would obtain a zigzag picture similar to that shown in Fig. 2-4.

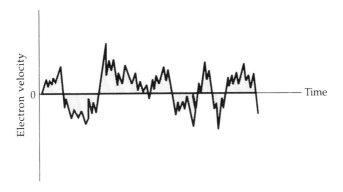

Figure 2-4   Random electronic motion.

By velocity, we mean not only how fast the electron is moving (its speed) but also in which direction. For example, we might define positive velocity to be that of the electron moving from left to right and negative velocity to be that of the electron moving from right to left. As you might expect in such random motion, each electron will be moving backward as much as it is moving forward, and its average velocity should be zero.

Another important thing to know about the motion is how much of the time the electron is moving slowly and how much rapidly. To arrive at this information, we imagine another hypothetical experiment. Instead of concentrating on the wanderings of a single electron, we make simultaneous measurements of the velocities of a very large number of electrons, all of which behave the same way statistically, and plot the result as in Fig. 2-5. The curve has a bell shape that is called *normal* or *Gaussian.* While most of the electrons have low speeds, some smaller number in the "tails" of the curve have higher speeds. Note also that the curve is symmetrical about zero, agreeing with our previous observation that the average velocity is zero.

Many statistical phenomena in nature are Gaussian, due to the *Central Limit Theorem* of probability theory which states that the more observations you make of a random process, the more the distribution of these observations tends toward the Gaussian. The fortunate aspect of this is that the Gaussian distribution is amenable to mathematical analysis.

In a communications receiver, the huge number of electrons in all the constituent components are in random motion, and this motion is super-

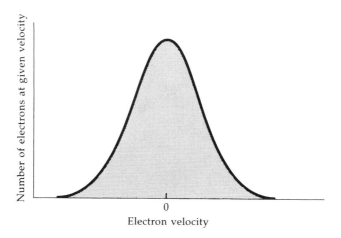

Figure 2-5   Velocity distribution of electrons in a material.

imposed upon the deterministic (nonrandom) motion caused by signals. This random motion of the electrons is the source of thermal noise (sometimes called Gaussian noise, from the shape of the curve in Fig. 2-5).

We call this noise thermal because the average electron kinetic energy is determined by the temperature. The higher the temperature, the higher the energy. The temperature at which all motion stops defines the lowest possible temperature, called *absolute zero*. This is the basis for the *absolute* or *Kelvin* (K) temperature scale. It is the same as the familiar Celsius (C) scale, but displaced by 273.2°, so that 0 °C is 273.2 K.

Our understanding of thermal noise is derived from statistical mechanics, the same branch of physics from which the entropy formula in Eq. 2-2 was first derived. From this point of view, the properties of a large ensemble of electrons in a material are similar to the properties of a large ensemble of oxygen molecules in a container. Early in the nineteenth century, it was discovered that the average energy of a molecule in thermal equilibrium is proportional to the absolute temperature, where the proportionality constant is 1.38×10^{-23} Joules per Kelvin (J/K). Like the speed of light and the electrical charge on the electron, this is a fundamental constant of nature, known as *Boltzmann's constant* after the famous nineteenth-century German physicist Ludwig Boltzmann. Thus, at normal room temperature of approximately 27 °C (300 K), the thermal noise energy is 4.14×10^{-21} J.

Anyone who studied elementary thermodynamics as part of a course in freshman physics will recall meeting Boltzmann's constant in the fundamental equation of an ideal gas. Suppose we have a container of volume V containing N_T molecules of gas at a pressure P. Then the gas equation

$$PV = N_T kT$$

says that the product of the pressure and volume is proportional to the number of molecules and the temperature, where Boltzmann's constant k is the proportionality constant. As previously noted, k has the dimension of Joules per Kelvin. Therefore kT has the dimension of joules and is interpreted as the kinetic energy per gas molecule. Multiplying this by N_T gives the total kinetic energy of all the molecules in the container, called the *internal energy* of the gas in thermodynamics. Of course, variables such as pressure, volume, and temperature are macroscopic ways of describing the average properties of a large number of molecules in constant motion; the higher the temperature, the more the energy of the molecules and the higher their average speeds. In the statistical picture the velocities of the molecules at any particular temperature are distributed as in Fig. 2-5. The equation governing this distribution

$$N(v) = N_T \sqrt{\frac{m}{2\pi kT}}\, e^{-mv^2/2kT} \tag{2-3}$$

is known as the *Maxwell distribution*. $N(v)$ is the number of molecules having the velocity v. When divided by the total number of molecules in the container, it becomes the probability that a molecule has the velocity v. As noted above, this Maxwell distribution is Gaussian in form.

The standard mathematical form of the Gaussian distribution of a variable x with mean 0 is given by

$$P(x) = \frac{1}{\sqrt{2\pi}\sigma}\, e^{-x^2/2\sigma^2}, \tag{2-4}$$

where σ, the standard deviation, is defined to be the square root of the average value of x^2 or, in other words, the root mean square (rms) value of x^2. Comparing Eqs. 2-3 and 2-4, you can see that σ^2 for the Maxwell distribution, the average value of the square of the molecule velocities, is kT/m. It follows from this that the average kinetic energy of the molecules is given by

$$\text{Ave. kinetic energy} = \tfrac{1}{2}m\,(\text{ave. velocity})^2 = \frac{kT}{2}.$$

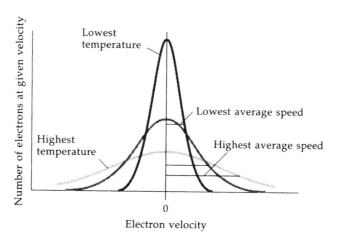

Figure 2-6   Electron velocites at different temperatures.

This random process when applied to the motion of the free electrons in a conductor is the source of what is called *thermal noise* and represents the fundamental limitation on the amount of energy required to communicate.

The curve of Fig. 2-5 was measured at a particular temperature. Figure 2-6 shows several similar curves at different temperatures. The lower the temperature, the lower the rms velocity and energy and the thinner the curve. In the limiting case at absolute zero, the curve degenerates to a line at zero velocity, reflecting the fact that all the electrons are motionless. The average value of the velocity in each case is still zero, since an electron is just as likely to be moving forward as backward, regardless of the temperature.

2.5   Communicating Digits

The dependency of communications performance on the ratio of signal energy to noise energy is universal, applying equally to analog and digital communications. The Jack and Jill example was of analog communications. We will now focus on digital data transmission.

Figure 2-7 shows an example of a binary communications system that might use any of the transmission media that have been mentioned. To send a 1 in this electronic system, we transmit a rectangular pulse of

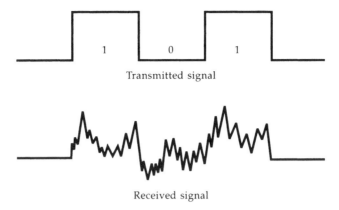

Transmitted signal

Received signal

Figure 2-7   Digital signals in the presence of noise.

energy in some time interval, and to send a 0, we transmit nothing during the time interval. At the receiver, the transmitted pulse is corrupted by thermal noise. A 1 is received as the pulse of energy with noise superimposed upon it. A 0 is received as a pulse of noise only. The receiver adds up all the energy received in the appropriate time interval and attempts to differentiate between 1s and 0s.

The noise fluctuations can either add to or subtract from the signal. If the signal is much larger than the noise, it does not matter very much how the noise behaves; the receiver will be able to distinguish between 1s and 0s almost all the time. However, if the signal and noise energies are close to the same strength, then fluctuations in the noise can cause a 0 to look like a 1 and vice versa. When this happens, the receiver can misidentify the signal. Note that even when the signal-to-noise ratio is very high, errors can still occur, albeit with a very low probability. This is because the noise is a statistical phenomenon, and there is always the chance that an improbable noise peak can occur that will cause the receiver to make an error.

Suppose that with a transmitted power level of 1 W and a pulse duration of 1 s—corresponding to a data transmission rate of 1 bps—the data transfer is not reliable enough. It is then necessary to increase the signal-to-noise ratio by either increasing the signal energy or decreasing the noise energy. Let's suppose that there is nothing we can do about the noise; this is often the case in practice. Therefore, we have no choice but to increase the signal energy. Since the signal energy depends upon the power and time duration, we can increase either one or the other, or perhaps both. Either approach will have the drawback of costing more money. But if we increase the time duration, we also reduce the rate at which bits are being transmitted. Figure 2-8 shows both approaches. The original signal from Fig. 2-7 is reproduced in Fig. 2-8(a). In Fig. 2-8(b) the energy in the signals is doubled by doubling their time durations to 2 s, while retaining the original power level of 1 W. In Fig. 2-8(c), the original power level is doubled, and the original pulse width is retained. In either case, doubling the signal energy for the same noise energy will decrease the chance that the receiver will make errors in identifying the received pulses.

Going back to our example of Jack and Jill in the park, as Jack walked away from Jill, he was able to compensate for the decreased signal level to some extent by shouting, the equivalent of increasing the signal power as in Fig. 2-8(c). While human physiology limits the amount of power increase that can be achieved in this way, there is much more latitude when we are dealing with electrical signals. Jack also could have compensated, again to some limited extent, by talking more slowly. Here,

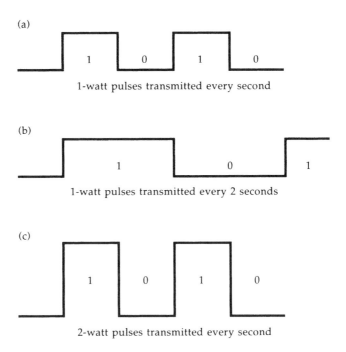

Figure 2-8   Doubling the transmitted energy.

too, there is a practical limit: if you talk too slowly, even when the noise level is very much lower than the signal, it is hard to understand the speech, since we are accustomed to hearing speech at rates within some normal bounds. But in digital transmission, there is no fundamental limit to how slowly the information can be sent to improve the reliability of the transmission. The slower the digits are sent, the more reliable the transmission should be.

In the foregoing discussion, we assumed that to improve the reliability of the communication, we had no choice but to increase the signal-to-noise ratio. That assumption is true only if we insist upon using the signals shown in Fig. 2-8. As it turns out, there are many different ways to choose the signals to be used, and some are better than others because they will achieve more reliability for a given signal-to-noise ratio. How do we find these better signaling schemes? It's easy to find some simple ones, and we will show examples later. But to do significantly better—in fact, to do the best that can possibly be done—is not an easy job at all. Shannon's work is so important to communications because it provided the insight needed to understand the best that can possibly be done. And even if the best is not achievable, it provides the yardstick for evaluating just what is achievable. We will have a great deal more to say about this later.

3

ANALOG COMMUNICATION

3.0 Introduction

The older telecommunications services—telephone, radio, and television—started out analog and have remained so, by and large, although digital transmission is finally making inroads into these services as well. Before the development of the computer, it would have been inconceivable for anyone to convert the human voice to a string of digits before transmitting it over a wire or through the air. Even today, when digital communication is commonplace, converting an audio or video signal to a stream of 0s and 1s and then sending the digits is not the first thing that comes to mind, since transmitting the audio as it comes in analog form is such a natural thing to do. But the success of the compact disc has already demonstrated the power of going digital, and the next century will surely see digital telephone, radio, and television taking over the marketplace. But it should never be forgotten that analog came first, laying both the practical and theoretical foundations.

3.1 Talking over the Telephone

The telephone line is the most familiar communications channel. It is also the simplest conceptually. Your local phone company provides a connection between your telephone and its *end office* (the name given to the switching center or *central office* closest to the subscriber) in the form of a pair of wires. When you talk into the microphone built into the telephone handset, your voice signal is converted from acoustical to electrical form and is carried in this way to the end office. From there it goes through an elaborate network of transmission and switching facilities (largely digital) until it reaches another pair of wires leading to the telephone of the person to whom you are talking. Despite the complexity of this network, we can think of the telephone line as a long pair of wires connecting the two telephones.

This circuit delivers a distorted version of your voice to its destination. We can gain some insight into the nature of this distortion by comparing telephone communication with some other higher-fidelity audio systems. Figure 3-1 shows a succession of audio communication channels of decreasing fidelity. The top picture (a) shows the best of all possible channels, the standard against which every other channel must be

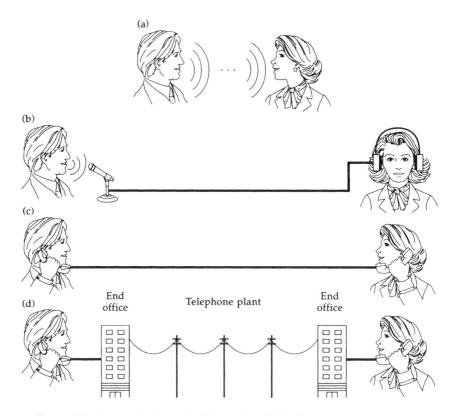

Figure 3-1   Four audio channels of decreasing fidelity from (a) to (d).

compared: the pure acoustical channel with no intrusion of electrical signals at all. The next picture (b) shows a representation of the best of all possible electrical channels: a high-quality microphone, a short pair of wires, and a pair of high-fidelity earphones. The microphone and earphones represent the best achievable transduction (conversion from acoustical to electrical form and back again), and the wires connecting them are short enough so that they do not introduce degradation. The sound quality that results from this channel is very good but still is not quite as good as that of the purely acoustical channel, because even the best microphone and speaker introduce some degradation. In the next picture (c), the high-quality microphone and earphones are replaced by the lower-quality devices found in the ordinary telephone handset; but, as before, the handsets are connected with a short pair of wires. The telephone transducers themselves are significantly poorer than the high-fidelity equivalents in the previous example. Thus, even though the circuit connecting them does not introduce any degradation, the resulting audio quality is significantly lower than it was in case (b). The final picture (d) shows a telephone circuit with telephone handsets connected by a realistically long pair of wires. As you would expect, the resulting quality is still worse, because of the circuit degradations.

The physical properties of the telephone channel that influence its capacity and, hence, degrade its quality are signal-to-noise ratio and bandwidth, that is, the extent of the band of frequencies passed by the channel. In all but the top example in Fig. 3-1, transducers are used to convert the audio signals from acoustical form to electrical and back again. These transducers, the microphone and the earphone, distort the speech signals in a frequency-sensitive way. We can see what this means from the following hypothetical experiment: generate a pure acoustic tone or sine wave, play it through the channel, and measure its amplitude. Then repeat the measurement many times, each time using as the source a tone at a slightly different frequency, but with the same amplitude, until the entire audible frequency band of signals from 0 to over 20,000 Hz has been covered. We plot the results of this hypothetical experiment in Fig. 3-2 for each of the channels of Fig. 3-1.

Graphs such as these are called *frequency-response* curves. Trace *a* is the frequency response of the reference acoustic channel corresponding to trace *a* in Fig. 3-1. As one would expect, this ideal channel has no frequency limitations whatsoever—the only frequency limitations are in the acoustical source and in the ears of the listener, both of which are external

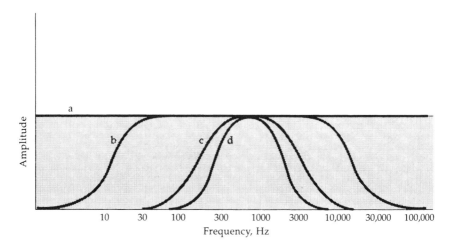

Figure 3-2   Frequency response of the audio channels of Fig. 3-1.

to the channel itself. Traces *b* and *c* show the frequency-response characteristics of the corresponding channels of Fig. 3-1. The differences are
readily apparent and are due to the effects of the different microphones
and speakers. In both cases, the channel passes a particular band of frequencies and rejects all others. The high-fidelity channel in trace *b* has a
frequency response that passes a wide band between 30 and 20,000 Hz.
The lower-fidelity channel in trace *c* passes the much narrower band between 250 and 4250 Hz. Or, in terms of bandwidth, the high-fidelity
channel has a bandwidth of 19,970 Hz, and the lower-fidelity channel has
a bandwidth of 4000 Hz. When you buy a microphone or a loudspeaker,
the manufacturer usually provides a frequency-response curve similar
to the curves shown in Fig. 3-2. These curves describe the performance of
the item.

   Any device that exhibits the characteristics of these channels—that
is, that treats the different frequencies selectively—is called a *filter*. All
our examples have been of *bandpass* filters, which *pass a band* of frequencies within a total frequency band of interest and reject frequencies
above and below that band. There are other common varieties of filters.
For example, a *low-pass filter* passes all frequencies below some threshold frequency, and a *high-pass filter* passes all frequencies above a
threshold frequency. Ordinary walls are low-pass acoustic filters, since
they attenuate treble tones much more severely than they do bass tones.

   Clearly, the narrow bandwidth of the telephone channel shown in Fig.
3-2(d) distorts the audio band a great deal. Every once in a while when

you call some business establishment and are put "on hold," you are forced to listen to music through the telephone system, under the misguided notion that the music will soothe you while you wait. If you have been subjected to this, you know that the quality of the music is poor, at best, and downright unpleasant, at worst. This is because the telephone system was not designed to transmit music. Its bandwidth of around 3000–4000 Hz is considerably narrower than that needed for most kinds of music. The telephone system was designed to carry the human voice, and it does a reasonably good job. But even in this case, we know from experience that the bandwidth is narrower than what is needed for complete intelligibility. For example, it is hard to distinguish an *f* from an *s* since these sounds have significant energy above the cutoff frequency of telephone circuits.

The other effect introduced by a real telephone line is noise. Many phenomena in the complex telephone plant introduce noise into the circuit. A sine wave, transmitted within the bandwidth of the circuit, is received at the other end with random variations superimposed upon it. Some of these variations are small and some are large. The audible effect is the presence of extraneous sounds that, if large enough, mask speech either partly or totally. Large impulses make a "popping" sound; continuous low-level thermal noise makes a "hissing" sound. When the noise level is low, it does not interfere with speech intelligibility; the primary limitation is the bandwidth. But when the noise level is high enough, its effects combined with those of the frequency limitations make some or all of the speech unintelligible. As we indicated in chapter 2, the words "high" and "low" make sense only when related to the signal amplitude. A voice signal loses strength as it travels over a long phone line. The telephone company amplifies the signal to compensate for this loss. The resulting signal, as it appears in your earphone, is usually in the correct loudness range for your ears. But whether you can understand what is spoken is determined, in part, by the signal-to-noise ratio.

3.2   Radio Broadcasting

The long-distance portion of the telephone plant uses a variety of media to transport telephone signals. Some are cables, either electrical or optical, and some use radio or *wireless* techniques. Indeed, the evolution of these transmission facilities in the public networks can be characterized as the search for more economical sources of the bandwidth required to satisfy the ever-increasing telecommunications demand. But since the ordinary analog circuit with a bandwidth of around 3–4 kHz is the commodity that the subscriber sees, the fact that wideband media exist is largely invisible. They are simply vehicles for carrying bundles of these narrowband circuits over long distances. The broadcast media are another matter entirely. The various radio and television channels have wider bandwidths that are evident to all. While many of the characteristics of these broadcast channels are similar to those of the telephone circuit, there are some significant differences.

The steps involved in transmitting audio by radio are shown in Fig. 3-3. Note that we cannot simply talk into a radio transmitter as we can into a telephone or tape recorder, both of which are designed to accept audio signals and transmit them as they are. In contrast, before an audio signal can be broadcast over the radio, it must be moved to a higher-frequency range by a process called *modulation*. The two common forms of modulation used in broadcasting, *amplitude modulation* and *frequency modulation*, are familiar to us by their respective abbreviations, AM and FM. These higher-frequency electrical signals are fed to an antenna that converts the signals to electromagnetic waves that are radiated out into space. When these waves are received by another antenna, they are converted back to electrical signals. The audio waveform is then extracted from the high-frequency electrical signals by the inverse process, called *demodulation*, and then played for the listener.

The conversions from electrical energy to electromagnetic energy and back represent another form of transduction where now the transducers are the antennas. Electrical signals propagate through a material by the transfer of energy from electron to electron. For example, copper wires contain large numbers of electrons that are free to move about. In contrast, electromagnetic signals can travel through space, empty or not, as well as through some matter. Electromagnetic waves propagate by

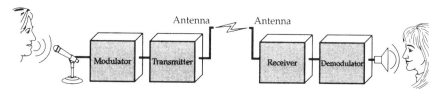

Figure 3-3   Broadcasting audio signals.

themselves, unaided by matter of any kind in contrast to sound waves, which depend upon the mechanism of pressure variations within the materials to propagate.

All wave phenomena, whether they be acoustic or electromagnetic have as their source a vibration or oscillation. If the electrical signals in an antenna were not oscillatory, no radiation of radio waves would take place. The oscillating electrical signals give rise to electromagnetic signals oscillating at exactly the same frequency.

The only thing that distinguishes light from radio waves is its frequency. However, even though light and radio are conceptually the same, for practical reasons it has not always been possible to generate light waves from oscillating electrical signals by a transduction. Until the latter part of this century, the generation of light always required an intermediate step—as, for example, heating a filament in a light bulb. It was only with the invention of the laser that it became possible to generate light waves with all the flexibility of the other form of electromagnetic waves that we call radio.

Electromagnetic transmission is a phenomenon that is hard to understand intuitively. How can one send signals into the air at one location and pick them out of the air at another? Light is so familiar that we take it for granted. We see it because its reflections from objects are visible. Part of the mystery surrounding radio waves that propagate in exactly the same way is the fact that their reflections are invisible. It may be easiest to resign yourself to the fact that the phenomenon is difficult to understand intuitively, and simply recognize that in some respects they behave like water and sound waves, spreading out as they propagate.

In the nineteenth century it was commonly believed that electromagnetic waves had to propagate like sound waves by the vibration of some substance. This led to the conclusion that space was filled with an invisible material called *ether* that made electromagnetic wave propagation possible. It is now known that the ether does not exist, although some continue to use the term in a metaphoric sense.

Our modern understanding of the nature of electromagnetic radiation is based primarily on the work of the great Scottish physicist, James Clerk Maxwell. Maxwell was one of those extraordinary geniuses of the caliber of Newton and Einstein who appear on the scene at rare intervals. While he made significant contributions to many branches of physics in his relatively short lifetime (including the statistical mechanics that we discussed in chapter 2), he is known primarily for his monumental *Trea-*

tise on Electricity and Magnetism published in 1873. Maxwell was the first to recognize that light is electromagnetic in nature—that is, that it consists of related electrical and magnetic vibrations. He also recognized that all electromagnetic waves, radio and light, propagate at the same speed, the *speed of light*, which is 186,000 miles per second or 300 million (3×10^8) meters per second. Maxwell predicted from purely theoretical arguments that it should be possible to generate electromagnetic radiation, and Heinrich Hertz, the German physicist, was the first to exhibit the phenomenon and thereby demonstrate conclusively the electromagnetic nature of light. The idea of communicating by wireless radio fascinated many people—by far the most successful was Guglielmo Marconi—from the mid 1890s on. By great ingenuity and drive they were able to develop practical devices to transmit and receive radio waves, and by the beginning of this century, radio communication had become a reality.

3.2.1   Radio Propagation and Frequency

Maxwell's theory of electromagnetic radiation is independent of the frequency or wavelength of the waves from the lowest-frequency radio waves to light and above. But, as we all know, real world radio propagation is highly dependent on frequency. The reason for this, of course, is that the atmosphere is not a vacuum. It contains various materials that can absorb, reflect, and refract the radiation, and these effects are all frequency dependent.

All electromagnetic waves, regardless of their length, travel in a straight line unless something is interposed that bends them. However, radio waves at some frequencies or wavelengths propagate differently than at others. This is because the earth is surrounded by a belt of electrically charged atoms (ions) known as the *ionosphere*. This belt, which extends from an altitude of 50 to 200 miles, has a large effect on radio waves with frequencies below 30 MHz. Above 30 MHz, however, the ionosphere has little or no effect.

Radio waves with frequencies up to around 3 MHz (just above the AM broadcast band that extends from 0.535 to 1.6 MHz) effectively hug the surface of the earth as they propagate. This is due in part to refraction at the surface of the earth and in part to a kind of channeling of the waves between the earth and the ionosphere. These effects permit the waves to propagate over very long distances, limited by losses at the boundaries.

These losses increase with frequency so that in the AM broadcast band they limit the effective propagation range to about a few tens of miles. In the *shortwave* band, between 3 and 30 MHz, the ionosphere reflects the waves very much like a mirror reflecting light, thereby permitting the spanning of long distances by successive reflections by the ionosphere and the earth.

Marconi and his contemporaries used primarily the low-frequency end of the band permitting them to astound the world with their long-distance transmissions. By the 1920s radio users began the move to the shortwave band. Until the development of the technology of satellite communications in the 1960s, shortwave radio remained as the only way of sending voice signals to places where wires could not be strung, for example, from ship to shore. It is still the principal vehicle for amateur radio operators or Hams.

Because the FM and television bands are above 30 MHz, these waves propagate in straight lines largely unaffected by the ionosphere. Their range is limited to about 30 – 40 miles by geometrical considerations (the heights of the transmitting and receiving antennas and the curvature of the earth), commonly called *line-of-sight*. Similar limitations apply to cellular radio and the newer personal communications systems that use still higher frequencies.

3.2.2   Amplitude Modulation

Radio broadcasting began in 1920 using the AM frequency band. This band is divided into 107 channels, each with a bandwidth of 10 kHz. Broadcasters are assigned one of these channels by the Federal Communications Commission (FCC) in the United States and similar authorities elsewhere for their exclusive use in a particular location. Broadcasters must confine their signals to their own 10-kHz channel to keep from interfering with other broadcasters in the same location assigned to nearby channels. Since the range of an AM station is limited, the same channel can be reassigned to another station in a location that is far enough away to avoid interference between the two stations.

Once an AM broadcasting station is assigned a channel, it must shift its audio signals from their normal frequency range to fit within the bandwidth of the assigned channel. As we noted earlier, this process of introducing audio variations into a high-frequency radio signal is called *modulation*.

The term *amplitude modulation* is very descriptive of the process by which this is done. The broadcast station generates a sine wave at the center of its assigned channel—say at 1000 kHz—called the *carrier frequency*. This term is used because this frequency carries or supports the information contained in the modulated audio signal. Amplitude modulation impresses the audio signal to be broadcast upon the carrier frequency and makes the *amplitude* of the carrier frequency vary with the amplitude of the audio signal. Figure 3-4 shows amplitude modulation when the audio signal is itself a single sine wave. Note that both the top and the bottom of the wave carry the audio information.

Amplitude modulation is generated by a simple multiplication. The modulator is, in essence, an electrical circuit that multiplies the carrier sine wave by the audio signal to be broadcast. You can see the result of this multiplication from the elementary trigonometric identities:

$$\cos (a + b) = \cos a \cos b - \sin a \sin b,$$
$$\cos (a - b) = \cos a \cos b + \sin a \sin b.$$

Adding the two equations and dividing by 2, we obtain the following:

$$\cos a \cos b = 1/2 \, [\cos (a + b) + \cos (a - b)].$$

Now substitute $2\pi f_c t$ for a, where f_c is the carrier frequency, and $2\pi f_m t$ for b, where f_m is the modulating frequency, and we get

$$\cos 2\pi f_c t \, \cos 2\pi f_m t = 1/2 \, [\cos 2\pi \, (f_c + f_m)t + \cos 2\pi \, (f_c - f_m)t]. \qquad (3\text{-}1)$$

Thus multiplying a carrier sinusoid by a modulating sinusoid gives us the sum and difference of the two frequencies. To take an example, multiplying an audio signal at 440 Hz by a carrier frequency at 1000 kHz is exactly the same as adding two sine waves at frequencies of 1,000,440 and 999,560 Hz. The resulting amplitude-modulated signal is shown in Fig. 3-4.[1] The top and bottom envelopes of the modulated wave are the result of these sum and difference frequencies. To simplify the receiver, a third sine wave at the carrier frequency of 1,000,000 Hz is also added in; the signal shown in Fig. 3-4 contains all three frequencies.

---

[1] Strictly speaking, what we are calling amplitude modulation should be called *double-sideband* amplitude modulation to distinguish it from other forms of amplitude modulation that do not use both the sum and difference frequencies.

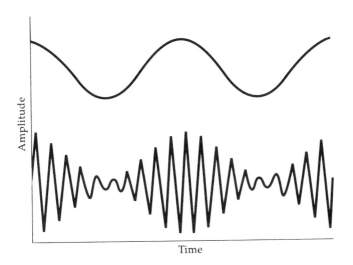

Figure 3-4   Amplitude modulation.

In the next chapter we address the fact that any audio signal can be expressed as a sum of sinusoids at the various frequencies making up the signal. Therefore, multiplying this audio signal by the carrier frequency will result in the sum and difference frequencies of the carrier and each of the components of the modulating signal. And the picture of Fig. 3-4 carries over; the overall audio signal rides on the top and bottom of the carrier.

Since the effect of amplitude modulation is to add frequencies both above and below the carrier frequency at a distance equal to the modulating audio frequency, we can transmit at most a 5-kHz audio band in the 10-kHz AM channel. (It actually has to be a bit less than that to eliminate any chance of interference with adjacent channels.) This explains why AM broadcasting is low fidelity. The demand for channels is so great and the width of the band so limited that only 10 kHz can be allocated to a channel.

3.2.3   Frequency Modulation

Of all the inventions in the area of communications, none had the popular impact of radio broadcasting. Within a few years following the first broadcast in November 1920, broadcasting stations had sprung up all over the country and the world. All the patterns that have characterized first radio and later television developed during that first decade. By 1930 the National Broadcasting Company (NBC) had become dominant in the United States, though it was being challenged by the upstart Columbia Broadcasting System. The dominant broadcast executive was David Sarnoff who headed the Radio Corporation of America (RCA), NBC's parent company.

It's not that there were no technical problems. One of the most irritating things was the poor quality of the average broadcast. Of course, there was the severe bandwidth limitation referred to earlier in the chapter that limited the fidelity of music broadcasts. Even more irritating was the noise background that could even be debilitating when strong interfering sources were in the neighborhood and especially during thunderstorms. Sarnoff commissioned a friend and colleague, Edwin Armstrong, to see if he could devise a way of diminishing the effect of interfering noise. Armstrong succeeded brilliantly with a novel modulation technique called frequency modulation or FM.

But invention is one thing and entrepreneurship quite another. Armstrong's view was that Sarnoff should set about to replace AM with FM to achieve the improved quality. But when he demonstrated his new scheme to Sarnoff, his friend was no longer as interested as before. To be sure, converting the world from AM to FM would have resulted in a greatly improved NBC radio network. But it would be a very expensive change, and it was not clear that the large investment would pay off. As ingenious as FM was, there was another new invention coming to fruition that had the potential to vastly increase RCA's business. This invention was, of course, television, and that was where Sarnoff chose to put his investment dollars. Modest investments were made in FM by many people, enough to start FM radio broadcasting at a modest level in parallel with AM. Frequency modulation was also adopted for the audio portion of television broadcasting. But Armstrong considered Sarnoff's rejection as the great disappointment of his life. The feelings between the two men grew so bitter that when RCA developed its own FM scheme for the television application, Armstrong sued for a patent violation. Armstrong ultimately won; however, it was his estate that collected the damages. Armstrong took his own life before the trial concluded.

Figure 3-5 shows a comparison of the two modulation processes. The FM waveform looks quite different from the AM waveform. In frequency modulation, the frequency rather than the amplitude of a carrier sine wave is modified in proportion to the amplitude of the audio signal. At

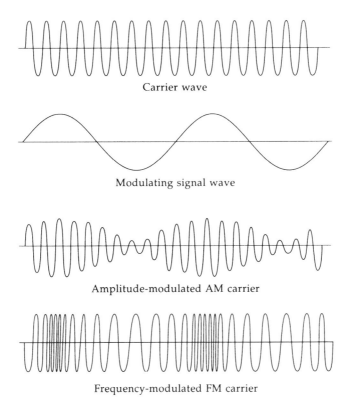

Carrier wave

Modulating signal wave

Amplitude-modulated AM carrier

Frequency-modulated FM carrier

Figure 3-5   Comparison of amplitude modulation and frequency modulation.

the peak of the modulating audio signal, the carrier frequency is increased by the largest amount, and at the trough of the modulating signal, the carrier frequency is decreased by the largest amount. Thus, the size of the maximum frequency deviation is an important contributor to the amount of bandwidth necessary to transmit the signal. For example, in the standard broadcast FM system, the carrier frequency is deviated on either side by 75 kHz to support the maximum amplitude of the audio. In a narrower bandwidth system, a carrier deviation of 10 kHz might be used to support the same audio amplitude.

The FM system achieves its improved performance over AM in both fidelity and noise resistance by using more bandwidth per channel. The band dedicated to FM radio broadcasting is 20 MHz wide, extending from 86 to 106 MHz. The channels in this band are 200 kHz wide, twenty times wider than the 10-kHz channels in the AM band. If we were to use

AM in this frequency band, we would only need 40-kHz channels to permit the broadcasting of full-frequency audio. Frequency-modulated channels are so much wider because the noise resistance of FM depends upon the amount of bandwidth used—the more the better.

The bandwidth determines the effect of noise on the system. The farther the radio receiver is from the broadcasting transmitter, the weaker the received signal. Since the receiver thermal noise level tends to remain constant, the signal-to-noise ratio at your receiver depends upon how far away the transmitter is from your home. Therefore, the acceptability of a broadcasting system depends to a large extent upon how well the system performs in the presence of noise over the entire geographic area that it is intended to serve, including the fringe areas.

Noise generally is additive. The signal in the receiver is a reduced-energy replica of the signal that was broadcast from the transmitting antenna with noise, sitting on top of it. In an AM system, this noise is added directly to the modulating signal sitting on top of the carrier, and it is not surprising that its effect is readily apparent to the ears. But FM is quite different in that the audio information is carried not in amplitude but in frequency variations. You can see from the sketch in Fig. 3-5 that, in the absence of noise, a frequency-modulated signal has a constant amplitude envelope. Thus the noise variations on the signal amplitude are of no importance, and, in fact, FM receivers get rid of this noise by clipping off any amplitude variations from the tops and bottoms of the waveforms before extracting the audio from the frequency variations. They can do this because any amplitude variations have to be due to noise of some kind.

However, noise does affect frequency as well as amplitude, the greater the frequency deviation, the less the effect. The 200-kHz frequency band was chosen for this reason. Broadcasting within this range permits the transmission of audio with frequency deviations large enough to provide significantly more immunity from noise than does AM transmission. However, the greater the dynamic range (range of amplitudes) in the audio, the greater the required frequency deviations. Because of this, even with 200-kHz-wide channels, the frequency range of the audio must be limited to 15 kHz, and the amplitude range of audio signals must be compressed before modulation. For this reason, the fidelity achievable in FM broadcasting, while much better than that of AM, is still below that achievable with high-quality analog recording and certainly below that typically achieved with digital recording.

Many FM stations transmit stereophonic signals. This simply means that they broadcast two audio signals instead of one, each obtained from a different set of microphones placed to the left and right of the signal source. Interestingly, they are able to do this in approximately the same bandwidth. The two broadcast signals are the modulated versions of $L + R$ and $L - R$, where L and R are, respectively, the audio signals from the left and right microphones. A stereophonic receiver obtains the left audio signal by adding the two signals before the demodulation process and the right audio signal by subtracting them. It then directs the two audio signals to separate audio channels that drive separate loudspeakers. This scheme is called *compatible* because a monophonic receiver can also interpret the signal. It uses the sum signal only and, therefore, behaves as if both signals originated in the same microphone. The stereo effect, of course, is not present.

The audio in a television broadcast occupies even less bandwidth than does the FM broadcast; virtually all the bandwidth used for the television transmission is consumed by the video signals. This reduced bandwidth is the principal reason why the television audio is of lower fidelity than in FM radio. In addition, the television receiver manufacturers have generally used very low-quality audio components to keep the cost of the receivers as low as possible. The resulting quality is hardly better than that of a table-top radio tuned in to an FM broadcast. Initially, the audio was monaural. Today, however, most broadcasting is binaural, and most receivers have a stereo capability. Some of these stereo receivers have higher-quality built-in audio and, even if they do not, provide a convenient way of connecting the audio signals to a high-fidelity audio system.

Of course, low-quality audio is well matched to the vast bulk of today's television programming. After all, what benefit might be attached to the use of hi-fi audio with the average sitcom? But every once in a while, there is a televised musical event of such quality as to merit high-quality audio reception.

3.2.4   Frequency and Bandwidth

The bandwidth of a radio channel is highly dependent upon the frequency band in which the channel is located. For example, a single television channel has a bandwidth six times wider than that of the entire AM band. Similarly, the entire shortwave band—which can support long-distance transmission by ionospheric reflection—is only 27 MHz wide, less than that of five television channels. It was inevitable, then, that the search for more bandwidth led to the development of the technology that permitted the use of the higher-frequency bands: first the microwave regions [the frequencies above 1000 MHz, or 1 GHz (gigahertz)] of the spectrum and later the optical regions.

The development of radar during World War II provided the microwave technology that began to be applied to telecommunications soon after the war. AT&T covered virtually the entire country with microwave relay circuits to replace its lower capacity cables. (A microwave relay is a chain of individual line-of-sight microwave radio links spanning a long distance.) Later, when the communications satellite was developed, it was used to span even longer distances for both the telephone networks and television. The satellite made a spectacular difference for transoceanic transmission where microwave relay is not a factor. Until the first Intelsat in the 1960s, all overseas telephone traffic was carried by the relatively low-capacity undersea cables, and there was no way of supporting the large bandwidths required for television. The television networks were forced to carry tapes of fast-breaking news events by jet aircraft. The communications satellite using the microwave bands has had an enormous impact on the ability of the broadcast media to bring virtually instantaneous coverage of world events into our homes.

The optical band with its enormous bandwidth was next to be exploited. Since the atmosphere presents such a severe limitation to optical propagation, it was clear from the start that optical transmission had to be by cable. It has already had an enormous impact on the telecommunications networks, first for domestic and later for overseas routes.

3.3   Analog Recording

Recording is a special kind of communication—communication with delay, as opposed to live or *real-time* communication. The entire recording and playback process constitutes the communications channel. Like any other communications channel, the recording channel introduces distortions. It may introduce frequency limitations, and it may add noise. In the old-time vinyl record, a replica of the actual audio waveform is cut into the plastic. In an analog tape recording, the replica of the audio waveform is in the form of magnetization proportional to the audio amplitude. In both cases, the playback mechanism converts the frozen image on record or tape back into an audio signal that is ultimately reconverted to an acoustic signal through a loudspeaker.

We can think of the entire chain of equipment used in the recording/ playback process as having a frequency response, analogous to the way that a telephone line has a frequency response. This frequency response determines how much of the original waveform is passed on to the listener. Similarly, the recording channel introduces noise, most of which is introduced in the playback mechanism. In the case of a record, the principal source of noise is the record scratch caused by the pickup needle as it makes physical contact with the record surface and causes a slight amount of abrasion. The effect is cumulative, and after the record is played enough, the surface noise caused by the successive abrasions interferes with the pleasure of listening, which means it's time to buy a new record to create a new channel.

This connection between communications and recording, while only of academic interest in the analog case, has become of practical significance in the development of digital recording systems. We shall see this later on.

4

THE SYMMETRY OF
FREQUENCY AND TIME—
FOURIER ANALYSIS

4.0 Representing Digital Signals

Analog communication has the virtue of being highly intuitive. You can follow every step in the process and have a feel for what is happening. Take the medium that everyone is most familiar with—the telephone. When you talk you set up vibrations in the air. The telephone microphone converts these vibrations from acoustic signals to electrical signals which are close to proportional to the original sound waves. These electrical signals travel over a series of wires and, perhaps, radio circuits until they finally arrive at the destination telephone where they are converted back to sound waves in the earpiece. Within reason, proportionality holds during the whole process. To be sure, there is some distortion: the telephone system will cut off any frequencies above and below its range, and noise will be added. But this is all easy to understand conceptually. Very similar processes occur in broadcasting. The original audio signal is recognizable as it rides on top of the carrier in AM and only slightly less so in the frequency variations of FM.

Unfortunately, this is not the case when the transmission is digital. When the human voice is to be sent digitally, the electrical signals coming from the microphone have to be converted to a string of 0s and 1s, but a stream of digits is a stream of digits regardless of its origin. When you observe such a stream, you cannot tell whether it comes from the human voice or a violin, or whether it represents an E-mail message or a financial report. The signals carrying digital information represent simply numbers, 0s and 1s, mathematical abstractions. This very sameness in digital transmission blurs the connection between the transmitted signals and the source information always present in analog communications. Look how beautifully the cartoonist, Garry Trudeau, pokes fun at this in Fig. 4-1.

However, there are things that help bridge the gap between the faceless digits and the information they represent. We do not send mathematical abstractions over telephone lines and radio circuits. Real media require real signals. Therefore, we have to represent the digits by electrical signals or *waveforms*, before they can be transmitted. These waveforms have to obey certain fundamental laws if they are to represent the information adequately and conform to the requirements of the channel. This chapter begins the discussion of these fundamental laws. Understanding them will begin the process of making the transmission of digits more intuitive. You will never reach the point of swooning over a sequence of 0s and 1s as in the cartoon. But you will be on your way to understanding why digital transmission techniques have become so important in both the communications and recording industries.

Figure 4-1   A catchy digital tune. (DOONESBURY Copyright 1988 G.B. Trudeau. Reprinted with permission of Universal Press Syndicate. All rights reserved.)

4.1 Digital Waveforms

Digital transmission is similar to analog transmission in many ways. To communicate data in digital form over communications media such as telephone lines or radio circuits, the digits have to be represented by waveforms that are compatible with the transmission media. A stream of binary digits is converted to a stream of waveforms, one waveform representing a 1 and another representing a 0. These waveforms, like all waveforms in this world, have frequencies and bandwidths and are transmitted through the channel in ways that are similar to the transmission of analog voice signals.

Like an analog signal, a digital signal must also be tailored to the channel that will transport it. From the beginnings of telephony, the phone line's bandwidth was designed to be large enough to convey most of the intelligibility of the speech signals and a good deal of speaker recognizability. To send digits over these same phone lines, you have to use signals that occupy a band of frequencies that fit within the phone line passband.

An example of digital signals that might be used on a telephone line is shown in Fig. 4-2. It is the same scheme that was used in chapter 2 to introduce digital communications. In this scheme, a 1 is represented by a signal pulse T seconds long, and a 0 is represented by the absence of a pulse for the same T seconds. One binary digit is sent every T seconds, making the data rate $1/T$ bits per second (bps). Thus, if the pulse is 1 ms long, then the data rate is 1000 bps. The shorter the pulse interval T, the higher the data rate.

Sending Morse code over a radio circuit is similar. Figure 4-3 shows examples of the signals that are typically used. A long pulse of a radio-frequency carrier represents a dash, and a short pulse of the same carrier represents a dot. (We could substitute 1 and 0 for dash and dot, respectively.) In this case, too, the shorter the pulses the higher the data rate.

Figure 4-2 On/off signaling.

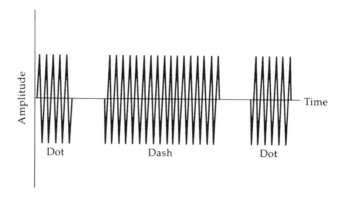

Figure 4-3   Radio telegraphy.

But changing the signal width to vary the data rate also changes the bandwidth of the signal. The nature of this relationship between pulse duration and bandwidth is at the heart of digital signaling.

4.2   Bandwidth and Signal Duration

The general rule that relates signal (pulse) duration and bandwidth is reciprocality: the bandwidth, suitably defined, is the reciprocal of the signal duration. If you know the duration of a pulse, then you also know its bandwidth. A signal 1 s long has a bandwidth of 1 Hz, and a signal ten times longer has a bandwidth $1/_{10}$ as large. This reciprocal relationship holds for signals of all shapes and sizes.

A signal 1 ms long with a bandwidth of 1 kHz will easily fit into a telephone line's bandwidth. In contrast, a signal 0.1 ms long has a bandwidth of 10 kHz, two to three times wider than a telephone line's bandwidth. Thus, when using the on/off signaling scheme of Fig. 4-2, we can easily signal at a rate of 1000 bps or 1 kbps, but not at a rate of 10 kbps. When these on/off signals are used, the bandwidth of the signals and the data rate are numerically the same. This has led to the use of the terms data rate and bandwidth interchangeably when speaking of digital channels. This loose terminology is neither accurate nor desirable because there are other signaling schemes and noise conditions in which the data rate, while always related to the bandwidth, does not equal it. Therefore, I will preserve the distinction between the two terms.

Reciprocal relationships like this one between time and frequency are found elsewhere. For example, the view angle of a lens is related to the diameter of the lens reciprocally. A large lens has a small view angle and vice versa. A large telescope such as the instrument on Mount Palomar obtains its power to see very distant objects at the cost of a very narrow field of view, just as communications signals obtain their ability to represent high-rate information at the cost of higher bandwidths. The same thing is true of dish antennas commonly used for communicating with satellites: the larger the antenna diameter, the greater its transmitting or receiving capability, but the narrower the beam formed by the antenna.

Quantum mechanics describes the motion of atomic particles. Heisenberg's famous uncertainty principle states that it is impossible to measure the position and velocity of a particle *simultaneously* with perfect accuracy. The greater the accuracy by which the position is measured, the poorer the accuracy by which the velocity can be determined, and vice versa. The two accuracies or uncertainties are related reciprocally.

All these examples of the reciprocality relationship obey the same kinds of mathematical formulas, even though the physical principles seem markedly different. The mathematics has its origin in the work of the nineteenth-century French mathematician, Jean-Baptiste Joseph Fourier. This mathematics, called *Fourier analysis*, describes the behavior of signals.

Fourier's mathematics was motivated by his interest in explaining heat conduction phenomena. In contrast, most pure mathematics in the latter half of the twentieth century has been an intellectual pursuit inspired by its inherent interest rather than motivated by the need to solve physical problems. Indeed, David Hilbert, one of the giants of early twentieth century mathematics, when asked to address a Joint Congress of Pure and Applied Mathematics to break down the supposed hostility between the two groups, began his talk in the following way:

> We are often told that pure and applied mathematics are hostile to each other. This is not true. Pure and applied mathematics are not hostile to each other. Pure and applied mathematics have never been hostile to each other. Pure and applied mathematics will never be hostile to each other. Pure and applied mathematics cannot be hostile to each other, because, in fact, there is absolutely nothing in common between them.

Not so in previous generations. Before the modern age of specialization, mathematicians and physicists were often indistinguishable. Fourier contributed to both fields. It is also of interest that he was not only a brilliant and eclectic scientist but also a man active in the affairs of the world. He lived in a time of great political and military turmoil in his native country, and he participated in these events as they unfolded both in the early days of the French revolution (to his credit, he is said to have opposed its bloodier aspects) and later during the reign of Napoleon.

4.3 Introduction to Fourier Analysis: Musical Waveforms

Our task at hand is to gain an understanding of these reciprocality relationships in waveforms that might be used to represent digital communications signals. A good place to begin to build up intuition about these relationships is with musical waveforms. The role of frequencies and harmonics in describing musical sounds is something well known. For example, you can sound the same note on the piano and oboe, recognize them as the same note, but, at the same time, recognize that they sound different. The reason, of course, is while both sounds have the same pitch or fundamental frequency, they also have distinct patterns of the harmonics of this fundamental frequency. In principle, one could compute the pattern of harmonics for each instrument by analyzing the sound production mechanisms of each. However, these mechanisms are generally too complex to do much analytically. What Fourier's mathematics allows you to do, however, is to analyze the waveform that each instrument produces when it sounds the note, and from this analysis you can determine the relative amounts of each harmonic constituting the sound.

According to Fourier's theory, a periodic waveform is a periodic waveform regardless of its origin. Periodic waveforms that arise from nonmusical sources have the same characteristics as periodic musical waveforms. Because the underlying mathematics is the same, we can take principles that apply to music and apply them elsewhere beyond the acoustical realm, using the insights derived from the musical connection. These principles provide the link connecting digital to analog communications. But even aside from this, Fourier's analysis has an esthetic appeal that transcends any application to specific practical problems.

4.3.1 Pulsing a Tuning Fork

We will begin to make these notions more concrete by applying them to an idealized musical instrument—a tuning fork that we pulse on and off. I have chosen the tuning fork because its sound is close to that of a single frequency without harmonics. This is, of course, the property that makes it so useful to a piano tuner.

Let's imagine an idealized experiment in which we sound a 100-Hz tuning fork for precisely 1 s, stop it for 1 s, restart it for 1 s, and so forth. The result is a rhythmic sequence of tone pulses that, when played on a violin or other stringed instrument, is called *tremolo*. Its waveform, shown in Fig. 4-4, looks very much like the Morse code waveform of Fig. 4-3. What can we say about its constituent frequencies? We know that there must be frequency components in addition to 100 Hz, because it sounds different from the sound produced when the tuning fork is allowed to vibrate indefinitely. While the tuning fork is being sounded, its frequency is 100 Hz, but it is only being sounded half the time.

The waveform shown in Fig. 4-4 is very similar to the waveform in Fig. 4-2. It is periodic with a fundamental frequency of 0.5 Hz, since the pulses occur at the rate of 1 every 2 s. The higher harmonics in hertz are 1, 1.5, 2, 2.5, and so forth. These harmonics must continue at least up to 100 Hz, the tuning-fork frequency, and even beyond, because the rapid beginnings and endings of the pulses must indicate the presence of some much higher frequencies.

But we can make another important observation: turning the tuning fork on and off is exactly equivalent to multiplying the 100-Hz tuning-fork sine wave by a square wave that is 1 for 1 s, then 0 for 1 s, then 1 for 1 s, and so on, that is, the waveform in Fig. 4-2. This is an example of

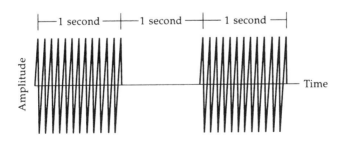

Figure 4-4 Pulsed tuning-fork waveform.

amplitude modulation, as defined in the last chapter. The difference is that now we are modulating the tuning-fork carrier frequency by a square wave instead of a sine wave. Figure 4-5 shows the result of modulating or multiplying the tuning-fork sine wave by a sine wave with a frequency of 0.5 Hz, the fundamental frequency of the square wave. While you could not do this with an actual tuning fork, you could do it with an electronic music synthesizer, which can create any combination of tones. The modulated tone would sound like a 100-Hz tone with a pulsating wobble, similar, perhaps, to an electronic version of Bert Lahr's singing as the Cowardly Lion in *The Wizard of Oz.*

As we saw in chapter 3, when a carrier frequency's amplitude is modulated by a sine wave, the resulting waveform contains three frequencies: the carrier frequency and the frequencies obtained by adding and subtracting the modulating frequency from the carrier. Since, in this case, the carrier is the 100-Hz tuning-fork tone and the modulating frequency is the 0.5-Hz sine wave, the waveform contains the frequencies 99.5 and 100.5 Hz in addition to the 100-Hz carrier frequency.

As we also saw in chapter 3, when you amplitude-modulate a carrier with an audio signal containing any number of different frequencies, you obtain the sum and difference frequencies of the carrier and all the audio components. For this reason, an audio band containing all the frequencies up to 5 kHz, when amplitude-modulating a carrier, produces all the frequencies 5 kHz above and below this carrier, thereby filling an entire allocated AM channel of 10 kHz. This gives us a clue to the nature of the frequency components of the pulsed tuning-fork waveform. According to Fourier, the modulating square wave will contain all the harmonics of its

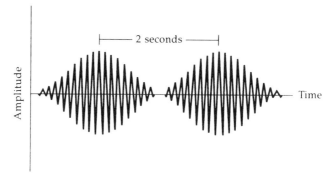

Figure 4-5   Tuning-fork waveform modulated by a sine wave.

0.5-Hz fundamental. Thus the pulsed tuning-fork waveform should contain, in addition to the 100-Hz carrier, all the sum and difference frequencies of the carrier and each of these harmonics. The relative amplitudes of these various frequency components can be determined by Fourier's analysis.

4.3.2   Fourier Analysis of Periodic Waveforms

Fourier's fundamental theorem for periodic functions says that a periodic time function $h(t)$ of period T can be expressed as a sum of sine and cosine waves multiplied by appropriate coefficients, where the frequencies of the sines and cosines are the harmonics of the fundamental frequency $1/T$. Thus if $h(t)$ represents the piano sounding middle A (440 Hz), Fourier's theorem provides a way of computing the amount of each of the harmonics of 440 Hz constituting the sound. Similarly, if the function represents the oboe sounding the same note, the theorem does the same thing. And, of course, in the very special case where the function represents a tuning fork sounding 440 Hz, the coefficients of all but the fundamental frequency have to be 0.

The way this goes in mathematical form is shown in Eq. 4-1:

$$h(t) = a_0 + \sum_{n=1}^{\infty} a_n \cos \frac{2\pi nt}{T} + \sum_{n=1}^{\infty} b_n \sin \frac{2\pi nt}{T}, \qquad (4\text{-}1)$$

showing explicitly $h(t)$ as a constant term plus a sum of cosines and sines of the harmonics of the fundamental frequency each multiplied by a specific coefficient. Having both sines and cosines complicates the equation a little, but they are both necessary if we want to describe a function with arbitrary phase. However, if $h(t)$ is an *even* function—that is, one in which $h(-t) = h(t)$—then only the cosines are needed. Similarly if it is *odd* —one in which $h(-t) = -h(t)$—then only the sines are needed.

There is an equivalent formulation of Eq. 4-1 in terms of complex numbers that is useful in some cases:

$$h(t) = \sum_{n=-\infty}^{+\infty} c_n e^{j\frac{2\pi nt}{T}}, \qquad (4\text{-}1a)$$

where $j = \sqrt{-1}$ and the coefficients c_n are complex numbers. This form, while more compact, hides the explicit dependence on the phase.

The Fourier series has a geometric interpretation. You know that a vector in space can be represented by its components along the coordinate axes, or as the vector sum $a_x\mathbf{i_x} + a_y\mathbf{i_y} + a_z\mathbf{i_z}$, where the $\mathbf{i}$s are unit vectors along the three coordinate axes and the as are the components of the vector along the axes. In the Fourier series, the function plays the role of the vector, the sines and cosines (or complex exponentials) play the role of the unit vectors, and the coefficients are like the vector components. This so-called *function space* has an infinite number of dimensions, not just three, but the principles are the same. The analogy becomes a little clearer when you consider the way the coefficients are computed.

$$a_0 = \frac{1}{T}\int_0^T h(t)\,dt,$$

$$a_n = \frac{2}{T}\int_0^T h(t)\cos\frac{2\pi nt}{T}\,dt, \quad n = 1, 2, \ldots, \qquad (4\text{-}2)$$

$$b_n = \frac{2}{T}\int_0^T h(t)\sin\frac{2\pi nt}{T}\,dt, \quad n = 1, 2, \ldots,$$

The coefficient a_0 is simply the average value or direct-current (DC) component of the function. The integrals for computing the other as and bs are now the equivalent of computing the components of the vector along the coordinate axes.

In order for the analogy to be complete, the sines and cosines must be *orthogonal* to one another, just as the unit vectors along the coordinate axes are perpendicular to one another. Equations 4-3 show that this is, in fact, the case:

$$\frac{2}{T}\int_0^T \cos\frac{2\pi mt}{T}\cos\frac{2\pi nt}{T}\,dt = \begin{cases}1 & n = m \\ 0 & n \neq m\end{cases}, \qquad (4\text{-}3a)$$

$$\frac{2}{T}\int_0^T \sin\frac{2\pi mt}{T}\sin\frac{2\pi nt}{T}\,dt = \begin{cases}1 & n = m \\ 0 & n \neq m\end{cases}, \qquad (4\text{-}3b)$$

$$\frac{2}{T}\int_0^T \sin\frac{2\pi mt}{T}\cos\frac{2\pi nt}{T}\,dt = 0 \quad \text{all } m,n. \qquad (4\text{-}3c)$$

That is to say, the only integrals (components) that are not 0 are those for which both the functions and the frequencies are the same.

4.3.3   Fourier Analysis of a Square Wave

Let's take an example of the square wave of Fig. 4-2 to obtain more insight into the way all this works. To make life a little simpler, let's assume that the square wave is an even function, so that all its frequency components are cosines. That is, the wave has amplitude 1 from $t = -T/4$ to $t = T/4$ and amplitude 0 from $t = T/4$ to $t = 3\,T/4$, and then keeps repeating itself. If $T = 2$ s, the square wave has a fundamental frequency of 0.5 Hz and harmonics at 1, 1.5, 2 Hz, and so forth.

The frequency components can be calculated using Eq. 4-2 as follows:

$$a_n = \frac{2}{T} \int_{\frac{T}{4}}^{\frac{3T}{4}} h(t) \cos \frac{2\pi n t}{T}\, dt =$$

$$a_n = \frac{2}{T} \int_{-T/4}^{T/4} \cos \frac{2\pi n t}{T}\, dt = \tag{4-4}$$

$$\frac{1}{\pi n} \sin \frac{2\pi n t}{T}\bigg]_{-T/4}^{T/4} = \frac{1}{\pi n}\, 2 \sin \frac{\pi n}{2} = \frac{\sin \pi n/2}{\pi n/2}, \quad n = 1, 2, \ldots.$$

The first observation to be made from Eq. 4-4 is that coefficients for all the even harmonics are 0. Then the odd harmonics alternate in sign, positive for $n = 1, 5, 9, \ldots$, and negative for $n = 3, 7, 11, \ldots$. And, of course, since n appears in the denominator, the successive coefficients decrease in amplitude. Note also the form $\sin x/x$. As we shall see shortly, this form is characteristic of a rectangular pulse, but not necessarily a square one as in the example.

The most illustrative way of viewing the Fourier coefficients is to plot them against frequency as in Fig. 4-6. We call this plot the *spectrum* of the square-wave function of Fig. 4-2. It contains the same information as the function itself but in the frequency as opposed to the time domain. We also show on the graph the function $\sin x/x$ that forms the envelope of the Fourier coefficients. It has a large positive half lobe beginning at the left end with subsidiary full lobes alternating in sign and decreasing in

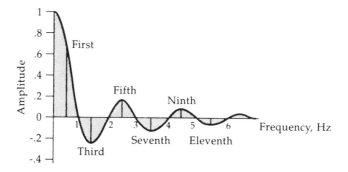

Figure 4-6   The frequency components of a square wave.

amplitude as the frequency increases. The amplitude of any particular harmonic of the square wave is given by the height of the curve at the frequency of that harmonic. The fundamental frequency of 0.5 Hz falls in the middle of the first lobe, and the second harmonic occurs at the junction of the first and second lobes. From then on, the odd harmonics fall at the peaks of the lobes and the even harmonics at the lobe junctions. This shows us in pictorial form what we have already calculated: that the even harmonics all have zero amplitude, and that the odd harmonics have alternating signs and decreasing amplitudes. While the exact relationship of the various harmonics is a consequence of the pulse being square, the shape of the envelope is more general. As we shall see in a moment, if the on and off times of the tuning fork are not the same, the positions of the harmonics will change, and the even harmonics will play a role, but the envelope remains.

The fact that the amplitudes of the lobes decrease fairly rapidly as the frequency increases means that the low-numbered harmonics, with their larger amplitudes will contribute most to the square wave, and we can probably neglect most of the higher harmonics.

Now let's return to our on/off tuning-fork waveform. The preceding discussion tells us that the square-wave modulating signal can be represented by a few of the lower harmonics of 0.5 Hz. It follows that modulating the tuning-fork sine wave with the square wave is just the same as modulating it by the sum of these few harmonics. We would therefore expect the frequency components of the tuning fork modulated by the square wave to be the sum and difference frequencies of the carrier and these harmonics. Thus, the frequency components of the pulsed tuning fork are

Carrier 100 Hz

First harmonic 99.5 and 100.5 Hz

Second harmonic 99.0 and 101.0 Hz

Third harmonic 98.5 and 101.5 Hz

Fourth harmonic 98.0 and 102.0 Hz

Fifth harmonic 97.5 and 102.5 Hz

(etc.)

I have used the word *harmonic* in the table above somewhat loosely. The first harmonic is the sum and difference of the carrier and the fundamental (first harmonic) of the square wave. And the table includes the even harmonics even though we know that their amplitudes are zero. The reason for this will become clear a little later.

The amplitudes of these modulated harmonics are shown in Fig. 4-7. The curve looks similar to the curve in Fig. 4-6 because it is obtained by laying the curve of Fig. 4-6 on either side of the 100-Hz carrier, the pictorial equivalent of taking the sum and difference frequencies. Now the initial half lobe of Fig. 4-6 becomes a central lobe in Fig. 4-7, and the subsidiary side lobes appear symmetrically on either side of the carrier. Since the Fig. 4-7 picture is another view of Fig. 4-6, the harmonics fall at the same places on the curve *relative* to the carrier frequency. The first harmonic frequencies fall within the central lobe. All the other odd harmonics fall on the peaks of the successive side lobes, and the even harmonics,

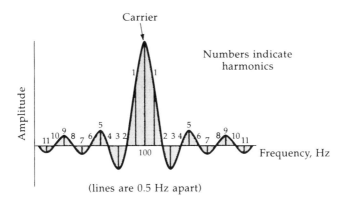

Figure 4-7 Amplitudes of the harmonics of the pulsed tuning fork of Fig. 4-4.

as before, fall on the lobe junctions. These junctions are commonly called *zero crossings* for obvious reasons. The positions of these zero crossings are of very great significance. The first occur 1 Hz (the reciprocal of the pulse width) on either side of the carrier tone. This means that the central lobe has a width from zero crossing to zero crossing of 2 Hz or twice the reciprocal of the pulse width. The other lobes have widths one-half that of the central lobe.

If the tuning fork were allowed to sound indefinitely, its waveform would contain a single frequency of 100 Hz, a single line at the peak of the central lobe in the picture of Fig. 4-7. Thus, the effect of the pulsing is to replace the single line with a sequence of lines clustered around the tuning-fork frequency. The width of the central lobe is, in some sense, representative of the bandwidth of the pulse.

The waveforms shown in Fig. 4-8 are obtained by synthesizing the pulsed tuning-fork waveform from its constituent harmonics with the am-

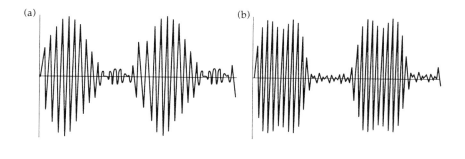

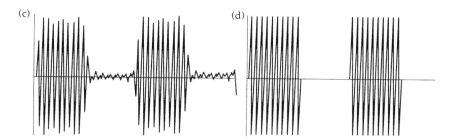

Figure 4-8   Reproduction of the pulsed tuning-fork waveform synthesized from its Fourier components. (a) Sum of the carrier and first harmonics; (b) third harmonics added; (c) all harmonics up through the fifth; (d) all harmonics.

plitudes as given in Fig. 4-7. Trace (a) shows the sum of the carrier and the first harmonics; in trace (b), the third harmonics are added; and in trace (c), all the harmonics up through the fifth. Note that with as few as three frequency components, the general shape of the square wave becomes evident. As more harmonics are added, a better approximation of the square wave is obtained. If we were to use all the harmonics, we would reproduce the original waveform shown in trace (d).

4.3.4 Pulsing a Tuning Fork: Unequal On/Off Times

Now let's modify our hypothetical tuning-fork experiment slightly. Instead of sounding the tuning fork for 1 s at 1-s intervals, we will sound it for 1 s and leave it off for 3 s, producing the waveform shown in Fig. 4-9. It is similar to the original waveform shown in Fig. 4-4. But now the 1-s pulse is followed by 3 s of off time, resulting in a rectangular wave with a period of 4 s instead of a square wave with a period of 2 s. With these modified parameters, the fundamental frequency of the waveform is now 0.25 Hz instead of 0.5 Hz. Using the same rule as above, the frequency components are

First harmonic	99.75 and 100.25 Hz
Second harmonic	99.5 and 100.5 Hz
Third harmonic	99.25 and 100.75 Hz
(etc.)	

The amplitudes associated with each frequency component are also shown in Fig. 4-9. The envelope of the curve is identical to that shown in Fig. 4-7. But now the spacing of the frequency components is half that in the first example, because the period of the wave has doubled. The first three pairs of harmonics occur within the central lobe, as compared to the first pair in the previous example. And the fourth, eighth, twelfth, and so forth, harmonics, rather than all the even harmonics, occur at the zero crossings. If we attempted to synthesize the waveform by adding up its constituent harmonics, as we did before, we would have to use twice as many to obtain the same degree of approximation.

If we repeat the experiment, each time separating the pulses of tuning-fork vibration by greater and greater intervals, the harmonics of the waveforms would move closer and closer together—but always with the

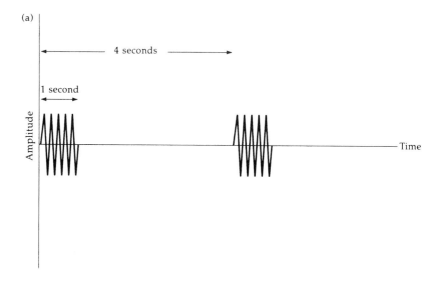

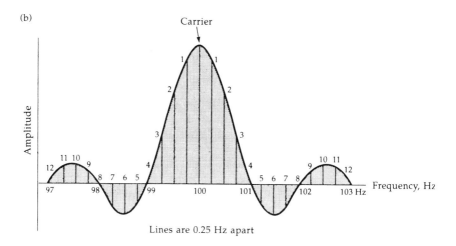

Figure 4-9   Pulsed tuning-fork waveform with 4-s period. (a) Sounding the tuning fork for 1s every 4s. (b) Amplitudes of the harmonics.

same envelope shown in Fig. 4-7. In the extreme case where the pulses are very far apart, the frequency components are so close to one another that they form a continuum completely covering the envelope of Fig. 4-7.

In each experiment, the location of the harmonics depends upon how often the tuning fork is sounded—the more often, the farther apart the successive harmonics. However, the curve (the *spectral envelope*) that determines the amplitude of the harmonics, wherever they occur, is the same, because this curve depends only upon the *shape* of the pulse and not at all upon how often the pulse occurs. This allows us to separate the effects of pulse width from the effects of pulse periodicity. The harmonics of a rectangular pulse of length T always have the same spectral envelope, regardless of how often the pulses occur. The periodicity of the pulse lets us locate the harmonic lines on this spectral envelope.

4.4   The Fourier Transform

There is a mathematical way of showing the effects due to pulse width divorced entirely from the effects of pulse periodicity. This technique lets us compute the spectra of pulses that are not necessarily periodic. Of course, this technique has to be related in some way to the Fourier series that we have been dealing with up to now. It is also due to Fourier and is called the *Fourier transform*. The construction of the last section in which we pulse a tuning fork at increasingly large intervals is a physical way of demonstrating the mathematical process of letting the time between successive pulses increase indefinitely, taking us from the Fourier series to the Fourier transform.

To see how this works mathematically, let $h(t)$ be a time function, not necessarily periodic, and let $H(f)$ be its Fourier transform. The two functions are then related in the following way:

$$H(f) = \int_{-\infty}^{+\infty} h(t)e^{-j\,2\pi ft}dt, \qquad (4\text{-}5a)$$

$$h(t) = \int_{-\infty}^{+\infty} H(f)e^{j\,2\pi ft}df. \qquad (4\text{-}5b)$$

The beauty of these relationships lies in their symmetry: You can go either way, from frequency to time or vice versa, with almost the same expression. Note the analogy with the Fourier series. Equation 4-5(b) is analogous to the series itself, while Eq. 4-5(a) is analogous to the expression for the coefficients of the series, especially evident in the exponential form shown in Eq. 4-1(a).

To see how this goes, let's go back to the example of Fig. 4-2, only instead of considering a periodic train of pulses, we take only the one at the origin and call its width τ. Substituting this value for $h(t)$ in Eq. 4-5(a), we can evaluate $H(f)$ as follows:

$$H(f) = \int_{-\infty}^{+\infty} h(t)e^{-j\,2\pi ft}dt = \int_{-\tau/2}^{+\tau/2} e^{-j\,2\pi ft}dt =$$

$$-\frac{1}{2\pi jf}(-2j)\sin \pi f\tau = \tau \frac{\sin \pi f\tau}{\pi f\tau}.$$

(4-6)

This gives us the characteristic expression of sin x/x, the envelope of the functions that we derived before using the Fourier series, interpreted as the spectrum you obtain as the separation between pulses increases indefinitely.

Now suppose we let the pulse width τ decrease and, at the same time, let its amplitude be $1/\tau$ so that the area under the pulse stays constant. Substituting these values into Eq. 4-6, $H(f)$ becomes sin $\pi f\tau/\pi f\tau$, which goes to 1 as τ goes to 0, showing that the spectrum of a very narrow pulse is flat in frequency. Equation 4-5(b) tells us that if we substitute this value for $H(f)$, the result should be $h(t)$. In other words, the value of the integral

$$\int_{-\infty}^{+\infty} H(f)e^{j\,2\pi ft}dt = \int_{-\infty}^{+\infty} e^{j\,2\pi ft}dt \equiv \delta(t)$$

(4-7)

should be a time pulse of zero width and infinite height that we call $\delta(t)$. The physicist Paul Dirac ran into the same function in his pioneering work in quantum mechanics in the 1930s, and we now call the function the Dirac *delta function* or the *impulse function* with the symbol $\delta(t)$. This function has the following properties:

$$\delta(t) = \{ \begin{array}{ll} 1 & \text{for } t = 0, \\ 0 & \text{for } t \neq 0, \end{array}$$

$$\int_{-\infty}^{+\infty} \delta(t)dt = 1,$$

(4-8)

which is simply a symbolic way of stating what we expressed previously in words. We arrived at the delta function by taking a rectangular pulse and letting its width go to 0 while keeping the area under the curve constant. There are many other ways of doing it, but, no matter how, the basic properties of the function are the same.

A useful property of the delta function is shown in Eq. 4-9.

$$\int_{-\infty}^{+\infty} \delta(t - t_0)y(t)dt = y(t_0), \qquad (4\text{-}9)$$

allowing the delta function to select out a particular value of some arbitrary function y. This property makes it very convenient to go from the time to the frequency domain and vice versa. In particular, it helps us connect the Fourier transform to the Fourier series. To see this, suppose we have a periodic function $h(t)$ that has a Fourier series

$$h(t) = \sum_{n=-\infty}^{n=+\infty} c_n e^{j2\pi nt/T}, \qquad (4\text{-}10)$$

where we are using the complex formulation of Eq. 4-1(a) rather than the formulation in terms of sines and cosines. The time function $h(t)$ has a Fourier transform $H(f)$ given by

$$H(f) = \int_{-\infty}^{+\infty} h(t)e^{2\pi jft}dt = \int_{-\infty}^{+\infty} \sum_{n=-\infty}^{+\infty} c_n e^{2\pi jnt/T} e^{2\pi jft}dt$$

$$\qquad (4\text{-}11)$$

$$= \sum_{n=-\infty}^{+\infty} c_n \delta(f - n/T).$$

This expression states explicitly that the frequency function or spectrum has a series of lines at the harmonics of $1/T$ with the amplitudes given by the coefficients c_n. If $h(t)$ is a periodic sequence of delta functions, then all the cs are unity and the spectrum $H(f)$ is also a set of delta functions with equal amplitudes.

4.4.1 Interpretation of Pulsed Waveforms from Their Fourier Transforms

There is a great deal that we can infer from the discussion in the previous sections. First, we have demonstrated the promised reciprocal relationship: a pulse T seconds long has a bandwidth of approximately $1/T$ Hz. This follows directly from Figs. 4-6 and 4-8, as well as Eq. 4-6. I used the qualifier *approximately* because the width can be estimated in different ways. The width between zero crossings is one way. Another, perhaps more reasonable, way approximates the effective width of the spectrum by half the total width of the central lobe in recognition of the fact that the amplitudes of any harmonics occurring near the zero crossings are small. Whatever the particular definition of bandwidth, a very long pulse has a very narrow spectrum, and vice versa. A very long pulse would result from striking a tuning fork and allowing it to vibrate for a long time before stopping it. In this case, the spectrum of the waveform is the frequency of the tuning-fork vibration with a very narrow envelope—in essence, the single tuning-fork frequency that a piano tuner finds useful.

By the same token, if a pulse is very narrow (say, approximating a delta function), its spectrum is very wide. A periodic series (or train) of very narrow pulses results in a spectrum wide enough for a very large number of harmonics to fit in the central lobe. Figure 4-10 shows this pictorially. Figure 4-10(a) shows the pulsed tuning-fork waveform with pulses 0.1 ms wide occurring every 10 ms, corresponding to a 100-Hz rate. Figure 4-10(b) shows the spectrum of this pulse train. The central lobe has a total width (zero crossing to zero crossing) of 20 kHz (2/0.0001 s). Therefore, the first one hundred harmonic pairs of the waveform fit in this central lobe. The spectrum of these pulses is a train of harmonic frequencies of about the same amplitude.

Every pulse shape has a particular spectral envelope associated with it, determined by the Fourier transform of the particular pulse. The specific spectral envelope of Fig. 4-7 that we have been using for all our examples to this point applies only to rectangular pulses. These contribute the high-frequency components of the beginning and end of the pulse. Such pulses have an idealized shape with perfectly vertical sides, which implies that the tuning fork is turned on and off instantaneously. In musical terms, it implies infinitely fast *attacks* and *releases*, the terms commonly used to characterize the beginnings and ends of musical phrases. It is easy to see that the steeper the sides of these waveforms, the greater their high-frequency content. These high frequencies appear in the spectral envelope as the long train of side lobes. If the pulse is not rectangular, the shape of its spectrum will be different from that shown in Fig. 4-7. For example, if the tuning fork is turned on and off with sloppy rather than sharp attacks and releases, there will be fewer high-frequency com-

(a)

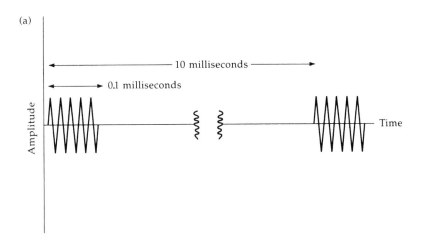

(b)

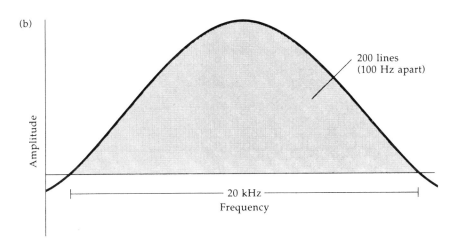

Figure 4-10   Spectrum of widely separated narrow pulses. (a) Time waveform. (b) Spectrum of waveform in (a).

ponents, and the resulting spectrum will have reduced side lobes. In the extreme case where the pulse of tone has a bell shape, the frequency spectrum has a single lobe that is also bell shaped; the side lobes disappear. You can show this for yourself by evaluating Eq. 4-6. The bell-shaped or Gaussian function is one whose spectrum can be evaluated in closed form. As you can well imagine, most of the pulse shapes that you can imagine are not amenable to such evaluation.

Regardless of the detailed shape, the reciprocality relationship still holds: if you define the width of the pulse in some reasonable way, its spectrum will have a width approximately equal to the reciprocal of the pulse width.

Figure 4-11 summarizes the reciprocal properties of time and frequency that we have just been discussing. Figures 4-11(a) through 4-11(c) describe the general properties of the spectra of waveforms independent of the detailed shape of the spectra. Note that Fig. 4-11(c) indicates that a sequence of narrow pulses has a spectrum that is a sequence

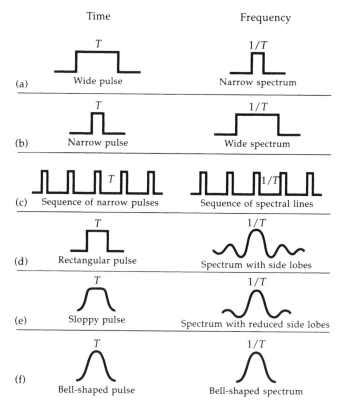

Figure 4-11   Time and frequency reciprocality. (a) through (c) General properties of the spectra of waveforms. (d) through (f) Dependence of the shape of the spectrum on the steepness of the waveform.

of narrow functions in the frequency domain—a fact that follows directly from Eq. 4-12. Figures 4-11(d) through 4-11(f) show the dependence of the shape of the spectrum on the steepness of the waveform. This figure can serve as a useful reference when we discuss waveforms of various kinds in later chapters.

4.5   Sending Signals over Wires at Baseband

The relationships between the shapes of waveforms and their spectra are perfectly general. They apply to all sorts of waveforms, not simply those that are related to the pulsed tuning fork or ones like it. Knowing these properties of waveforms permits the design of waveforms suitable for transferring digital signals either within computers or between computers located at great distances from each other.

The process is conceptually simple. The basic digital communications task is to transfer a number from one place to another. It does not matter whether that number is a piece of data stored in a computer or a number derived from the conversion of audio sounds. This number can be thought of as a sequence of binary digits, and the first step in the process is to convert the digits into a sequence of pulses as in Fig. 4-2. We call these *baseband* pulses; they have no carrier associated with them. These may then be moved up in frequency as the circumstance demands.

Baseband pulses, representing 0s and 1s as in Fig. 4-2, transport signals from one place to another within a computer. These signals are transferred at very high speeds with timescales quite different from our audio examples. Computer pulses are usually measured in minute fractions of microseconds, rather than in seconds or milliseconds. For example, a personal computer may use a pulse rate of 100 million per second, corresponding to a period of 10 ns (10^{-9} s). The pulses themselves must be considerably narrower with correspondingly wider bandwidths. But, despite the wide difference in scale between these pulses and the audio scale of our examples, all the principles are the same.

Whatever their speeds, these baseband signals have spectra analogous to that shown in Fig. 4-6 for the square wave of Fig. 4-2. This particular spectrum shows only the "positive" frequency components derived from the Fourier series. A negative frequency is just the same as a positive frequency with a 180-degree phase change; this will not affect any

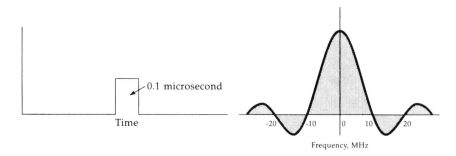

Figure 4-12   A baseband pulse and its spectrum.

of our discussions. (Note that the Fourier transform includes negative frequencies, as does the complex formulation of the Fourier series.) Just imagine this spectrum reflected about the vertical axis to get the full sin $^x/x$ function including the negative frequencies. Another way of obtaining this spectrum is to take the pulsed tuning-fork spectrum shown in Fig. 4-7 and imagine that the carrier frequency is 0 Hz rather than 100 Hz. Of course, when you do this, the spectrum loses the significance of being representative of a tuning fork. We show this explicitly in Fig. 4-12 for a single pulse 0.1 μs wide.

Baseband pulses at very high speeds are practical only for transmission over short distances, say, within a computer chip or between close neighbors. To transmit pulses over longer distances, modulation is almost always required, analogous to the way analog waveforms are modulated for AM or FM transmission. When it comes to telephone line transmission, however, there is a difference: When we talk on the telephone, the audio signals coming out of the telephone microphone are fed directly to the telephone line with no modulation interposed. In contrast to such analog audio transmission, digital transmission over telephone circuits does require a carrier. The reason for this, shown in Fig. 4-13, is that the phone line has a passband between about 300 and 3000 Hz, while a baseband waveform is centered at 0 Hz. Therefore, the pulse spectrum must be translated so that the center frequency of its main lobe is near the center of the phone line passband at 1650 Hz. Also, the width of the lobe has to be small enough so that it fits within the phone line passband. Practically speaking, the maximum data rate that a phone line can support with the binary signaling that we have been discussing is in the vicinity of 2400

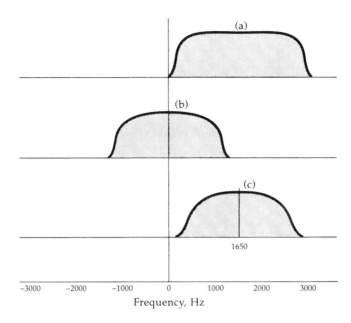

Figure 4-13 Sending pulses over telephone lines. (a) Telephone line passband; (b) spectrum of pulse at baseband; (c) pulse spectrum translated to center of telephone line passband.

bps. At this rate, most of the significant portion of the center lobe of the pulse spectrum is contained within the phone line passband. If you are accustomed to using a computer on-line, you most likely send and receive your data at many times that rate. This requires different modulation techniques that we discuss later.

5

INFORMATION THEORY, MODULATION, AND CODING

5.0 Introduction: The Goals of Information Theory

"The fundamental problem of communication is that of reproducing at one point either exactly or approximately a message selected at another point." Thus states Claude Shannon in the introduction to his revolutionary paper in 1948. In what he called the *Mathematical Theory of Communication*, subsequently called *Information Theory*, he went on to quantify the problem of communicating with high efficiency and accuracy, and, in so doing, converted the art of communications into a science. His approach was to address an abstraction of the practical problem faced by the communications professional on an everyday basis in having to transport data *sufficiently rapidly, sufficiently accurately,* and *sufficiently economically.*

Of course, the quantification of the adverb *sufficiently* depends upon the context of each individual application. "Sufficiently rapidly" depends crucially upon the nature of the data. Live voice or video at one extreme must be delivered in real-time, that is, as it happens with a minimal delay. At the other extreme, bulk transfer of computer files can often be delayed for overnight delivery. Similarly, "sufficiently accurately" is also dependent upon the nature of the data. When the data represents voice, music, or television, their accuracy need not be as great as when they represent financial balances sent from a member bank to the Federal Reserve or a set of program instructions sent from one computer to another.

What represents "sufficient economy" is, of course, even more sub-jective and, as we have seen, is time dependent. For economy has two as-pects: the computational approach and the implementation technology.

Shannon's seminal papers established the performance bounds gov-erning this threefold tradeoff. Those who followed developed mathemati-cal techniques for application of the theory. But widespread application of these techniques to practical problems had to await the revolution in digital component technology that led to the microprocessor and the desktop computer.

5.1   Channel Capacity

Shannon defines the *capacity* of a communications channel as the maxi-mum amount of information that can be transported through the channel with the stipulation that the information must be transferred perfectly ac-curately. If we assume that the data stream delivered to the channel by the source is, in fact, an information stream, then the capacity becomes the highest data rate that the channel can sustain with *perfect* accuracy. A concept defined in this way with these idealized attributes is not some-thing that can ever be achieved practically. Nevertheless, the concept is a useful benchmark against which to compare the performance of channels when they are used with practical signaling schemes. Shannon went on to show that it is possible to achieve a balance of high data rate, high accu-racy, and acceptable cost as long as the data rate is below the maximum represented by the channel capacity.

A surprising aspect of capacity is the fact that it is not zero. It is not obvious that a channel can support any transmission rate at all under the stipulation that the accuracy is perfect. Indeed, the notion of being able to transport data at an arbitrary rate and with arbitrary accuracy as long as the rate is less than some threshold value was startling when first intro-duced.

Fundamental to Shannon's computation of the capacity is his concept of information as the measure of the amount of choice inherent in a fam-ily of signals. For example, a transmitted sequence consisting of three bi-nary digits, each of which can be 0 or 1 with equal likelihood, designates one of eight equally likely things and therefore carries three bits of infor-mation. But all this information reaches the recipient only if the channel supports the transmission perfectly accurately. Whenever the channel is noisy, the amount of information that is transferred is reduced commensurately. However, if the effect of the noise can be mitigated, then the *information* transfer rate can become the same as the *data* transfer rate.

Shannon's methodology in developing his theory was based upon this concept. He defined the capacity as the maximum *information* rate that the channel could support. Then he found that if the data was represented by increasingly long signals, the effect of noise in reducing the information flow became increasingly small provided that the rate at which the information was being sent did not exceed the channel capacity. The key to Shannon's methodology was the use of very long signals. Capacity itself is achieved when the signals representing the data become infinitely long. Thus, achieving capacity demands infinite complexity. The closer the communicator attempts to approach capacity, the longer the signals he must use and the more expensive his system.

5.1.1   How Capacity Depends on Bandwidth and Signal-to-Noise Ratio

We have already seen that the two fundamental parameters that determine the properties of a communications channel are its signal-to-noise ratio and its bandwidth. Shannon's capacity must also depend upon these parameters, and the higher the signal-to-noise ratio and the wider the bandwidth, the greater the capacity of the channel ought to be.

As you can well imagine, calculating the capacity of a channel is a complex process, depending in detail on the characteristics of the noise. There is one case, fortunately, where the calculation can be performed. This is the Gaussian channel that we met in chapter 2. Even more fortunately, there are practical situations in which the noise behaves, at least approximately, in this way. The most important of these situations, from our point of view, is the noise produced by thermal agitation of electrons in a resistor that is the dominant noise source in a communications receiver. As we saw in chapter 2, the essential reason why the noise statistics in situations such as these are Gaussian is because they are representative of the motion of very large numbers of electrons in the material. It follows that the channel in which the only noise is thermal is called the *Gaussian* channel.

Just as we can speak of the spectra of the signals that are used to communicate, so we can speak of the spectra of the noise that impedes the communication. But since noise is a random process, so are the spectra of the noise signals. In particular, we can think of the spectrum of Gaussian noise as the average of the spectra of the pulses representing the electron motion that give rise to the noise. These electronic pulses are extremely short. Recall from chapter 4 that the shorter the pulse width, the wider the spectrum of the pulse—in the extreme, the spectrum of an impulse is constant over an infinite band of frequencies. The pulses due to electronic motion are short enough to be considered impulses for practical purposes, in that their spectra are constant over all frequencies of interest. We can also speak of the *power spectrum* of each pulse as the spectrum of the square of its amplitude, and this power spectrum is likewise constant over all frequencies of interest. Since the waveform of Gaussian noise is the sum of a very large number of these pulses, it too has a very broad spectrum—so broad that it makes sense to speak of it as *white* by analogy with light. This white Gaussian noise also has a power spectrum. We call the amplitude of its power spectrum the *noise spectral density* N_0, measured in watts per Hertz. This noise spectral density N_0 has the dimensions of energy and is, in fact, equal to the noise energy kT that we introduced in chapter 2. It follows that in any finite bandwidth W the total noise power is N_0W or kTW.

In his fundamental paper, Shannon computed the capacity C of the Gaussian channel of bandwidth W with a signal-to-noise ratio P_s/P_n to be

$$C = W \log (1 + P_s/P_n). \qquad (5\text{-}1)$$

In the equation, the logarithm is taken to the base 2, and, therefore, the capacity is expressed in units of bits per second.

In Fig. 5-1 we plot the capacity against the signal-to-noise ratio for bandwidths of 1000, 3000, and 10,000 Hz. All three curves coincide at very low power levels. We can see why this is so by looking at the behavior of Eq. 5-1 when the signal-to-noise ratio is small and the argument of the logarithm is close to 1. In this case we can use the approximation for the logarithm

$$\log (1 + x) = \log e \left[x - \frac{x^2}{2} + \frac{x^3}{3} + \ldots \right], \qquad (5\text{-}2)$$

where $\log e$ is the logarithm to the base 2 of $e = 2.718\ldots$, the base of natural logarithms. Representing the logarithm by the first term of the expansion, Eq. 5-1 reduces to

$$C = W \log (1 + P_s/P_n) \rightarrow WP_s/P_n \log e. \qquad (5\text{-}3)$$

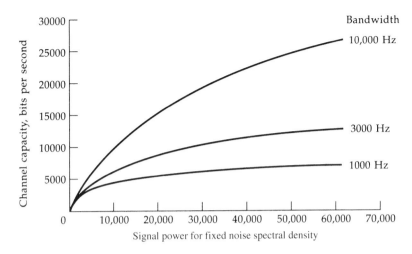

Figure 5-1   Capacity of the Gaussian channel.

Since $P_n = N_0 W$, Eq. 5-3 becomes

$$C = W P_s / P_n \log e = P_s / N_0 \log e, \qquad (5\text{-}4)$$

showing that when the signal-to-noise ratio is small, the capacity is proportional to the ratio of signal power to noise power density and is independent of bandwidth.

As the signal-to-noise ratio increases, the three curves in Fig. 5-1 begin to diverge from one another as each slopes up at a value related to the bandwidth in accordance with Eq. 5-1. Communications engineers often refer to the left portion of the curves as the *power-limited* or *noise-limited* region and to the right portion as the *bandwidth-limited* region. At low values of power, the achievable data rate is determined primarily by the available signal-to-noise ratio and only minimally by the bandwidth. Once the power is high enough, increasing the signal-to-noise ratio by adding more power has increasingly less effect as bandwidth becomes the limiting factor.

We can gain some insight into the significance of power and bandwidth limitations from the behavior of radio broadcast channels. For example, within the 10-kHz channel provided to the AM radio broadcaster, his radio transmitter must generate a signal powerful enough to provide a high enough signal-to-noise ratio for all listeners within the normal broadcasting range. The capacity of the radio channel to a receiver at a particular location depends upon the amount of the station's radiated power that reaches that receiver. Thus, at the fringes of the broadcast range, the reception sounds noisy, evidence of the power limitation that results in an inadequate signal-to-noise ratio.

Similarly, the wider the bandwidth of the channel, the more information can be transmitted. Imagine that an AM broadcaster obtained the FCC's permission to transmit in the 20-kHz band of two adjacent channels. Since amplitude modulation can support the transmission of an audio signal bandwidth half as wide as the available radio bandwidth, doubling the bandwidth of the AM channel would enable it to transmit an audio signal with twice the bandwidth, 10 kHz instead of 5 kHz. The added bandwidth would result in added signal fidelity, a form of information. But what if we tried to double the information content by doubling the bandwidth without transmitting more power to strengthen the signal? Listeners close to the transmitting station would have a very high-capacity, bandwidth-limited channel that could easily benefit from the increased information flow. In contrast, listeners on the fringe who are power limited would find that the reception was worse because of the lower signal-to-noise ratio. This example shows qualitatively that a communications channel not only must have enough bandwidth to support the transmission of information but also must have a sufficiently high signal-to-noise ratio to render the bandwidth useful.

A frustrating aspect of Shannon's work was that he proved the existence of channel capacity without providing a methodology for achieving it. His method of proof was to consider all possible ways to send the information using progressively longer signals and then to compute the average amount of information transferred using all of these signals. Since we know that some of these schemes give very poor results and that these schemes are also included in the averaging process, it follows that some schemes must exist that are better than average. But how do we find them? Unfortunately, the general problem of finding signals that permit communication close to capacity has resisted solution. However, we are able to do this in the power-limited extreme, and it is illustrative to examine this special case.

5.2   Transmitting at Rates Approaching Capacity

In the next several sections we outline a theoretical way of achieving capacity in one special case: when the bandwidth is infinite or, equivalently, when the channel is at the power-limited extreme. The word *theoretical* is important because the argument to be presented illustrates the meaning of capacity and why it is so difficult to achieve in practice. Later sections and the two chapters that follow continue the argument by outlining practical ways of signaling efficiently.

5.2.1   Families of Digital Signals

The theoretical argument depends on the use of what are called *families* of signals. What do we mean by a family of signals? In the simplest case of binary signaling, the family consists of two waveforms, one to represent the digit 1 and the other to represent a 0. At any given time, one of these waveforms is transmitted depending upon which digit is to be sent. The process of associating waveforms with digits at a transmitter is called *digital modulation*. The signal that is finally received at the destination is a corrupted version of the transmitted waveform. The receiving processor knows precisely what the uncorrupted waveforms are like. Its job is to *demodulate* the received signal—that is, to infer from the corrupted waveform received which transmitted waveform was more likely to have been sent. If its inference is correct, a correct digit is passed on to the user. If its inference is incorrect, an error is made. The ratio of digits in error to the total number of transmitted digits is the measure of accuracy. It is usually referred to as the *error probability*, the *error rate*, or sometimes the *bit error rate* (BER).

Most communications are two-way. Because of this, each end of a communications link requires a modulator to send and a demodulator to receive. For practical reasons, the modulator and demodulator are built into a single piece of equipment called a *modem*, the abbreviation for *mo*dulator/*dem*odulator.

Since an error is made whenever the demodulator misidentifies the received waveform, one way to reduce the possibility of confusion is to make the waveforms as different as possible. There are many ways to do this, and three possibilities are shown in Fig. 5-2. In each case, the waveform is T seconds long, so that the data rate is $1/T$ bps. The first waveform (Fig. 5-2, top) is the one introduced earlier: a 1 is represented by a pulse of carrier, and a 0 is represented by no pulse. This is simply a kind of amplitude modulation in which only two amplitudes are allowed. By examining the amplitude of the received waveform that has been corrupted by noise, the demodulator's job is to infer whether the transmitted

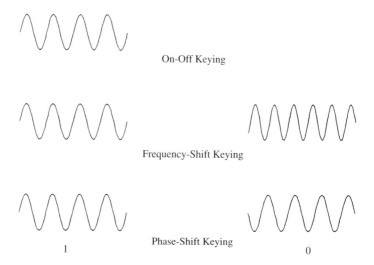

On-Off Keying

Frequency-Shift Keying

Phase-Shift Keying

1   0

Figure 5-2   Pairs of waveforms for binary signaling.

amplitude was 1 or 0. The second waveform pair (Fig. 5-2, middle) is the digital equivalent of frequency modulation and is called *frequency-shift keying* (FSK). The pair is a constant-amplitude pulse of one of two carrier frequencies. In this case, the demodulator's function is to examine a band of frequencies $1/T$-Hz wide centered on each of the two possible carriers and infer which one of the frequencies was sent. If there were no noise, then the output of each band is either something or nothing depending on which frequency was sent. Thus, these FSK waveforms are examples of functions that we saw in the last chapter that were orthogonal to each other. Another pair of orthogonal signals that might be sent are sine and cosine waves. This pair of signals would achieve the same results. This type of signaling is the digital equivalent of phase modulation. However, there is a more effective form of phase modulation called *binary phase shift keying* (BPSK) that is shown in Fig. 5-2 (bottom). Rather than using the orthogonal sine and cosine functions, BPSK uses the *antipodal* sine and its negative. It should be evident that the performance of antipodal signals should be better than that of orthogonal signals since the two signals are more different from each other. In the next chapter we quantify these statements.

In each of the three cases, it is possible for noise to confuse the receiver. The more noise energy there is relative to signal energy, the more often this will happen. Which pair of signals is best? There is no single answer for all circumstances. It depends on a number of factors—the nature of the noise, the signal-to-noise ratio, and the bandwidth of the channel, among other things. For the discussion that follows, we use FSK signaling.

5.2.2   How to Approach Capacity by Using Large Families of Long Signals

Having chosen the signals, the first thing to be examined is how the error rate depends upon the signal-to-noise ratio. We would expect that the higher the signal-to-noise ratio, the lower the error rate. This expectation is confirmed in Fig. 5-3 that shows the error rate plotted against the signal-to-noise ratio for these FSK signals. The general shape of this curve is characteristic of all curves of error rate versus signal-to-noise

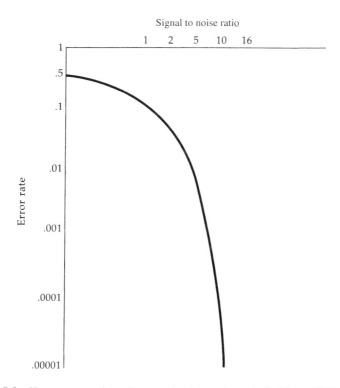

Figure 5-3   How accuracy depends upon signal-to-noise ratio for binary FSK modulation.

ratio, whatever the signaling scheme. At very low values of signal-to-noise ratio, the error rate approaches $^1/_2$, since, in the extreme of no signal energy at all, the received signal carries no information and thus cannot shed any light on whether the transmitted digit was a 0 or a 1. Indeed, if you knew ahead of time that as many 0s as 1s were being sent, you could make your decision on each digit by flipping a coin, and on the average you would be correct half the time. As the signal-to-noise ratio increases, the accuracy increases, slowly at first and then more rapidly as the signal-to-noise ratio becomes large.

Now we introduce the issue of complexity. We saw earlier that Shannon's technique for finding the capacity was to use increasingly long families of signals, and long implies complex. Let's see what this means by generalizing the binary FSK example. In the binary scheme, the transmitter accepts the bits from the data source one at a time, and for each bit it assigns one of two frequencies, depending upon whether the bit is a 0 or a 1. Now we extend the concept. Instead of accepting the bits one at a time, the transmitter will now accept them two at a time. Since there are four possible combinations of values for two bits, it will assign one of four frequencies, depending upon which combination is received:

> 00   frequency 0
>
> 01   frequency 1
>
> 10   frequency 2
>
> 11   frequency 3

This scheme is called 4-ary FSK. The signals for the binary and 4-ary cases are compared pictorially in Fig. 5-4. If the bits are delivered by the

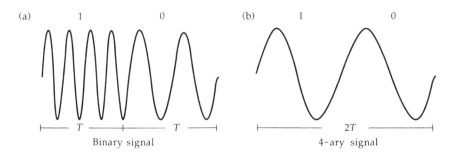

Figure 5-4   (a) Binary and (b) 4-ary FSK signals.

source at the same rate in both cases, we see from the figure that the 4-ary signals must be twice as long as the binary signals. Therefore, if we hold the transmitter power (energy per second) constant, each 4-ary waveform has twice the energy of each binary waveform. But that is just what we want for a fair comparison of the two cases, since each of the double-energy signals contains two bits of information and thus has exactly the same energy per bit as in the binary case. The receiver's job is now to determine from a corrupted received waveform which of the four transmitted waveforms is most likely to have been sent. When it makes this identification, it sends on to the user the two bits of data associated with the waveform. Note that the receiver's job is more complex in the 4-ary case than in the binary case, since for every decision, it must deal with four possibilities instead of two.

Now let's continue the process by taking the bits from the source three at a time instead of two at a time. By analogy with the previous example, we now need eight frequencies to correspond to the eight combinations possible with three bits. This gives us an 8-ary frequency modulation system:

000	frequency 0
001	frequency 1
010	frequency 2
011	frequency 3
100	frequency 4
101	frequency 5
110	frequency 6
111	frequency 7

Each of these signals is now three times as long as the binary signals, with three times the energy per signal, but the *same* energy per bit, since each contains three bits of information. To take one more example: if the receiver accepts the bits from the data source ten at a time, it requires 1024 frequencies to be able to assign a unique frequency to each of the 10-bit combinations. Again holding the data rate constant, these 10-ary FSK signals are ten times longer than the binary FSK signals.

We can continue this process indefinitely. As the number of signals increases, the receiver must compare the received waveform with more possibilities. One would think that, other things being equal, the more

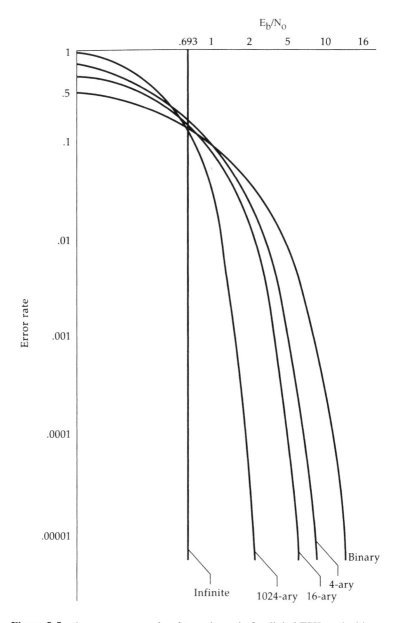

Figure 5-5   Accuracy versus signal-to-noise ratio for digital FSK modualtion using different signal lengths.

choices, the greater the chance of making an error. But other things are not equal, since, by way of compensation, each 8-ary waveform has three times the energy of the binary waveform, and each 1024-ary waveform has ten times the energy of the binary waveform. It is not at all obvious which scheme is best and under what circumstances.

But Fig. 5-5 shows us. Before comparing the different signaling schemes, we have to be sure that the comparison is fair. When an error is made in the binary case, only a single bit is involved. But in the 8-ary case, an error means that three bits can be in error. Therefore to put all the signaling schemes on an equal basis, the vertical axis is the probability of error per bit. We also need a parameter on the horizontal axis that provides a fair comparison. That parameter is the ratio of the signal energy per bit, E_b, to the noise power density N_0, an expression that is related to but not identical to the signal-to-noise ratio. The problem with the signal-to-noise ratio, P_s/P_n, is that the noise power depends on the bandwidth, and, as we have seen, the different signal families have different bandwidths. The ratio E_b/N_0 does not have this limitation. Equation 5-5 shows how the two ratios are related:

$$\frac{P_s}{P_n} = \frac{E_b}{T_b} \frac{1}{N_0 W} = \frac{E_b}{N_0} \frac{1}{T_b W}. \tag{5-5}$$

In the equation the signal power is expressed as the signal energy per bit E_b divided by the time duration of a bit T_b, and the noise power as its spectral power density N_0 is multiplied by the bandwidth W. Regrouping the variables, the signal-to-noise ratio is expressed as the product of the two factors, E_b/N_0 and $1/T_b W$. In the binary case that we plotted in Fig. 5-3, the signal duration is the reciprocal of the bandwidth, and so E_b/N_0 is exactly equal to the signal-to-noise ratio. More generally, for M-ary signals, the bandwidth is $1/T_b \log M$, and Eq. 5-5 is reduced to

$$\frac{P_s}{P_n} = \frac{E_b}{N_0} \frac{1}{T_b W} = \frac{E_b}{N_0} \log M. \tag{5-6}$$

Note also that since E_b/N_0 is dimensionless, N_0 can also be interpreted as the noise energy that the receiver observes during the duration of the signal pulse. Figure 5-5 plots the bit error rate against E_b/N_0 for the 4-ary, 8-ary, 16-ary, and 1024-ary cases along with that for the binary case, repeated from Fig. 5-3. Although each of the curves shows the same qualitative behavior, there are some differences that become progressively more pronounced as the signal set becomes increasingly large. The most evident difference is that, as the signal duration gets longer, the successive curves become squarer in shape. At very low values of signal-to-noise ratio, the longer the signals, the worse the performance. However, once some threshold signal-to-noise ratio is exceeded, the error rate decreases very rapidly, and the longer the signals, the faster the rate of decrease.

This result is extremely significant. When the signal-to-noise ratio is decreased slightly in an analog system, the result is a slight degradation in quality, so slight that it may not even be noticed. A digital system is fundamentally different. A small change in signal-to-noise ratio can produce a large change in performance that becomes readily detectable. A properly designed digital system will give very good results. However, the more sophisticated the system, the squarer will be its characteristic performance curve. And if something goes wrong, its performance can degrade very rapidly.

This property of digital signaling always reminds me of the old nursery rhyme:

> *There was a little girl*
> *Who had a little curl*
> *Right in the middle*
> *Of her forehead.*
>
> *And when she was good*
> *She was very, very good,*
> *But when she was bad,*
> *She was horrid.*

Keeping in mind that achieving capacity requires the use of signals that are infinitely long, the next step is to carry this process to an extreme and let the FSK signals become infinitely long. We can never do it practically, but the consideration of this hypothetical case provides us with a great deal of insight. As you might expect, in this extreme case, the curve of error rate versus signal-to-noise ratio is perfectly square. As shown in Fig. 5-5, the result is either "horrid" with an error rate of $1/2$ (a coin toss) when the signal-to-noise ratio per bit is less than some threshold value or perfectly "good" with an error rate of 0 for values above the threshold. The threshold signal-to-noise ratio per bit is $1/\log e = 0.693$.

We can see where this limit comes from by interpreting Eq. 5-4, which we repeat for convenience as Eq. 5-7:

$$C = W \frac{P_s}{P_n} \log e = \frac{P_s}{N_0} \log e. \tag{5-7}$$

Since C is, by definition, the maximum possible data rate for error-free performance, any other rate R must obey the inequality

$$R \leq C = \frac{P_s}{N_0} \log e. \tag{5-8}$$

Turning this around and dividing both sides by R, we obtain

$$\frac{1}{R} \frac{P_s}{N_0} \geq \frac{1}{\log e}. \tag{5-9}$$

Since the quantity $P_s/N_0 \times 1/R$ is just E_b/N_0, we obtain

$$\frac{E_b}{N_0} \geq \frac{1}{\log e} = 0.693. \tag{5-10}$$

The reason for the appearance of this particular number, 0.693, is a mathematical consequence of taking logarithms to the base 2, which, in turn, is a consequence of using the bit as the unit of information. If, instead, we measured information in another unit that we might call the *nat* in which the logarithms are taken to the base e, then we would obtain the result that the minimum amount of energy to noise density required to send one nat is 1. Similarly, the minimum energy to noise ratio required to send a decimal digit is $1/\log_{10} e$ or 2.3028.

This threshold given in Eq. 5-9 represents an absolute lower limit on the amount of energy relative to the noise needed to send a bit of data with perfect accuracy and infinite complexity. It is called the *Shannon limit*, and it tells us that we will never be able to communicate absolutely accurately with less energy. In fact, most practical systems use at least ten times that much energy. Since the thermal noise power density at room temperature is about 4×10^{-21} J, then this is the minimum amount of energy required to send a nat. The minimum amount of energy required to send a bit is 0.693 times as large or about 2.9×10^{-21} J.

Communications engineers usually express the various factors that make up a transmission link in decibels rather than in absolute units, where the decibel value of a ratio r is expressed as

$$r \, (\text{dB}) = 10 \log r. \tag{5-11}$$

This is convenient because it converts the various multiplicative factors that determine the properties of a link into additive terms. Thus, rather than expressing the Shannon limit as 0.693, it is typically expressed as 10 $\log_{10}$ (0.693), which is -1.6 dB.

The infinitely long signals that lead to the Shannon limit also require that the channel have infinite bandwidth. We can understand this by examining the bandwidth requirements for the various FSK signals. In the binary case each waveform is T seconds long, and it occupies a bandwidth of $1/T$ Hz centered on the frequency used for the pulse. Since two frequencies are used, one to represent a 0 and one to represent a 1, we know immediately that the channel must have a bandwidth of at least $2/T$ Hz to support communications using these waveforms. To take an example, if T is 1 ms, then each waveform will have a bandwidth of about 1000 Hz, and both together occupy 2000 Hz. The other families behave similarly:

Signaling Scheme	No. of Waveforms	Bandwidth per Waveform	Total Bandwidth
2-ary	2	$1/T$	$2/T$
4-ary	4	$1/2T$	$2/T$
8-ary	8	$1/3T$	$2.67/T$
16-ary	16	$1/4T$	$4/T$
24-ary	1024	$1/10T$	$102.4/T$

Thus, increasing the number of signals from 2 to 1024 increases the bandwidth about a factor of 50. If we continued to fill in the table for longer and longer signals, the total bandwidth would become larger and larger. In the limiting case when the signals are infinitely long, an infinite bandwidth is required.

5.2.3   Attaining Capacity in the Power-Limited Channel

Figure 5-5 shows how the FSK family of signals approaches channel capacity as the size of the family of signals increases. However, it does this indirectly by showing how the value of E_b/N_0 approaches the Shannon limit as the signals become infinitely long. Figure 5-6 is a way of showing the same thing more qualitatively but a little more directly. It plots data rate against the ratio of received signal power to the noise power density (P_s/N_0) for several sets of conditions. The bottom three curves are for binary, 16-ary, and 32-ary FSK signaling in a channel bandwidth of 5000 Hz. Each of the curves has two regions: a power-limited region in which the rate increases linearly as the power is increased and a bandwidth-limited region in which the rate remains constant as the power is increased. In the power-limited region, the error probability is held at a fixed value of 10^{-4} using the appropriate value of E_b/N_0 from Fig. 5-5. In each case the rate is increased by decreasing the signal pulse width and increasing the signal power proportionately. The system makes an abrupt transition to the bandwidth-limited region when the signal pulse width becomes narrow enough for the bandwidth occupied by the signal family to equal the channel bandwidth. As we showed earlier, the rate at which this transition occurs decreases as the family size increases.

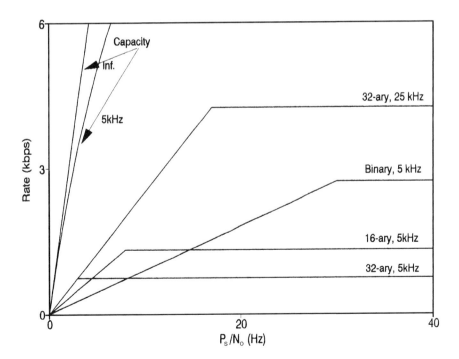

Figure 5-6   Approaching capacity in the power-limited channel.

It is easy to show that in the power-limited region the slope of each curve is inversely proportional to the value of E_b/N_0. Thus, the curves become steeper as the family size increases. Of course, as long as the system remains power limited, these slopes do not depend on the bandwidth. We can see this in Fig. 5-6 from the curve for 32-ary FSK with the increased bandwidth of 25,000 Hz. It coincides with the 32-ary curve at 5000 Hz in the power-limited region but the increased bandwidth allows it to flatten out at a rate five times as high.

We also show two capacity curves in the figure. The curve on the right is for a bandwidth of 5000 Hz and that on the left for infinite bandwidth. The two capacity curves virtually coincide at very low power levels and then begin to diverge as bandwidth begins to play a role. It is also evident that the FSK curves approach the capacity curves in the highly power-limited region as the family size increases. Note also that in the bandwidth-limited region the FSK curves diverge rapidly from the capacity curves. Thus FSK signaling, when carried to the limit, achieves channel capacity in the extreme of power limitation but is very inefficient everywhere else. According to Shannon's theorem, there must be similar families of signals that approach capacity in the other regions. Unfortunately, we do not know how to find them. Ever since Shannon's pioneering work in 1948, communications scientists and engineers have been searching for schemes that are efficient and also practical. While general results have not been achieved, over the years a set of techniques have been developed that have made controlled-accuracy digital communications economically possible.

5.3   Getting Practical—Division of the Problem into Modulation and Coding

As beautiful as Shannon's theory is, there is something unsatisfying about the way it tantalizes us with what can be done without showing us how to do it except in special cases. The one bit of guidance that the theory provides is to use the "right" kind of long signals. And as already noted, the problem of finding such signals has two separate facets. The first is the mathematical problem of finding families of signals that achieve the desired results, and the second is the engineering problem of finding economical ways of implementing these signals. Not all long signals are equally effective, and there is no general way to find signals that are optimum even if implementation cost is ignored.

Of course, complexity and cost cannot be ignored. We can gain some appreciation for the complexity problem by returning to the FSK example, which we know is a theoretically good approach when power limited. Suppose that, for some application, we have computed that 1024-ary FSK will perform acceptably. The method of generating the signals requires that the modulator accept the data 10 bits at a time and associate a waveform with each of the 1024 possible combinations of 10 bits. The demodulator compares the received waveform with replicas of the 1024 waveforms that could have been transmitted. A number of this size is always a concern since, no matter how simple an individual comparison, a computer fast enough to perform 1024 of them might be complex. But what if, later, the engineer should conclude that 10-bit signals are not long enough to achieve the required performance? Increasing the number of bits by only one doubles the number of waveforms and the number of receiver comparisons. Qualitatively, it means that a small increase in the dimensions of the problem can lead to a very large increase in complexity. Much of the research that has been done in communications has aimed to find clever ways around this problem of exponential growth.

One thing is clear: We cannot transmit and receive waveforms of increasing length in the straightforward way described up to now. We must devise schemes that are clever enough to defeat the exponential problem if we are to obtain the benefits of long signals.

The first and most fundamental step is to divide the problem into two parts. The first part is to define a manageably small set of basic waveforms. Then we generate the very long signals needed to come close to Shannon's results as *sequences* of these waveforms called *codes*.

5.3.1   Coding

Here is an example. It is the result of work done in the 1950s by Richard Hamming at Bell Laboratories, who discovered a systematic class of codes that would correct a single error. In the example, we are going to generate 16-ary signals. Instead of using sixteen amplitudes, frequencies, or phases, we will use two channel waveforms designating binary 0 and 1 and then generate sixteen different sequences of these waveforms. The sequences are shown in the following table:

1	0	0	0	0	0	0	0
2	0	0	0	1	1	1	1
3	0	0	1	0	1	1	0
4	0	0	1	1	0	0	1
5	0	1	0	0	1	0	1
6	0	1	0	1	0	1	0
7	0	1	1	0	0	1	1
8	0	1	1	1	1	0	0
9	1	0	0	0	0	1	1
10	1	0	0	1	1	0	0
11	1	0	1	0	1	0	1
12	1	0	1	1	0	1	0
13	1	1	0	0	1	1	0
14	1	1	0	1	0	0	1
15	1	1	1	0	0	0	0
16	1	1	1	1	1	1	1

Each sequence contains a distinct pattern of seven 0s and 1s. The first sequence is transmitted as a succession of seven of the 0 waveforms; the second sequence as a succession of three 0 waveforms followed by four 1 waveforms, and so forth. A comparison of these numbers gives us an initial inkling of what the process is. There are 128 possible sequences of 7-bit numbers. But since we are using only sixteen of them, each sequence carries only 4 bits of information. Therefore, if we assume that 0s and 1s are equally likely, each transmitted binary digit is carrying $4/7$ of a bit of information, a degree of redundancy that potentially can be exploited.

In order for sets of signals to be useful for communication, they must be different from one another. If you examine the set of sequences, you will see that every sequence differs from every other sequence in at least three places. Suppose that the first sequence is transmitted and is received with an error in the fourth digit. The receiver will declare that it received the sequence 0001000. Here is where the redundancy comes in. There is no transmitted sequence corresponding to this received sequence. But the first sequence, 0000000, differs from this received sequence in only one place. If you look through the table, you will see that there is no other sequence differing from the received sequence in only one position. The next closest are sequences 4, 6, and 10, all of which differ from the received sequence in two positions. All the other sequences differ in more than two places. Since it is more likely that a single error was made in the receiving process than two or three errors, the receiver has no choice but to conclude that the first sequence was the most likely to have been transmitted.

This code corrects a single error in any digit. Its purpose is to reduce the probability of error in the transmission, and it pays for this with a reduction in data rate. If we make certain simplifying assumptions about the channel, we can easily compute the resulting probability of error.

The first simplifying assumption is that each transmitted bit, whether a 0 or a 1, has a probability p of being received in error, and the second is that this probability is independent from bit to bit. The resulting channel is known as the *binary symmetric channel*. Then the probability of a 7-bit sequence being received in error, P_e, is just the probability that two or more digits in the sequence are received in error, or 1 minus the probability that one or no digits was received in error. The probability of no errors is just $(1 - p)^7$. Since an error can occur in any position of the sequence, there are seven ways of making a single error. The probability of each of them is the probability of one digit being in error, p, multiplied by the probability that six digits are correct, $(1 - p)^6$. We therefore obtain the following expression for the probability of error:

$$P_e = 1 - \text{prob of 0 errors} - \text{prob of 1 error} = 1 - q^7 - 7pq^6, \qquad (5\text{-}12)$$

where $q = 1 - p$ *is* the probability that a bit is received correctly. If p is 10^{-2}, then P_e is 2×10^{-3}, a small improvement. If the channel is a little better with $p = 10^{-3}$, then P_e is 2×10^{-5}, a greater improvement. On the other hand, if p is very much larger than 0.01, then the coding makes a bad situation worse.

What we have done is to divide the transmission and reception process into the two processes shown in Fig. 5-7. We take four information bits and associate a sequence of seven *channel bits* with each information bit combination in a device called a *coder*. Each channel bit is then associated with one of two waveforms in the modulator. The received corrupted waveforms are then reconverted to channel bits in the demodulator. These bits, some of which may be in error, are then processed in a *decoder*, which will do all it can to correct the errors coming from the demodulator and then send the hopefully correct set of information bits to the recipient. By splitting the process, the complexity of the modulation/demodulation process is deliberately limited, and the en-

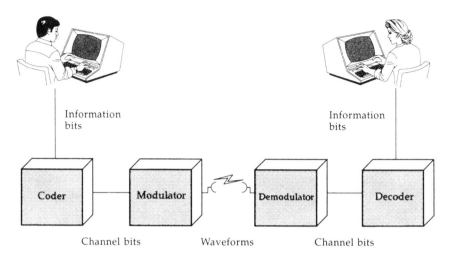

Figure 5-7   Modulation and coding.

tire scheme depends on the complexity of the inherently digital coding/decoding process. Thus, the practical successes of the technique depend upon our ability to conceive of and implement effective coding/decoding schemes.

Dividing the communication problem into the two areas of modulation and coding was an essential step on the road to achieving any of the benefits of Shannon's theory. Beyond that there are no easy approaches applicable to all cases. We can simply look at these coding and modulation techniques as part of the communicator's bag of tricks to be used in individual circumstances as warranted.

But we can categorize the applications to gain some insight into the kinds of things that do make sense in practical situations. At the lowest level of sophistication, modulation techniques alone without coding may be sufficient to achieve the communicator's objectives. At the next level of sophistication, the modulation techniques are almost sufficient, but a coding applique is applied to reduce the error rate. At this level, there is no attempt to improve the efficiency of the channel by increasing the data rate. In fact, using coding in this way must decrease the data rate to obtain the benefit of improved reliability. This was the case in the earlier example of the Hamming code in which seven channel bits were used to transmit one of sixteen waveforms or four information bits, almost 50% overhead. If this were applied to a modulation system for error reduction, the penalty would be almost a factor of two in data rate.

The highest level of sophistication, in the spirit of Shannon's original work, attempts to decrease the error rate and to increase the data rate simultaneously, or to use the metaphor of the old adage, to allow you to have your cake and eat it too. To achieve the benefits that Shannon's theory predicts, you must be prepared to apply a suitable marriage of the two techniques of modulation and coding. There is an intuitive way to see what this means. Instead of applying coding to a modulation/demodulation system that is already moderately accurate to improve the accuracy at the expense of data rate, you increase the channel data rate with the modulation system. This leads inevitably to increased errors, which are corrected with a coder/decoder of the right kind. The coding process will add overhead, but if the marriage is a good one, the increased modulation rate will more than compensate for the rate decrease in the coding process. The net result is an increased rate at an acceptable level of accuracy. The penalty in this case is simply the cost of the modulation and coding equipment.

5.3.2 Error Detection

There is one particularly useful special case that falls within the intermediate category cited above. Suppose you wish to transfer a data file from your personal computer to that of a colleague. The telephone line connection at the selected data rate of, say, 28,800 bps yields an error rate of 1 in 100,000 bits, but the parameters of the application demand an error rate of no more than 1 in 100 million or more digits. You might think that, in accordance with Fig. 5-3, a slight increase in signal-to-noise ratio could reduce the error rate to the desired level. But this curve is for the idealized case in which the only noise is thermal. No real system noise is ever purely thermal; there are always other perturbations. Because of this, it is very difficult, in practice, to achieve extremely low error rates in real systems by the use of modulation alone.

A very practical way to cope with this problem is to use a code that detects errors but cannot correct them. If that were the end of it, then the data stream passed on to the user would have almost no errors, but it would have some number of blanks or erasures representing digits that were received in error but could not be corrected. A common way of filling in the blanks is to take advantage or the fact that channels are usually two-way and send a request back to the sender to repeat the block of data in which the erasures occurred. Since the channel is pretty good to start with, then the probability of a second erasure is very small, and a virtually error-free bit stream is passed on to the user.

Such error-detecting codes are of minimal complexity and add a minimum of overhead (perhaps 10%) to the bit stream. Often, error-correcting codes have some error-detection capability over and above their correction capability, and the erasures so obtained can be used in the same way. In fact, many telephone line modems include this kind of error-detect-and-repeat protocol as a low-cost option. Such devices can be very useful provided that errors are rare, and correspondingly not too many blocks must be repeated. They are typically used when files are transferred from one personal computer to another.

But the way one treats erasures depends upon the application. Detect and repeat protocols make a great deal of sense when the transmitted information is computer data or the equivalent. But the situation is quite different when the transmissions are time sensitive, voice, for example. In such a case it makes sense to ignore the erasures and fill in the blanks from the adjacent bits rather than repeat the data, which would lead to delays that might be unacceptably long. And, as we shall see later, the codes used in compact discs correct some errors and detect others. The playback equipment then fills in the blanks from the adjacent bits.

5.3.3   To Code or Not to Code

The question of whether to use sophisticated signaling systems including coding so as to use the channel more efficiently or to use simple signaling without coding and to increase the channel capacity is largely a matter of economics. For example, is it cheaper to push up the rate on a telephone by the use of sophisticated signaling or to buy a second phone line and use the two lines less efficiently? Or, in a power-limited situation, is it cheaper to double the data rate on a satellite communications circuit by using powerful coding or to install a larger antenna that increases the capacity of the channel? During the 1950s and 1960s when powerful coding schemes were being developed, the economics were usually on the side of increasing the capacity. But this situation began to change in the 1970s with the continued refinement of integrated circuit technology. When the compact disc system was being designed during the 1970s, the decision was made to use a very sophisticated coding technique that would have been quite out of the question economically only a few years earlier. As time went on, the balance was shifted increasingly toward the signal-processing approaches. We only have to observe the great strides in the design of telephone-line modems where the rates have gone from 2400 bps to beyond 28,800 bps costing in the $100 range in a relatively small number of years.

Thus, with the increasing digitization of communications, the issue has not become whether to use sophisticated signal processing. Rather the issue has become which of the many techniques available should be used. The next two chapters explore these questions.

6

MODULATION AND CODING— POWER-LIMITED CHANNELS

6.0 Introduction

We are now ready to see how the principles brought out in the last chapter are actually used in real situations. The last chapter referred to a few particular modulation and coding schemes. In point of fact, there are many such schemes. How does one decide which ones to use in which situation? There are no hard and fast rules, only guidelines. Yet there are a few broad principles, based primarily on the nature of the communications channel.

Recall that the two dominant channel parameters are the signal-to-noise ratio and the bandwidth. Sometimes the channel is power limited; that is to say, the signal-to-noise ratio that the communicator has to work with is low enough so that it limits the data rate for any bandwidth. The other extreme is when the communicator has all the power he needs to operate at the full bandwidth of the channel. Consideration of these two extreme cases illustrates the range of possibilities inherent in the various modulation and coding schemes.

Radio channels such as those found in most satellite communications and personal communications systems are good examples of power-limited systems. In both cases transmitter power is expensive in one or more dimensions. In a satellite system, the power source is a spacecraft power amplifier, a very expensive component. Moreover, the higher the power of this amplifier, the greater the drain on the satellite's solar cells and battery backups, also very expensive commodities. In a personal communications system, it is desirable to keep the transmitter power low for another reason: the lower the power of the portable radio, the lighter and hence more portable it becomes. As we shall see, there is a direct trade-off between transmitter power and the efficiency of the modulation/ coding system that can be taken advantage of in these cases.

There are similarly many examples of the bandwidth-limited extreme, where it is economical to provide enough transmitter power to take advantage of all the inherent bandwidth of the channel. In a line-of-sight microwave link, for example, the most precious commodity is the bandwidth assignment. It therefore makes sense to do everything possible to maximize the data rate through the choice of modulation system and by providing as much power as necessary; fortunately, the cost of a high-power microwave transmitter mounted on a tower is relatively modest. An even better example is the common telephone line where it is easy to supply enough power to make the signal-to-noise ratio almost as high as desired. The important thing is to squeeze as much data as possible through this relatively narrowband pipe by the choice of modulation and coding. Anyone familiar with computer networks is aware of how important the data rate is in taking advantage of all that the networks have to offer. This has given the impetus to the development of the improved modem technology that has increased the allowable data rates by many factors during the 1980s and 1990s.

In this chapter we consider the power-limited case, beginning with modulation techniques suitable for such channels and continuing with the various kinds of coding schemes that are commonly used with these modulation systems. Then, in the next chapter, we go on with a discussion of the bandwidth-limited channel with emphasis on the telephone line. Even though the details of the modulation and coding schemes used in these situations differ substantially from those used in the power-limited case, the principles established in the earlier discussion carry over.

6.1   Modulation for Power-Limited Channels

We showed earlier that there is a direct trade-off between the efficiency of a modulation-coding system and the data rate achievable for a given amount of transmitter power. We can easily quantify this with the following simple equation that was introduced in the last chapter. It is applicable to any communications link.

$$\frac{P_r}{N_0} = \frac{E_b}{N_0} R. \tag{6-1}$$

In the equation, P_r is the received signal power; N_0 is the receiver thermal noise power density; and the ratio of the two quantities, P_r/N_0, the power-to-noise density ratio, defines the physical parameters of the link itself. It is not the same as the signal-to-noise ratio; you would have to multiply the denominator by the bandwidth for that. Thus the power-to-noise density ratio has the dimensions of inverse seconds, rather than being dimensionless. E_b/N_0 is the energy-to-noise ratio that the modulation/coding system requires for an acceptably low error probability and is a dimensionless quantity. Finally, R is the data rate. If you imagine a link with a fixed value of P_r/N_0, then you can maximize the data rate through that link by minimizing E_b/N_0. You can also look at it another way: Hold the data rate constant; the lower the value of E_b/N_0, the lower the transmitter power can be. In a power-limited system, the modulation system has to reflect the fact that we are fighting hard for every watt of transmitter power. Therefore, a modulation system such as amplitude modulation that does not use the maximum power all the time is a power waster. Thus it makes sense to use a scheme such as frequency or phase shift keying in which all the available power is used all the time. As it turns out, the most popular scheme is phase shift keying—you will see why later—and that is what we consider next.

6.1.1 Binary Phase Shift Keying

There are many variations of phase shift keying (PSK). The simplest of these is called *binary phase shift keying* (BPSK), and that is what we consider first. As we saw in Fig. 5-2, in BPSK a 1 is distinguished from a 0 by a 180-degree phase shift. An easy way to think of this is to imagine a modulator that generates a positive rectangular pulse at baseband for transmission of a 1 and a negative rectangular pulse for a 0. The signal at baseband then becomes a sequence of positive and negative pulses, each $T = 1/R$ s long. Since the systems we are interested in are radio systems, these pulses have to be translated from baseband to a higher carrier frequency. In order to do this, the sequence of positive and negative pulses multiplies a constant-frequency carrier signal. Multiplying the carrier sign wave by this sequence is equivalent to changing the phase of the carrier by 180 degrees whenever the sequence changes from positive to negative and vice versa. The multiplication process, therefore, produces a carrier signal in which the binary digits are represented by phases 180 degrees apart.

The job of the demodulator is to determine the transmitted bit sequence by examining the phase of the received waveform in the presence of noise. The intuitive thing for the demodulator to do is to multiply the received waveform over the interval T by replicas of the two possible transmitted waveforms. In the absence of noise, multiplication by the correct waveform would yield a large positive signal, while multiplication by the incorrect waveform would yield a large negative signal. Of course, noise can alter these results. Every once in a while, depending on the signal-to-noise ratio, the output of the multiplier with the incorrect signal replica can exceed the output of the correct multiplier, causing an incorrect digit to be passed on to the data destination.

The optimum detector is along the same lines as this intuitive picture. It is what is called a *matched filter* receiver. But before describing this optimum detector, it is important to review the general operation of any linear filter, and Fourier transform theory is very useful for this description. The usual way of describing a filter is through its frequency response $H(f)$. If a signal $x(t)$ with a spectrum $X(f)$, given by its Fourier transform, is passed through the filter as in Fig. 6-1, the output of the filter $y(t)$ has a frequency response or Fourier transform $Y(f)$ given by

$$Y(f) = X(f) H(f). \tag{6-2}$$

We can express the same relationship in the time domain. The filter with frequency response $H(f)$ has what is called an *impulse response* $h(t)$ that is the inverse Fourier transform of $H(f)$. The reason for the name impulse response is easy to understand. In chapter 4 we introduced the impulse function $\delta(t)$, and we showed from the definition of the function that its Fourier transform was 1 for all frequencies. Equation 6-2 tells us that when the input to the filter $x(t)$ is the impulse function $\delta(t)$, the filter

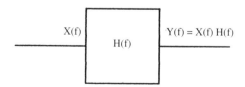

Figure 6-1 Behavior of a filter in the frequency domain.

output $Y(f)$ has the frequency response of the filter $H(f)$, which means that the output in the time domain is $h(t)$.

The equivalent of Eq. 6-2 in the time domain is the following form known as a *convolution*:

$$y(t) = \int_0^t x(\tau)h(t - \tau) \quad d\tau.$$
(6-3)

Because of the symmetry of the Fourier transform, these relationships also work the other way around. If you multiply two time functions together, the spectrum of the product function is obtained by convolving the spectra of the individual time functions, a property that we will find useful when we discuss the sampling theorem in chapter 8.

These relationships apply to any functions that have Fourier transforms. Now we introduce the concept of a filter that is *matched* to an input signal $x(t)$. This so-called *matched filter* has the impulse response

$$h(t) = x(-t),$$
(6-4)

the input itself with time running backward. For the matched filter, Eq. 6-3 then becomes

$$y(t) = \int_0^t x(\tau)x(\tau - t) \quad d\tau.$$
(6-5)

Thus, matched filtering is equivalent to sliding the input signal across a delayed replica of itself, continuously multiplying the two signals, and adding the results. Clearly, this sum increases steadily until the two pulses exactly overlap, and then it begins to decrease. The output is obtained by sampling this sum function at the peak.

Returning now to the BPSK example, suppose that the signal $x(t)$ represents a 1 and $-x(t)$, a signal with the opposite phase, represents a 0. Assume first that there is no noise in the channel. Then the received signal is a replica of the transmitted signal. Suppose also that the receiver knows exactly when to sample the matched filter output to maximize the signal. Then the sampled output of the matched filter has a value proportional to the amplitude of the received signal when $x(t)$ is transmitted, $+\sqrt{E_b}$, where E_b is the received signal energy. Should the received signal be 180 degrees out of phase, then the sampled output of the filter is the negative of the signal amplitude, $-\sqrt{E_b}$. These two possible outputs appear as two lines in Fig. 6-2(a).

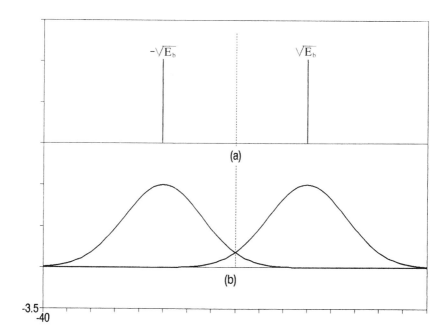

Figure 6-2   Output of BPSK receiver: (a) no noise and (b) Gaussian noise.

We can see the same thing in the frequency domain. The matched filter has a frequency response

$$H(f) = \int_{-\infty}^{+\infty} h(t)e^{-j2\pi ft}dt = \int_{-\infty}^{+\infty} x(-t)e^{-j2\pi ft}dt = X^*(f), \quad (6\text{-}6)$$

where $X^*(f)$, the complex conjugate of $X(f)$, has the same real part and the negative of the imaginary part of $X(f)$. In this case, Eq. 6-2 reduces to

$$Y(f) = X(f)\, H(f) = X(f)\, X^*(f) = |X(f)|^2, \quad (6\text{-}7)$$

which is proportional to the signal amplitude.

When noise is present, the matched filter has noise superimposed on its output. Instead of having two precise values as in the no-noise case, the output follows one of two probability distributions, depending on whether a 1 or 0 was transmitted. When the noise is white Gaussian, as in a channel in which receiver noise is dominant, the matched filter output is as shown in Fig. 6-2(b): the values of Fig. 6-2(a) with Gaussian distributions centered on each.

The demodulator's decision is conceptually simple: It observes whether the filter output is positive or negative. The figure also shows us that a decision error can occur in one of two ways: when a 1 is transmitted and an improbable noise event causes the matched filter output to be negative or when a 0 is transmitted and the noise produces a positive output from the matched filter. It is easily seen that the probability of an incorrect decision is given exactly by the area of those portions of the tails of the distributions that cross the axis. Clearly, the greater the signal-to-noise ratio, the skinnier the distributions and the smaller the areas representing the probability of an incorrect decision.

To compute the value of the probability of error, we have to compute the area of the tails of the distributions in Fig. 6-2(b). The symmetry of the situation tells us immediately that the two tail areas are equal, so it is sufficient to compute one of them, say, the probability of detecting a 1 when a 0 is sent, the tail of the left curve. The probability density function for the Gaussian process is given by

$$p_0(x) = \frac{1}{\sigma\sqrt{2\pi}} e^{-\frac{(x+A)^2}{2\sigma^2}},$$

$$(6\text{-}8)$$

where the mean of the distribution is $-A$ and its standard deviation *is* σ. The area under the entire curve is 1. In our case, A has the same value $\sqrt{E_b}$ as in the noiseless case shown in Fig. 6-2(a). The standard deviation σ is the noise power density that, in this case, has the value $N_0/2$. Why the factor of $1/2$? It is because in all our Fourier transform calculations, we have been using negative as well as positive frequencies. As a result, the noise power density has to be halved, so that the noise power in a band W (including both positive and negative frequencies) becomes $(2W)(N_0/2)$, the same value as when the frequencies are restricted to be positive. All of which goes to demonstrate that mathematics cannot change physical reality.

To obtain the desired probability of error, we compute the area of the tail of the distribution to the right of the origin. Thus,

$$P_e = \frac{1}{\sigma\sqrt{2\pi}} \int_0^\infty e^{-\frac{(x+A)^2}{2\sigma^2}} \, dx = \frac{1}{\sqrt{\pi N_0}} \int_0^\infty e^{-\frac{(x+\sqrt{E_b})^2}{N_0}} \, dx. \quad (6\text{-}9)$$

We will designate this function as $Q\left(\sqrt{E_b/N_0}\right)$. Unfortunately, this function cannot be evaluated in closed form. However, it is closely related to

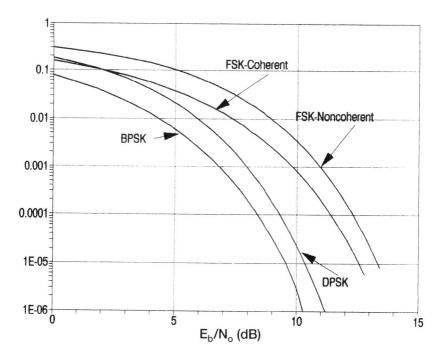

Figure 6-3   Performance of several modulation systems.

a common function among statisticians called the *complementary error function,* which is widely tabulated. Clearly, the larger the value of E_b/N_0, the smaller the error probability. Figure 6-3 shows a plot of P_e vs. E_b/N_0. The figure also shows several other binary modulation systems that we discuss in the following sections.

6.1.2   Limitations of BPSK

Binary phase shift keying is a very efficient modulation technique. However, it has certain practical difficulties. Probably the most important of these is the fact that the phase of the carrier frequency has to be known precisely in order to build the matched filter that is the key to the demodulator. Before demodulation can begin, this phase has to be determined through the transmission of some sort of preamble known to the receiver. Then the phase has to be tracked all during the transmission to keep the performance from degrading as the phase shifts while the information is being transmitted. This drawback is particularly severe if one or both of the ends of the link is mobile and only transmits or receives spasmodically.

There is another practical difficulty, called *intersymbol interference*, that has to be watched out for in many modulation systems, including but not restricted to BPSK. If the received signal pulses have tails on them that last for an appreciable length of time, then the samples obtained at the output of the matched filter can be contaminated by remnants of pulses transmitted previously. In the example of the previous section, the transmitted pulses were perfectly rectangular with no tails. Recall, however, that such a pulse has a spectrum with *sinx/x* shape that requires a significant amount of bandwidth before the tails die out. If you cannot afford all the bandwidth needed to pass most of the significant harmonics, and pass the signal waveforms through a filter, then the filtering process will insert potentially harmful tails on the pulse shape.

However, there are remedies. One approach is to soften the edges of the pulses. This reduces the tails of the frequency spectrum at the cost of reducing the signal energy slightly. A more sophisticated approach is to use one of a family of pulse shapes known as *Nyquist* pulses. Pulses in this category have a confined spectrum that produces tails in the time waveform. However, these tails are guaranteed to have zero crossings at the sampling times of other pulses and hence do not contribute unwanted components to the matched filter outputs.

Even with the most carefully designed pulse shapes, the channel can distort the signals so as to introduce intersymbol interference, and any matched filter has to take this into account to be effective. High-frequency radio channels are notorious for introducing such dispersion in the form of *multipath*, the reception of delayed copies of the transmitted signals that result from multiple reflections. The "ghosts" that sometimes appear on television screens when indoor antennas are used are caused by similar reflections. Such multiple signals have to be tracked to allow the matched filter to compensate for them.

In some situations, the problem of acquiring and maintaining the receiver phase in synchronism with the phase of the received signal is more trouble than it is worth. It is preferable, in such situations, to use a slightly different modulation technique known as *differential phase shift keying* (DPSK). DPSK is substantially easier to synchronize than BPSK, and the small loss of efficiency suffered in its use is sometimes worth the simplicity.

6.1.3   Differential Phase Shift Keying

The chart that follows illustrates the difference between BPSK and DPSK. In BPSK the sequence of 0s and 1s in the data stream is mapped into a sequence of opposite phase pulses. In DPSK a negative phase is transmitted when the current data bit is the same as the previous one and a positive phase when the current bit differs from the previous bit. Obviously, something has to be done to start the process. Here we have assumed a start-up bit set to 1 preceding the data stream. Since the first data bit is 0, the first transmitted phase is + reflecting the change.

Data bits	0	1	1	0	0	1	0
BPSK	–	+	+	–	–	+	–
DPSK	+	+	–	+	–	+	+

In BPSK all the demodulator has to do is pass the received signal through a matched filter and then measure the polarity of the sampled output to determine whether a 0 or 1 was transmitted. In DPSK the signal has to be passed through the matched filter and compared with the previous signal. Then the polarity of this differential sample has to be examined. But since the DPSK demodulator is not presumed to know the absolute phase, it has to match filter the signal in two separate channels using local oscillator phase references 90 degrees out of phase with each other ($\sin 2\pi f_0 t$ and $\cos 2\pi f_0 t$). Then the sine and cosine channels are combined using envelope detectors before the final polarity determination can be made.

The computation that determines the performance of DPSK differs from that for BPSK primarily because when Gaussian noise is passed through an envelope detector, its statistical behavior changes. The mathematics involved is fairly complex, and I will simply quote the result:

$$P_e = 1/2\, e^{-\frac{E_b}{N_0}}. \qquad (6\text{-}10)$$

It is remarkably simple, despite the complexity of the computation. This expression for the error probability is also plotted in Fig. 6-3. In the range of interest, it differs from BPSK by 2 dB at most.

The other two curves in Fig. 6-3 are labeled FSK with coherent detection and FSK with noncoherent detection. As it turns out, the computation for these two cases are simple variants of BPSK and DPSK, and we discuss these in the next section.

6.1.4 Orthogonal Signaling—FSK

When one gets into the mathematics of either form of FSK, it is immediately evident that we are dealing with the mathematics of orthogonal signals. FSK is simply the most common form of implementing such signals. Orthogonality is the same here as when we defined it in chapter 4 during the discussion of Fourier series and transforms. It means that the product of the functions integrated over the appropriate interval is zero.

Coherent detection means that the demodulator knows the phase of the received signals and can maintain this phase. It therefore contains two filters matched to each of the frequencies. For each transmitted signal, one of the filters should have a large output and the other no output. Of course, noise can corrupt the signal and, on occasion, the "incorrect" filter will yield a larger output than the "correct" filter and an error will occur. In the absence of noise, the sampled output of the matched filter is $\sqrt{E_b}$, as with BPSK. But unlike BPSK, in which the polarity of a single matched filter output was used to identify the received signal, in coherent FSK the outputs of two matched filters are compared. This effectively doubles the noise, giving us the result that for coherent orthogonal signals, the error probability is

$$P_e = Q\left(\sqrt{\frac{E_b}{N_0}} \right), \tag{6-11}$$

the same expression as for BPSK but with half the E_b/N_0 value. This curve is, therefore, 3 dB worse than for BPSK.

With noncoherent FSK signaling, the receiver is assumed to have no knowledge of the phase. All it can do is detect the envelope of the received signals in the two filter bands and see which is larger. The process is similar to that used in DPSK, and the result is the same with a 3-dB degradation as follows:

$$P_e = 1/2\, e^{-\frac{E_b}{2N_0}}. \tag{6-12}$$

The 3-dB degradation results from the fact that in DPSK, as opposed to noncoherent FSK, each received pulse is used twice. This means that the noise is correlated on successive decisions and is effectively divided in two.

   The following table summarizes the error probabilities for the four binary modulation techniques that we have just discussed.

BPSK $P_e = Q\left(\sqrt{\dfrac{2E_b}{N_0}}\right)$,

DPSK $P_e = 1/2\, e^{-\frac{E_b}{N_0}}$,   (6-13)

FSK/coherent $P_e = Q\left(\sqrt{\dfrac{E_b}{N_0}}\right)$,

FSK/noncoherent $P_e = 1/2\, e^{-\frac{E_b}{2N_0}}$.

6.2   Coding Considerations for the Power-Limited Channel

As we showed in the last chapter, the practical way to improve the efficiency of a communications system is to couple a code to the modulation system in order to make the signals longer and obtain the benefits of Shannon's theorem. Of course, such a process when realizable with practical equipment does not reach capacity. Still, in the power-limited case that we are interested in at the moment, it enables us to reduce the required E_b/N_0 value to bring it closer to the Shannon limit than practical by modulation alone. This allows the communicator either to reduce the power-to-noise density ratio for a given rate or to increase the rate for a given power-to-noise ratio in accordance with Eq. 6-1.

   We show what this means graphically in Fig. 6-4. The curve on the right is for an uncoded modulation system, and that on the left is for the same modulation system coupled to a rate $1/2$ code. At an error probability of 10^{-5}, the curves show an improvement of a little more than 3 dB in E_b/N_0. The figure also indicates that when coupled to the rate $1/2$ code, the modulation system has to run twice as fast as when uncoded or with a *channel-bit* energy-to-noise ratio of about 7.5 dB, yielding an error prob-

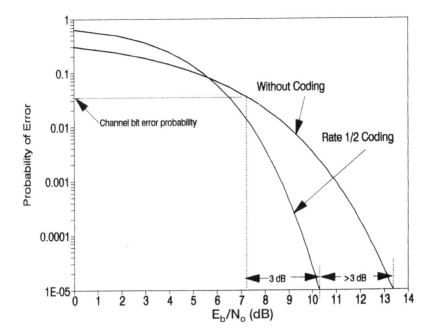

Figure 6-4   How coding improves system performance.

ability of about $3.5 + 10^{-2}$, illustrating our previous assertion that the way to improve performance is to push the channel rate up so that more errors are made and then correct the errors with a code.

Once the decision is made to use coding, choices have to be made:

- Should the modulation system be binary, or is a higher-order alphabet preferable?
- What kind of coding/decoding system should be used?

In the power-limited case, it turns out that there is not much to be gained by using a higher-order alphabet. This is because the coupling to a code means that the modulation system itself works at a relatively high error probability in the range where the alphabet size is not very important. As shown later in chapter 7, this situation is substantially different in the bandwidth-limited case. This conclusion is independent of which modulation system is used. Next comes the choice of coding/decoding scheme.

6.2.1   Coding and Decoding Classes

In chapter 5 we gave the example of the Hamming code. This code has two features that we emphasize at this point. It is a *block* code, and the way it is encoded and decoded is called *algebraic*. The encoder for a block code takes k information bits from the data source and performs a computation to convert them into n *channel bits* to be sent over the communications channel. The algebraic decoder accepts the (possibly corrupted) block of n channel bits and extracts the k information bits by some kind of arithmetic operation.

The family of Hamming codes was the first of many such algebraic block coding schemes to be developed. All are conceptually the same, although the way the codes are generated and decoded are different in each case. Most notable among these is the Reed–Solomon (RS) code family. Reed–Solomon codes have become well-known in recent years because they are fundamental to the way that data is stored on compact discs (CDs) and their cousins CD-ROMs. Both the Hamming and RS codes go back to the 1950s. But neither they nor any other coding systems were applied in any widespread way until the compact disc system was being designed in the 1970s. The engineers and mathematicians responsible for the development of these coding techniques used to lament the fact that their creations were not being of any use to anyone. Then along came the CD, and the coding world was a different place. The thing that made coding practical for the CD and later for communications systems was, of course, the integrated circuit. These same chips that made the desktop computer cheap enough for the home made the complex computations inherent to decoding cheap enough for the CD player in the living room.

There is another entire class of codes and decoders that the integrated circuit has also moved from the realm of the experimental to the practical. The coding scheme is called *convolutional,* and the decoding techniques are called *probabilistic.* Probabilistic decoding is, in principle, just as applicable to block as to convolutional codes. As with algebraic codes, a block encoder takes k information bits and maps these into n channel bits. But now the decoder, instead of solving a set of equations to extract the information, compares the received sequence of n corrupted channel bits with each of the 2^k possible transmitted sequences and delivers to the user the sequence that it judges was most likely to have been sent. This computation is the same, in principle, as that performed when a higher-order alphabet is used, and it suffers from the same defect: the exponential increase in the number of required computations as k increases. And that is precisely the reason why convolutional encoding was invented.

Let's take an example to show the difference between the two types of codes. Suppose we have a block code that takes $k = 20$ data bits and from these generates $n = 60$ channel digits. (The ratio of k to n is called the *coding rate r*. In this example, $r = \frac{1}{3}$.) The coder then moves on to the next 20-bit block and from these generates the next 60 bits to be transmitted. Clearly, the transmitted bits in successive blocks are independent of one another.

The convolutional encoder also takes a window of k data bits and from these generates k/r channel bits. But rather than doing it on disjoint blocks, it does it one (or, perhaps, a few) information bit(s) at a time. Using the same values of k and n as in the block case, for a given window of k bits, it generates three channel bits. It then discards the oldest bit in the window, takes in one new bit, and then generates another three channel bits. It continues in this way indefinitely. Thus, for the same values of k and n, the convolutional encoder slides across the input data bit by bit (or a few bits at a time) in contrast to the block decoder that jumps k bits at a time. Thus, successive channel bits from the convolutional coding process are related to the bits transmitted in the past in a continuous way.

The convolutional coding/probabilistic decoding combination has become more widely used in communications systems than has the block coding/algebraic decoding combination, both because of the convolutional rather than block coding and because of the probabilistic rather than algebraic decoding. An important advantage of probabalistic decoding over algebraic is the fact that the former allows the demodulator to furnish the decoder with information about a received digit above and beyond its decision as to whether the demodulated digit is presumed to be a 0 or a 1. This so-called *soft-decision* decoding can achieve as much as a 2-dB advantage in signal-to-noise ratio over *hard-decision* decoding. Once the decision is made to use probabilistic decoding, the convolutional coding approach usually wins out over the block approach because the sequential nature of the output of a convolutional coder allows certain efficient probabilistic decoding procedures, which we discuss later, not possible with block codes. For this reason, block codes are almost always algebraic.

6.2.2　Soft Decisions and Hard Decisions

An algebraic decoder is, in essence, a device that corrects errors. For example, the Hamming code that we described in chapter 5 had the power to correct a single error in any position. A probabilistic decoder is not an error corrector per se. Rather it computes the probability that a particular sequence was transmitted given the evidence of the received signal. You might consider this hair splitting, since a decoder that decodes a message correctly has to have corrected whatever errors were made by the demodulator. However, a demodulator can provide more information to the decoder than its hard and fast decisions about whether a received bit is a 0 or a 1. It can, as noted above, provide a digitized version of the output voltage of its matched filters to some degree of approximation—a so-called *soft* decision. Since anything that provides more information about the received signals cannot help but improve the determination of the most probable sequence, there is an advantage to using this additional information.

As an indication of the plausibility of this argument, consider a simple example involving two channel symbols sent by BPSK. Suppose the detection of the first symbol results in a small positive voltage from the matched filter and the second yields a large positive voltage. A hard-decision detector would call each of the bits a 1, disregarding the fact that one voltage was large and one small. Now imagine a soft-decision detector that delivers two bits to the decoder defined as follows:

00　large negative voltage

01　small negative voltage

10　small positive voltage

11　large positive voltage

with *large* and *small* defined by establishing a threshold at the matched filter output. In our example, the output would be 10 for the first bit and 11 for the second, telling the decoder that the first bit was a little more likely to be a 1 than a 0, while the second bit was a 1 with high probability. If the transmitted bits were 01, then the hard-decision decoder would simply have delivered the first bit incorrectly, while the soft-decision decoder would give the result that the first bit was probably a 1 but might be a 0 with somewhat lower probability. This information would be used in subsequent decisions based upon longer sequences of digits that followed these two.

The difference between hard- and soft-decision decoding is reflected in the capacity of the two channels. We saw in chapter 5 that in a Gaussian channel, E_b/N_0 cannot be less than $1/\log e = \ln 2$, which has the value of 0.693 or -1.6 dB. When the modulation process is restricted to hard decisions, then the bound on E_b/N_0 is $(\pi/2)\ln 2$, which has the value 1.08 or 0.4 dB, approximately 2 dB higher than when soft decisions are allowed.

It is important to note that this 2-dB differential for the bound on E_b/N_0 extends to practical modulation-coding systems and, as noted above, gives us a strong reason to prefer probabilistic decoding particularly for the power-limited channel. It should be mentioned that while a few algebraic codes have been developed that can take advantage of soft-decision coding, these have not been widely applied.

6.2.3   Block Codes

As stated earlier, a block code of coding rate r is one in which k information bits are mapped into $n = k/r$ channel bits. It is often called an (n,k) code. The mapping is usually expressed mathematically in matrix form. Let u be the k-bit input to the encoder expressed as a k-component vector, $u_1, u_2, \ldots, u_k$, and let v be the n-bit output expressed as an n-component vector, $v_1, v_2, \ldots, v_n$. Then k and n are related by the following matrix equation:

$$v = uG, \tag{6-14}$$

where G, a matrix with k rows and n columns, defines the code. In most cases, the elements of both vectors and the matrix are 0s and 1s. The following is an example of such an encoding matrix for $k = 3$ and $n = 6$:

$$G = \begin{bmatrix} 1 & 0 & 0 & 1 & 1 & 1 \\ 0 & 1 & 0 & 0 & 1 & 1 \\ 0 & 0 & 1 & 1 & 0 & 1 \end{bmatrix}. \tag{6-15}$$

The multiplication of u by G follows the rules of matrix multiplication that involve taking sums and products of the elements of the matrices. Since all these elements are 0s and 1s, the multiplications and additions follow the rules of Boolean algebra defined in accordance with the following tables. The symbol $\oplus$ in the table is called the *exclusive or,* the *sum modulo*-2, or the *parity* symbol.

x	y	xy	x	y	$x \oplus y$
0	0	0	0	0	0
0	1	0	0	1	1
1	0	0	1	0	1
1	1	1	1	1	0

To see how the matrix multiplication works, suppose the input vector u is 101, then the output vector v is obtained as follows:

1. To obtain the first bit of v, perform a bit-by-bit multiplication of u by the first column of the matrix in Eq. 6-15, obtaining 1×1, 0×0, 1×0. Then add the three products modulo-2, giving the result $1 \oplus 0 \oplus 0 = 1$.

2. To obtain the second bit of v, do the same as in step 1, using the second column of the matrix.

3. Obtain the remaining digits using the remaining columns of the matrix. The resulting sequence for v is 101010.

Note that the first three columns of the matrix have 1s along the diagonal. This means that the information bits themselves are the first three bits of the output sequence. Such a code is called *systematic*. It can be shown that there is no loss of generality in using systematic as opposed to nonsystematic codes, and, for reasons of simplicity, almost all the codes of interest are systematic. The remaining bits in the code, the so-called *check* bits, are determined by the pattern of 0s and 1s in the matrix. Obviously, not all patterns are equal. The essential task is to define a matrix that generates code words that are as *unlike* one another as possible.

Figure 6-5 shows a block diagram that implements the foregoing encoding process. The three information bits, u_1, u_2, u_3, are shifted into a register to which are connected three sum modulo-2 or parity circuits corresponding to the rightmost three columns of the matrix. Note that a connection into the parity circuit signifies that the matrix bit is a 1, and no connection signifies a 0. For example, the first check digit is formed by taking the sum modulo-2 of the first and third information bits. The outputs of these three parity circuits are, respectively, the check bits v_4, v_5, and v_6 of the output sequence. The first three bits of the output sequence, the information bits v_1, v_2, and v_3, are obtained directly from the shift register. Once this process is completed, the next three information bits are shifted into the register, and the process is repeated.

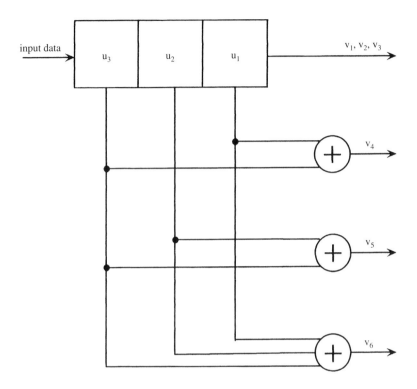

Figure 6-5   A block encoder.

In most cases in which such algebraic codes are used, the underlying assumption is that the channel is *binary symmetric,* that is, a channel in which the probability of a 1 being received as a 0 is the same as the probability of a 0 being received as a 1, with this probability of error independent from bit to bit. With this assumption, the number of places in which two *n*-bit code words differ from one another is a measure of the probability that noise will make one look like another. Thus the best codes are those whose code words differ from one another in as many places as possible. We refer to the number of places in which two *n*-bit vectors differ from one another as the *Hamming distance*, after R. W. Hamming, one of the pioneers in coding theory.

Hamming was the first to develop a systematic set of codes. These codes are of the form

$$n = 2^m - 1, \quad k = 2^m - 1 - m, \quad m \geq 3.$$

For example, the Hamming code introduced in chapter 5, repeated below in Table 6-1, is for $m = 3$, $k = 4$, and $n = 7$.

Table 6-1   The (7,4) Hamming Code

1	0	0	0	0	0	0	0
2	0	0	0	1	1	1	1
3	0	0	1	0	1	1	0
4	0	0	1	1	0	0	1
5	0	1	0	0	1	0	1
6	0	1	0	1	0	1	0
7	0	1	1	0	0	1	1
8	0	1	1	1	1	0	0
9	1	0	0	0	0	1	1
10	1	0	0	1	1	0	0
11	1	0	1	0	1	0	1
12	1	0	1	1	0	1	0
13	1	1	0	0	1	1	0
14	1	1	0	1	0	0	1
15	1	1	1	0	0	0	0
16	1	1	1	1	1	1	1

In all Hamming codes, the minimum Hamming distance between code words is 3. Note, for example, in the preceeding table that the first (all-0) sequence has seven nearest neighbors each with three 1s—sequences 3, 4, 5, 6, 9, 10, and 15. If sequence 1 is transmitted and a single error is made, the received sequence will be distance 1 from the transmitted sequence and distance 2 or more from any other. Thus, any Hamming code will correct all instances in which a single error is made. But whenever two or more errors are made, the received vector is closer to some incorrect sequence, and a decoding error is made.

In the most common decoding procedure for systematic codes, the first step is to re-encode the first k bits of the received sequence (the information bits of a systematic code) using the same encoding matrix G as that used in the coder. The check bits obtained in this way are called the *syndrome* of the received vector. This syndrome is then added modulo-2 bit by bit to the check bits in the received message. If no transmission errors are made, the result of this addition is a vector with $n-k$ 0s. If a correctable number of errors is made, then the sum indicates the places in which the errors occur. This indicates a simple decoding scheme: build a table addressed by the syndrome, storing at each address the sequence that when added to the received sequence will correct the errors. The following is such a table for the (7,4) Hamming code.

Syndrome	Correction
0 0 0	0 0 0 0
0 0 1	0 0 0 0
0 1 0	0 0 0 0
0 1 1	1 0 0 0
1 0 0	0 0 0 0
1 0 1	0 1 0 0
1 1 0	0 0 1 0
1 1 1	0 0 0 1

To see how this works, suppose the first sequence is transmitted and the received sequence is 0000100, with an error in the first check bit. The computed syndrome is 000 and the correction sequence is all 0s since the information bits were received without error. If, on the other hand, the first four bits of the received sequence are 0100, then the syndrome is 101, the check bits for sequence 5. In this case, the correction is 0100, which corrects the error in the second information digit.

6.2.3.1   *Cyclic Codes.*   Hamming codes, while simple conceptually, are not very powerful and are rarely used. It is also evident that decoding by computing the syndrome and then using a table lookup scheme becomes unwieldy when k and n become large. Of course, the Hamming codes were only the first to be discovered. Subsequently, other families of block codes were developed. Almost all the significant families belong to a sub-category called *cyclic* codes. Some of these cyclic code families have error-correction properties far more powerful than those of the Hamming codes. In addition, their cyclic nature introduces certain symmetries that simplify the decoding process. Most of the block codes that have been implemented are in this category.

To understand what cyclic codes are, we first need a definition of a cyclic shift. Suppose we have an n-bit code word. A cyclic shift to the right shifts every bit of the code word one place to the right with the rightmost bit shifted around to the leftmost position. A cyclic shift to the left does the equivalent. A cyclic code is defined as one in which all cyclic shifts of a given code word are also code words. For example, if a vector 0111001 is a code word, then so is 1011100, obtained by shifting all the bits to the right and cycling the rightmost bit around to the left end. Similarly, the vector 1110010, obtained by a cyclic shift to the left, is also a code word.

Like any other block code, a cyclic code can be specified by an encoding matrix with k rows and n columns that maps a k-bit information sequence into an n-bit output sequence. The following encoding matrix is for a cyclic (15, 11) code:

$$\begin{bmatrix} 1 & 0 & 0 & 0 & 0 & 0 & 0 & 0 & 0 & 0 & 0 & 1 & 0 & 0 & 1 \\ 0 & 1 & 0 & 0 & 0 & 0 & 0 & 0 & 0 & 0 & 0 & 1 & 1 & 0 & 1 \\ 0 & 0 & 1 & 0 & 0 & 0 & 0 & 0 & 0 & 0 & 0 & 1 & 1 & 1 & 1 \\ 0 & 0 & 0 & 1 & 0 & 0 & 0 & 0 & 0 & 0 & 0 & 1 & 1 & 1 & 0 \\ 0 & 0 & 0 & 0 & 1 & 0 & 0 & 0 & 0 & 0 & 0 & 0 & 1 & 1 & 1 \\ 0 & 0 & 0 & 0 & 0 & 1 & 0 & 0 & 0 & 0 & 0 & 1 & 0 & 1 & 0 \\ 0 & 0 & 0 & 0 & 0 & 0 & 1 & 0 & 0 & 0 & 0 & 0 & 1 & 0 & 1 \\ 0 & 0 & 0 & 0 & 0 & 0 & 0 & 1 & 0 & 0 & 0 & 1 & 0 & 1 & 1 \\ 0 & 0 & 0 & 0 & 0 & 0 & 0 & 0 & 1 & 0 & 0 & 1 & 1 & 0 & 0 \\ 0 & 0 & 0 & 0 & 0 & 0 & 0 & 0 & 0 & 1 & 0 & 0 & 1 & 1 & 0 \\ 0 & 0 & 0 & 0 & 0 & 0 & 0 & 0 & 0 & 0 & 1 & 0 & 0 & 1 & 1 \end{bmatrix} .$$

As before, the eleven columns on the left each contain a single 1 positioned along the diagonal. This forces the first 11 bits of the output sequence to be the information bits. The other 4 bits of the sequence, the parity check bits, are sums modulo-2 of these information bits as determined by the pattern in the rightmost four columns of the matrix.

You cannot tell that this code is cyclic by simply observing the pattern of 0s and 1s. It takes a little algebra to see that this is so. One way to give you confidence that this is so is to assume a particular input vector of 11 information bits, run them through the matrix, and compute the 15 output bits. Then cycle the bits, compute the parity bits for the cycled sequence, and check that the parity bits agree.

But there is a more analytical way to do this. In a cyclic code the general properties of encoding and decoding that we discussed earlier correspond to certain algebraic operations involving polynomials, and it is this algebraic structure that gives the codes their power. To see this, let's call the 15-bit codeword resulting from multiplying an information bit sequence by the foregoing matrix a_{14}, a_{13}, a_{12}, . . . , a_0. Then we form the polynomial

$$a(x) = a_{14}x^{14} + a_{13}x^{13} + \ldots + a_1x + a_0. \qquad (6\text{-}16)$$

Shifting the sequence to the left by one place is equivalent to multiplying the polynomial by x, converting it to the 15th-degree polynomial $a_{14}x^{15} + a_{13}x^{14} + a_1x^2 + a_0x$. When we cycle the leftmost bit to the rightmost position, we convert this 15th-degree polynomial to the 14th-degree polynomial $a_{13}x^{14} + a_1x^2 + a_0x + a_{14}$. This is equivalent to dividing the cycled polynomial by $x^{15} - 1$ and retaining the remainder. For example, take the information sequence 10001000100. When encoded, the sequence is transformed to 100010001000010, corresponding to the polynomial $x^{14} + x^{10} + x^6 + x$. A cyclic shift to the left gives us the sequence 000100010000101, corresponding to the polynomial $x^{11} + x^7 + x^2 + 1$, which is just what you get when you multiply $x^{14} + x^{10} + x^6 + x$ by x and then divide by $x^{15} - 1$.

The polynomial representation is used to simplify both the encoding and decoding operations. To see how this works for the encoding operation, we can rewrite the encoding matrix in polynomial form. We do this by expressing each row of the matrix by a polynomial in which the 1s are replaced by the associated power of 10 (from 14 to 0) and the 0s are left blank. When we do this, we get the following polynomial matrix:

$$\begin{bmatrix}
x^{14} & & & & & & & & & & x^3 & & & 1 \\
& x^{13} & & & & & & & & & x^3 & x^2 & & 1 \\
& & x^{12} & & & & & & & & x^3 & x^2 & x & 1 \\
& & & x^{11} & & & & & & & x^3 & x^2 & x & \\
& & & & x^{10} & & & & & & & x^2 & x & 1 \\
& & & & & x^9 & & & & & x^3 & & x & \\
& & & & & & x^8 & & & & & x^2 & & 1 \\
& & & & & & & x^7 & & & x^3 & & x & 1 \\
& & & & & & & & x^6 & & x^3 & x^2 & & \\
& & & & & & & & & x^5 & & x^2 & x & \\
& & & & & & & & & & x^4 & & x & 1
\end{bmatrix}.$$

The polynomial in each row of a cyclic code has a common factor called the *generator polynomial* for the code. For this particular code, the generator polynomial is

$$g(x) = x^4 + x + 1. \qquad (6\text{-}17)$$

For example, the first row of the matrix can be expressed as

$$x^{14} + x^3 + 1 = (x^4 + x + 1)(x^{10} + x^7 + x^6 + x^4 + x^2 + x + 1). \quad (6\text{-}18)$$

Writing each row in terms of its generator polynomial, the foregoing polynomial matrix can be expressed in the following form:

$$
\begin{bmatrix}
(x^{10} + & x^7 + & x^6 + & x^4 + & x^2 + & x + & 1) & (x^4 + x + 1) \\
 & (x^9 + & x^6 + & x^5 + & x^3 + & x + & 1) & (x^4 + x + 1) \\
 & & (x^8 + & x^5 + & x^4 + & x^2 + & 1) & (x^4 + x + 1) \\
 & & & (x^7 + & x^4 + & x^3 + & 1) & (x^4 + x + 1) \\
 & & & & (x^6 + & x^3 + & x^2 + & 1) & (x^4 + x + 1) \\
 & & & & & (x^5 + & x^2 + & x) & (x^4 + x + 1) \\
 & & & & & & (x^4 + & x + & 1) & (x^4 + x + 1) \\
 & & & & & & & (x^3 + & 1) & (x^4 + x + 1) \\
 & & & & & & & & x^2 & (x^4 + x + 1) \\
 & & & & & & & & x & (x^4 + x + 1) \\
 & & & & & & & & & x^4 + x + 1
\end{bmatrix}.
$$

Using this representation, we can obtain the parity check bits from the information bits by dividing the information polynomial by the generator polynomial. The remainder from this division indicates the parity bits. For example, the information sequence 10001000100 is expressed as the polynomial $x^{14} + x^{10} + x^6 + x$. Dividing this by the generator polynomial $x^4 + x + 1$ leaves the remainder x, which indicates that the third parity bit is 1 and all the others are 0, the same result that we obtained previously by a direct computation of the parity bits.

Figure 6-6 shows a coder structure based on these properties of cyclic codes. The top diagram (Fig. 6-6(a)) is of a generic encoder. The information bits are shifted into an $(n - k)$-bit register from the left. Then once the first $n - k$ bits have been shifted in, the switch at the right end of the shift register is then thrown to the top position. After each of the next k shifts, the rightmost digit is fed back to the earlier stages in accordance with the values of $g(x)$. After these k shifts, the parity bits are in the shift register. The switch is then thrown to the bottom position, and these parity bits are shifted out of the register as the first $n\text{-}k$ bits of the next block are shifted in. The encoder for the generator polynomial of our example, $g(x) = x^4 + x + 1$, is shown in Fig. 6-6(b). It is much simpler in form than would be the straightforward encoder that generates the parity check matrix as in Fig. 6-5.

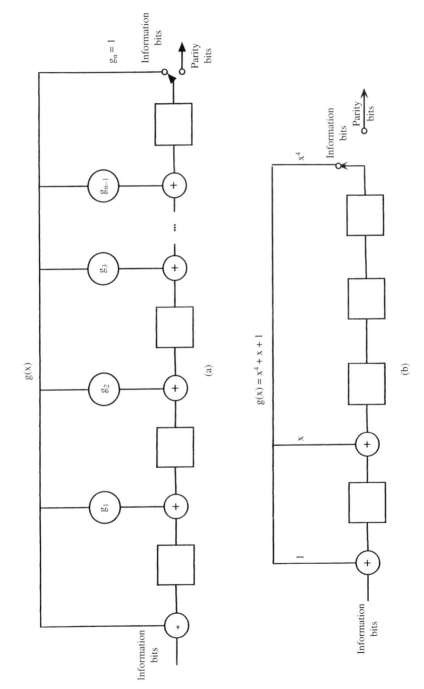

Figure 6-6 Encoders for cyclic codes: (a) generic encoder and (b) encoder for polynomial $g(x) = x^4 + x + 1$.

6.2.3.2   Families of Cyclic Codes—Reed–Solomon Codes. In the cyclic category is a well-known code family known as Bose–Chaudhuri–Hocquenghem (BCH) codes with the following properties.

$$m \geq 3, \quad n = 2^m - 1, \quad n - k = mt,$$

where t is the number of errors corrected. In these codes, the minimum distance between any pair of code words is $2t + 1$. For example, let $m = 3$, so that $n = 7$. If we want the code to correct two errors, then $n - k$ must equal 6, or k is 1. Note also that when $t = 1$, the values of k and n are the same as for a Hamming code.

The BCH family, developed in the 1950s, constituted a major step in understanding the limits of applicability of block coding. A few years later, Reed and Solomon took another major step when they succeeded in generalizing the BCH codes to higher-order alphabets, that is, numbering systems in which the base is larger than 2. They showed that all the above expressions for the BCH codes carry directly over to higher-order alphabets. This is an important step since, in many cases, the bits to be encoded are derived from the sampling and subsequent digitization of analog signals into multivalued symbols. For example, in the compact disc format, 16-bit samples of the source audio are taken. These 16-bit samples are each divided into two 8-bit units that are encoded by a Reed–Solomon code based on an eight-symbol alphabet.

As stated earlier, one of the main advantages of cyclic codes such as BCH and RS codes is the fact that they can be decoded by solving a set of equations rather than using the syndrome lookup table method, making them practical for larger values of k than otherwise possible. The mathematics underlying these codes, the algebra of finite fields, is too complex to present here, and references are provided for readers who wish to dig deeper into algebraic coding.

6.2.4   Convolutional Encoding

Figure 6-7 shows a convolutional encoder. It looks superficially the same as the block coder. The difference between the two has to do with the way information bits are introduced into the encoder. For block coding, the $k = 3$ bits are shifted into the encoder at a time. Then, once the $n = 6$ channel bits shown in Fig. 6-5 or Fig. 6-6 have been transmitted, the next three information bits are shifted into the register in place of the previous bits, and the process is repeated. Clearly, successive codings and hence decodings are based on disjoint sets of bits.

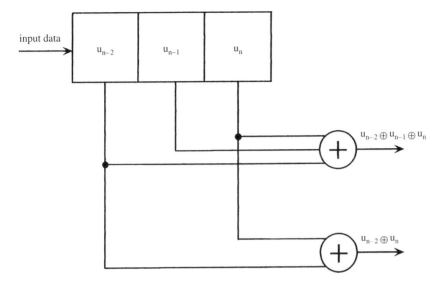

Figure 6-7   A convolutional encoder.

In the convolutional encoder of Fig. 6-7, the information bits are shifted into the register one at a time; at each shift the oldest bit is shifted out and a new one shifted in. The convolutional encoder in the figure has two parity check circuits. Each time a new bit u_n is shifted into the 3-bit register, 2 bits are sent out, v_{n1} and v_{n2}, one from each of the parity circuits. The code is, therefore, nonsystematic with rate $1/2$. Thus in this convolutional code, each pair of output bits depends on the last three information bits. The encoder can, therefore, be viewed as a window that slides across the information 1 bit at a time, with the corresponding output bits having a dependency that slides correspondingly. This is in contrast to the block code where the dependency in the output bits jumps from block to block.

This sliding dependency can be expressed in different ways. Perhaps the most useful way is the *trellis*. The trellis is a form of state diagram that shows the way the system progresses from one state to another as successive bits are shifted into the convolutional encoder. The states are characterized by the different combinations of bits in the shift register. Table 2 shows the combinations of states and input and output bits. In the table the current state S_n is determined by the two previous input bits u_{n-1} and u_{n-2}. Similarly, the next state S_{n+1} is designated by u_n and u_{n-1}. The channel bits designated v_n are the outputs of the two parity circuits, first the upper one and then the lower one.

Table 6-2   Inputs, Outputs, and States for the Convolutional Encoder
of Fig. 6-7

u_n	u_{n-1}	u_{n-2}	v_n	S_n	S_{n+1}
0	0	0	00	00	00
1	0	0	11	00	10
0	1	0	10	10	01
1	1	0	01	10	11
0	0	1	11	01	00
1	0	1	00	01	10
0	1	1	01	11	01
1	1	1	10	11	11

As seen before, each pair depends upon the current state and the current input bit. The elementary trellis, shown in Fig. 6-8, is a pictorial way
of showing the same information. The four system states are shown in
two columns. The column on the left designates the current state, and that
on the right shows the next state. The lines represent the paths from one
state to another. Two lines leave each of the current states, the upper

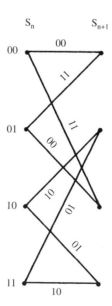

Figure 6-8   A four-state trellis.

when the current input bit is a 0, and the lower when it is a 1. Each line is labeled by the two output bits. Thus when the system is in state 01 and the current bit is a 0, the channel bits are 11, and the system moves to state 00.

But the trellis representation is more than an alternative to a state diagram. It is also a convenient pictorial way to show how the state changes from input bit to input bit, and it is helpful in showing how decoding works.

There are two decoding schemes customarily used with convolutional codes, called, respectively, Viterbi decoding (after Andrew Viterbi) and sequential decoding. Both are probabilistic in that they compare the received sequence of digits with sequences that could have been sent, rather than solve equations. Viterbi's method is to compare the received sequence with all possible transmitted sequences. While his searching technique is especially efficient, the fact that it is an exhaustive procedure means that ultimately the exponential problem will limit the constraint length of the code that can reasonably be handled this way.

Sequential decoding, in contrast, restricts its comparisons to the most probable transmitted sequences. This drastically reduces the number of computations, and so it allows very long constraint lengths. But it has other problems that we discuss later in the chapter.

6.2.4.1   Viterbi Decoding.   We show the essence of how Viterbi decoding works with an example derived from the convolutional encoder in Fig. 6-7. The trellis in Fig. 6-8 represents the behavior of the coder when a single information bit is shifted in. The cascade of identical trellis stages shown in Fig. 6-9 demonstrates how the encoder behaves as successive bits are shifted in. The figure starts out with the assumption that the system is in the 00 state and proceeds from there to build up the entire trellis. After the first information bit is shifted into the encoder, there are two possible states 00 and 10, and after the next bit all four states are possible. Any particular transmitted sequence is represented by a path through the trellis. For example, the path in bold represents the information sequence 101100 and the transmitted sequence 111000010111.

The Viterbi decoder contains an encoder identical to that at the transmitting end of the channel. The decoder receives a corrupted version of this transmitted message and, based upon the sequence, tries to find the path through the trellis that was its source. The way it does this is best explained with an example.

Just as the encoder at the transmitter traces out a path through the trellis one bit at a time, so the decoder works one bit at a time. Figure 6-10 contains a succession of diagrams that show how this is done using the basic trellis structure in Fig. 6-9. We label the stages or nodes of the trellis in sequence, and this is shown at the top of the diagram; for example, the trellis begins at node 0 and proceeds to node 1 after the first input digit. In this example, we assume for the sake of simplicity that the all-0 sequence is transmitted. We also assume that a single bit is received in error—the fourth bit—as shown in the received bit sequence above the trellis. As we go through the operation of the decoder, you will see how the decoder is confused at first by the error and then recovers.

Think of the decoder as laying a window on top of the received data and the trellis paths determined from this data. As the received digits pass through this window, the leftmost digit is decoded. The size of this window is typically a few times the constraint length, and, as shown later, the window used in the example has to be at least 8 nodes long.

Figure 6-10(a) shows the trellis up to node 3. Each path in the trellis is labeled by the *cumulative* Hamming distance between the received sequence and the path in the trellis. This Hamming distance is, of course, a measure of the probability that the path in question is correct based upon the received information. To make the diagram more legible, I have omitted the transmitted digits corresponding to the various paths that are shown in Fig. 6-9.

Once the decoder has reached node 2 of the trellis, all four states are possible. At node 3 we reach the steady-state configuration in which two branches terminate on each the four states. The decoder is now ready to begin eliminating trellis paths. At each state it discards the branch on the path with the larger cumulative Hamming distance (the less probable path) and retains the other branch. The diagram shows this by using a lighter line for the rejected path. As you can readily see by tracing back from the rejected branches, this selection process eliminates all paths stemming from the lower branch at node 0, indicating that the first information bit is a 0.

Figure 6-10(b) extends the trellis in Fig. 6-10(a) to four nodes. In this picture the paths that were rejected in the previous step are erased. As in the previous diagram, the less probable branch at each state of node 4 is rejected. But, unlike the previous step, no early paths are eliminated. At the five-node step shown in Fig. 6-10(c), some paths are rejected by the pruning process, but the correct path from node 1 to node 2 is still not de-

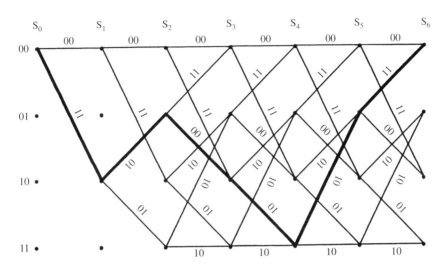

Figure 6-9 Cascade of trellis stages.

termined. Note that the two branches leading to the 10 state at node 5 have the same cumulative Hamming distance, and both these paths are retained at the next step. At node 6, shown in Fig. 6-10(d), three of the states have two equiprobable paths leading to them, and the identity of the second bit is still undetermined. This bit remains ambiguous through the seventh node in Fig. 6-10(e). But at node 8 in Fig. 6-10(f), the rejection process not only eliminates the lower branch at node 1 but also identifies the next four bits as well. Figure 6-10(g) is a cleaned-up version of Fig. 6-10(e) that shows this more clearly.

It is interesting to note that even in this relatively benign example in which only a single error occurs, it takes eight nodes to determine the identity of the bit involving the error. There will, of course, be instances in which the leftmost bit is still ambiguous when it passes out of the decoding window. There will also be instances in which the noise pattern is such that the decoder selects the wrong branch and an error is made. Of course, the larger the constraint length and decoding window, the smaller the probabilities of both these kinds of occurrences.

This example was a simple one; it used a small constraint length, and it shifted a single bit into the encoder at a time. None of these simplifications are essential, nor is the assumption of a hard-decision demodulator. Clearly, since the decoder makes its decisions by computing probabilities, soft decisions are ideal for such a decoding procedure and improve its

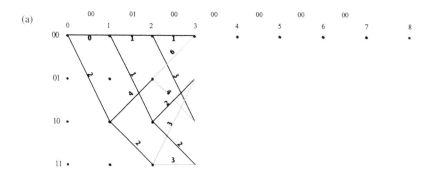

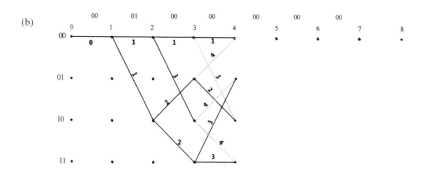

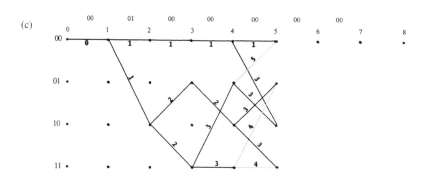

Figure 6-10 Viterbi decoding: (a) three nodes, (b) four nodes, (c) five nodes, (d) six nodes, (e) seven nodes, (f) eight nodes, (g) eight nodes (simplified).

(d)

(e)

(f)

(g)

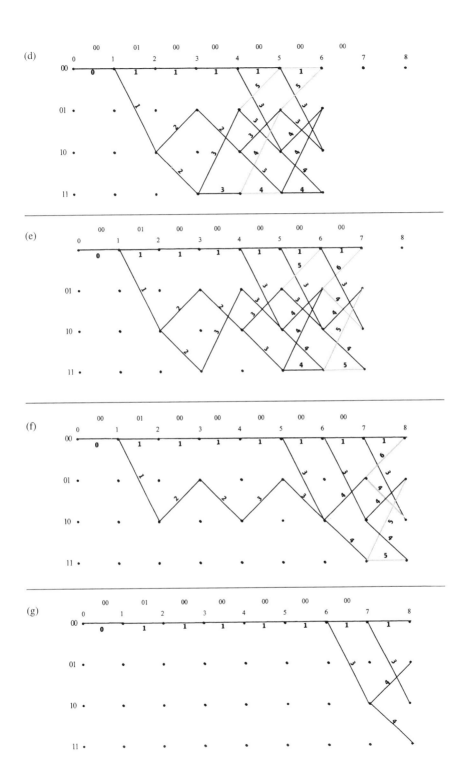

performance by about 2 dB. Viterbi decoders are applicable for constraint lengths up to 10 or thereabouts. For larger constraint lengths, the problem of examining all possible paths becomes just too time-consuming, and other techniques have to be used.

6.2.4.2 Sequential Decoding. Sequential decoding is just such a technique. Its inventor was Prof. John Wozencraft of MIT. Sequential decoding is a way of looking at the received digits so that they do not have to be compared with *all possible* transmitted sequences, but only with those sequences most likely to have been transmitted based upon inferences from previously decoded digits. This was the first technique that permitted communicators to make the sequences long enough to approach Shannon's results, although even this technique breaks down when the data rate is too close to capacity.

In 1961, my colleagues and I at MIT's Lincoln Laboratory built a system using Wozencraft's technique and succeeded in more than doubling the telephone-line data rates customary at the time. This machine was hardly practical, nor was it meant to be. Figure 6-11 shows Professors Shannon and Wozencraft with Paul Rosen, the Lincoln Laboratory project manager, in front of the two large cabinets full of electronics that constituted the system. We built another system in 1965 for use with one of the early satellite communications systems. This system achieved operation at E_b/N_0 of about 5 dB under power-limited conditions, a value only 5.6 dB above the Shannon limit. This system was much smaller physically, taking advantage of the improved component technology of the day (the first generation of small-scale integrated circuits) and also used a more efficient decoding scheme devised by Prof. Robert Fano, also of MIT. Nevertheless, the sequential decoding processing remained too complex for widespread application until the advent of the remarkably economical integrated circuits of the 1990s.

Recall that in Viterbi decoding the decoder proceeds through the trellis at each node by rejecting the less probable branch leading to each state at the node, retaining all the residual paths to each state until they are either eliminated or pass out of the decoding window. In contrast, the sequential decoder follows the single path that is locally most probable by comparing the cumulative distance between the received sequence and the possible transmitted sequences with a threshold value proportional to the length of the sequence being examined. When the distance remains under the threshold as the decoder proceeds to the right, it means that the

Figure 6-11 The first sequential decoder. (Reprinted with the permission of MIT Lincoln Laboratory, Lexington, Massachusetts.)

decoder is becoming more confident that it is on the right path. But when the distance exceeds the threshold, it can mean one of two things: (a) the decoder is on an incorrect path, or (b) the decoder is on the correct path, which an improbable burst of noise is making look incorrect. The decoder first assumes that (a) is the case and goes backward and then forward trying to find another path that looks better than the one it is on. If it fails to find one, then it returns to the original path under the assumption that hypothesis (b) is correct. If by going back far enough, the decoder finds a path that looks more probable, it proceeds forward on that path, making the assumption that this new path is the correct one. When the code constraint length is long, the decoder usually succeeds in finding the correct path in this way without having to retrace its steps far enough back to reach the boundary of the decoding window. Even if it does not run out of memory in this way, there are times when an improbable noise pattern forces the decoder to back up such a long distance that it is effectively examining such a large number of paths that the number of computations begins to climb exponentially just as with an exhaustive search scheme as in Viterbi decoding. As you would expect, the closer the rate is to the channel capacity, the more likely this is to happen. But it turns out that this exponential growth in the number of computations occurs at a rate below channel capacity, called the *computational cutoff* rate R_0. This rate, not the capacity, becomes the theoretical bound on the data rate achievable with sequential decoding.

A way of showing the relationship of R_0 to the capacity makes use of the following bound to the probability of error that is valid in all cases of interest:

$$P_e \leq A e^{-E(R)T}, \tag{6-19}$$

Where A is a constant, and T is the constraint length of the code measured in units of time. The function $E(R)$ known as the *error exponent* is plotted against the information rate R in Fig. 6-12. Note that for low rates the function decreases approximately linearly but then flattens out slowly to 0 as it approaches the horizontal axis at the capacity of the channel. Equation 6-19 therefore gives us an intuitive way of understanding the general meaning of the coding theorem and the channel capacity. The closer the rate is to capacity, the smaller the error exponent, hence the longer the

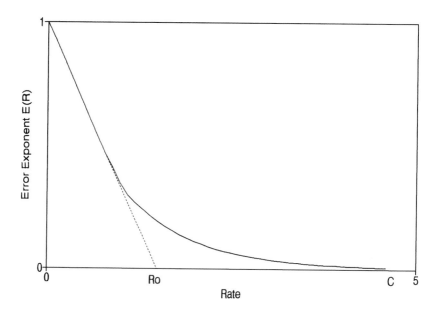

Figure 6-12   Error exponent vs. rate.

signals needed to achieve a given error probability. Capacity itself is the point at which the error exponent is 0, requiring infinitely long signals.

The computational cutoff rate R_0 appears in this picture as the extension of the straight-line portion of the curve to the horizontal axis. This theoretical limiting rate for sequential decoding is roughly one-half the channel capacity. In practice, the rate is kept below about $0.9R_0$. Thus, the price one pays for the advantages of sequential decoding is an effective limit on data rate to a value that, in most cases, is about one-half that of capacity.

The effect of this limitation is much more theoretical than real. For the Gaussian channel, this means a value of E_b/N_0 about 2.5 times the minimum of $1/\log e$ or 1.73, corresponding to about 2.4 dB, which is a remarkably low value. A more serious limitation is the fact that there are occasions in which the decoder has to go back farther than its memory allows in searching for the correct path. The lower the rate, the less frequently this overflow condition occurs, but it can occur at any rate. This means that from that point on the decoder has lost its way and will pass on incorrect digits until it is resynchronized. This can be accomplished by sending along resynchronization sequences periodically to permit the decoder to start afresh. The effect of the errors occurring in this way can be made less serious by scrambling the information digits before entering them into the convolutional encoder. In this way the contiguous errors resulting from an overflow become more like random errors. Another, perhaps more satisfactory, technique is to take advantage of a two-way channel and allow the search failure to trigger a signal to the transmitter to retransmit the last block of information. Either of these techniques results in a net decrease in data rate. Even with these limitations, sequential decoding remains as the most powerful coding technique available.

6.2.5 Concatenated Codes

There is still another interesting approach that combines block and convolutional coding in concatenated form. Recall that the most efficient way of coupling coding and modulation is to increase the modulation rate so that the resulting low value of E_b/N_0 is in the operating region of the modulation system where a significant number of errors are made and then correct the errors with a code. The result is a high rate (or low E_b/N_0) together with a low error rate. Of course, the higher the error probability at the operating point of the modulation system, the more powerful the code has to be to correct the errors. A concatenated scheme does the coding on two steps: (1) a modest code coupled to the modulation system corrects some of the errors, and (2) a second code completes the job of correcting the residual errors. If the residual error rate from the first code is not too high, then the second code can have a relatively high coding rate r so that the rate degradation is only slight.

A typical scheme is shown in Fig. 6-13. It is typical of the kind of modulation/coding systems used in small-antenna satellite systems—a so-called *very small-aperture terminal* (*VSAT*)—and hence are highly power limited. The diagram shows the two codes in tandem: an inner convolutional code with Viterbi decoding (rate $\frac{1}{2}$, constraint length 7) coupled to a BPSK modulation system with soft-decision demodulation and an outer Reed–Solomon block code with $k = 201$ and $n = 219$. Such a concatenated system delivers an extremely low error rate (10^{-10} under the most ideal conditions) at an E_b/N_0 of 4.3 dB. The inner code delivers an error probability of about 10^{-4}. The Viterbi decoder used by itself would require an E_b/N_0 of 7–8 dB to achieve such a low error rate. The manufacturer of this terminal also offers a system using sequential decoding with constraint length 32 that requires in excess of 6 dB to achieve this error rate. An alternative that could more than match the performance of the concatenated system would use sequential decoding with a larger con-

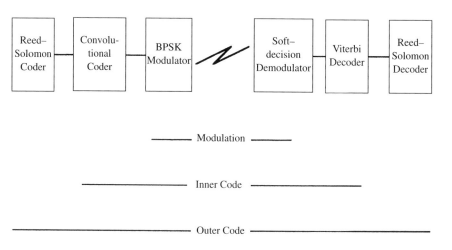

Figure 6-13   A concatenated code.

straint length. All of which goes to show that there is no unique solution to an engineering problem that is applicable to all situations.

6.3   Sharing Channels among Multiple Users

Throughout this chapter we have assumed communication to be between a pair of users through a well-defined channel. This is true in a literal sense in the case of a telephone line but not in most other situations. In the most familiar example, AM broadcasting is carried out in the band of frequencies between 500 and 1500 kHz. In any given locality, many radio stations share this bandwidth. The same thing is true in the other broadcasting bands used for FM radio and television. Other radio bands are designated for two-way communications of different kinds: microwave relay, satellite relay, cellular radio, and so forth. In all these cases many users share the band, and some rules have to be established to give each user or set of users a channel without interfering with other users of the same band. This channel sharing is known as *multiple access.*

6.3.1   Multiplexing

Multiple access is related to another simpler process called *multiplexing,* in which a single channel is shared by data streams from several sources. For example, a telephone company uses wideband trunks between its switching centers on which it bundles together a large number of telephone circuits. The most straightforward multiplexing technique for analog signaling is called *frequency-division multiplexing* (FDM). As the name implies, this describes a technique in which the wideband telephone trunk is divided into a number of frequency slots for the individual telephone circuits.

In digital trunks, the most common multiplexing scheme is in the time domain and is called, appropriately, *time-division multiplexing* (TDM). In this case a frame is established with time slots for each of the multiplexed signals. Then each of the digitized circuits is transmitted in bursts for a fraction of each frame. In the telephone networks, a single narrowband telephone channel is typically digitized into a 64 kbps data stream by a process known as *pulse code modulation* (PCM), which we describe at some length in chapter 8. These bits are then transmitted in

1.544 Mbps bursts in one of the slots of a twenty-four-slot frame, slightly more than twenty-four times the source rate.

6.3.2 Multiple Access

Multiple access techniques are similar to those used for multiplexing, but a little more complex because the users sharing the channel are separate entities located at different places. For example, the most common multiple-access technique for analog signals, called *frequency-division multiple access* (FDMA), simply divides the total spectrum into frequency bands and assigns each user circuit to one of these bands. Each user then has to be sure that his signal is confined to his assigned band and does not interfere with the signals in adjacent bands. The analog of TDM, called TDMA, assigns a time slot within a larger frame to sets of users, with the pulse rate within each slot no shorter than approximately the reciprocal of the bandwidth of the channel. In such a system the timing has to be monitored carefully to be sure that each user stays within his time slot.

It is interesting to note that both TDM and TDMA are often used in satellite communications, sometimes side by side in the same configuration. In a typical situation, for example, a network is established with one large station communicating with several smaller ones. The large station transmits to the small stations in one channel using a time-division multiplexed data stream with one slot in the stream assigned for transmissions to each of the small terminals. Then the small terminals respond to the large terminal in another channel using TDMA in which one TDMA slot is assigned to each of the small terminals.

But dividing up the frequency spectrum with FDMA or time with TDMA are not the only ways of assigning capacity to multiple users. There are different ways of combining the two that go under the name of *spread spectrum*. Spread spectrum communication was originally conceived as a way of protecting communications signals, especially in the military environment, against interference, either deliberate or inadvertent. One form of spectrum spreading illustrates the principle. Suppose we are communicating a narrowband signal using BPSK that uses a particular carrier frequency f_0. An interfering sine wave in the vicinity of f_0 entering the receiver with power comparable to that of the signal can completely disrupt the receiver. Suppose now that the BPSK signal is modified in accordance with Fig. 6-14. Instead of using a fixed carrier frequency, a different carrier is selected for each transmitted bit, with the

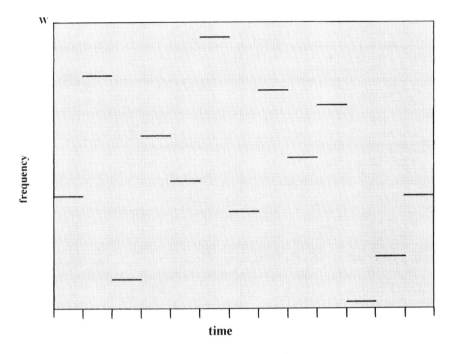

Figure 6-14   Spectrum spreading by frequency hopping.

choice of carrier made in a pseudorandom way anywhere in the overall channel band. Over time, the BPSK signal occupies the whole channel band. Under these circumstances, a narrowband interfering signal will only disturb the receiver during those times in which the frequencies overlap. Even this can be mitigated against if the signals are coded in such a way that decisions are made over several received bits. The overall effect of the spectrum spreading is to reduce the effective power of a jammer by the ratio of the signal bandwidth to the total bandwidth over which the frequency spreading takes place.

This property of spectrum spreading can be extended to provide a multiple access technique called *code-division multiple access* (CDMA) that combines some of the features of FDMA and TDMA. Suppose that several narrowband BPSK signals occupy the same wide band with each hopped in a pseudorandom way independently of one another. Then every once in a while one signal will interfere with another, but in a relatively harmless way provided that not too many signals are crammed into the same band. If the hopping is rapid, you can think of the signals as

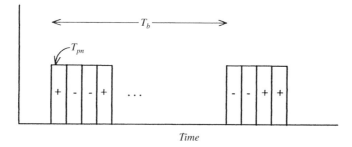

Time

Figure 6-15   Direct-sequence spectrum spreading.

contributing to the noise level seen by the other signals. The interference noise contributed by each user to each of the others is $P_s W_s / W_T$, where P_s is the power of each signal, W_s is the signal bandwidth, and W_T is the total bandwidth occupied by the hopped signals. You can think of this interference noise as having a density N_i that adds to the thermal noise density N_0 in the channel. Clearly, this is a way of sharing the spectrum among multiple users as long as the number of signals in the band is not large enough for the total power of all to interfere excessively with any given signal.

The most common form of spectrum spreading goes by the name of *direct sequence*. The principle behind it is shown in Fig. 6-15. Instead of hopping the carrier over the total band in a pseudorandom way, as previously described, the phase of the carrier is reversed (or not) rapidly every T_{pn} seconds, where T_{pn} is approximately the reciprocal of the bandwidth. There will be a large number of such phase changes in the time T_b required to send an information bit. Another way to look at this signal is to think of the carrier underlying the information bits as a BPSK signal, the bandwidth of which encompasses the entire channel band rather than as the usual sine wave. Further, if the carrier phase is changed in a pseudorandom way, the carrier has all the statistical properties of noise and is, in fact, called a *pseudonoise* carrier. The extension of this technique to multiple access follows immediately. The users sharing the band have only to use different pseudorandom sequences, and then each user appears as noise to each other user as with frequency hopping. It is a very powerful technique and remains along with TDMA as one of the primary means of channel sharing in digital communications systems.

7

MODULATION AND CODING FOR BANDWIDTH-LIMITED CHANNELS—THE TELEPHONE LINE

7.0 Introduction

A channel is bandwidth limited when it is possible to supply a signal-to-noise ratio as high as necessary to take advantage of all the available bandwidth. The most common example of such a channel is the ordinary telephone line. Coaxial cables used for television transmission are also close to bandwidth limited. These cables are customarily divided into 6-MHz channels as are over-the-air channels. When digital television broadcasting becomes more common, the cable operators may choose to carry more television signals of a given kind in a channel than is possible in broadcast channels of the same bandwidth because the higher signal-to-noise ratio in the cable gives them a greater capacity than the over-the-air channels. To do this, they will use modulation and coding techniques similar to those used on telephone lines. Some satellite channels are also close to being bandwidth limited. While, in most cases, the applications demand small-aperture terminals that make them power limited, high-capacity trunking applications demand high satellite power and large-aperture earth stations making them "cables in the sky" that are close to being bandwidth limited and that, accordingly, may also use techniques analogous to those that we describe in this chapter for the telephone line.

7.1 Sending Digits over a Telephone Line

The problem in a bandwidth-limited channel is how to generate and detect signals that make optimum use of the limited bandwidth. As we saw in the last chapter, it is easy to lay out the important issues in the power-limited channel. An efficient modulation and coding system can either increase the data rate or decrease the power requirements for a given data rate. In the bandwidth-limited channel, the task at hand is to maximize the data rate within a constrained bandwidth, generally using as much power as required.

An ideal bandwidth-limited channel is described by a filter with a well-defined bandwidth and Gaussian noise. Such a channel has a capacity given by Shannon's formula that provides the theoretical limit toward which the communicator sets his sights. A high-powered satellite channel probably comes closest to this ideal. The common telephone line deviates from this ideal in some major respects. This is not surprising considering the fact that the characteristics of the lines coming into our homes may distort the signals in ways that have little effect on the analog voice signals for which they were designed but have major effects on high-efficiency digital signaling. For one thing, a phone line's frequency response is usually far from square with wide phase deviations at the band edges, and, for another, the noise may be far from Gaussian, both of which factors are of considerably less concern for analog voice than for digital signals.

Nevertheless, over the years, engineers have done the best they could in the face of these less-than-ideal characteristics. The first digital transmission over telephone lines took place in the late 1940s at rates in the few hundred bit-per-second range. By the early 1950s, speeds of 2400 bps were achieved, and that remained the standard rate until well into the 1980s. To be sure, rates as high as 9600 bps could be transmitted over special lines with characteristics tailored to data transmission. But transmission over ordinary switched voice lines was, by and large, limited to lower rates. It is not that the technology needed for higher rates was not understood, but there were two major problems: (1) the average quality of the circuits in the switched network was relatively poor, and (2) implementation of sophisticated processing needed to squeeze higher rates out of the lines was too expensive for the market.

But then a massive change took place. As we all know, the same cheap component technology that revolutionized the computer made it advantageous to the telephone companies to begin the process of digitizing their networks and thereby to improve the general circuit quality. This technology also made it feasible to build very sophisticated modems to operate over these improved circuits and achieve the previously unheard of rates of 14.4 and 28.8 kbps. And the demand stemming from the surge in popularity of the Internet brought the price of these modems down to a range affordable to most individuals. With these high rates, the speed of navigating the Web becomes just acceptable for moderate-definition graphics transfer. However, anyone who has used the Web even at these rates would dearly love still higher speeds to make the system more responsive.

The digitization of the communications networks is so important that we describe something of this process before going on to the question of modulation and coding.

7.2   Trends in the Public Communications Networks

It is not that digitization is the only development in the evolution of the communications networks. There has been radical change in other, nontechnical aspects of the communications marketplace as well. All are the results of a complex combination of legal, entrepreneurial, economic, and technological factors. The dominant nontechnical trend has been the steady move from monopoly to competition, especially in the United States but also elsewhere in the world. It is hard to imagine that not too many years ago most Americans bought all their telephone service from one company, The American Telephone and Telegraph Company, known to all, with appropriate filial affection, as Ma Bell. Like a proper mother, Ma Bell took care of all the needs of her children, even down to the ubiquitous telephone instrument itself. It was considered a radical change when we were finally given the opportunity to buy our telephones from competing vendors. Now we have the choice of buying all kinds of sophisticated customer-premises equipment from a host of competitors and to obtain an increasing variety of services from various competing telephone companies. Elsewhere in the world, there has been a steady increase of private-sector competition to government-chartered telecommunications monopolies.

Of course, our concern is the technical trend from analog to digital. There is no better example of the mutual dependence and, perhaps, ultimate fusion of the disciplines of telecommunications and computing than in this digital evolution of the public networks. The immediate post-war AT&T provided analog services only, almost all of it voice, in an all-analog network. Now, many companies offer a variety of voice, video, and data services from a set of networks that are evolving from analog to digital. But just to say the networks are moving from analog to digital tells only part of the story, because in something as complex as a communications network, the words analog and digital mean different things to different people. It is therefore important to have our definitions of analog and digital straight.

7.2.1 Circuits: Analog and Digital

It is only natural to think of a circuit as a physical connection, a piece of copper wire, between a pair of subscribers. Often, this is indeed the case. When your local telephone company installs service in your home or business, it literally runs a pair of copper wires between its end office and your premises. Long-distance circuits are not quite so straightforward. They may be microwave radio circuits spanning hundreds or thousands of miles in a sequence of relays, satellite circuits spanning thousands of miles, or fiber-optic cables. Or they may be a combination of several such media. While each of these circuits has its advantages and disadvantages in different circumstances, from the subscriber's point of view they are equivalent: Each provides a way to deliver signals from one place to another.

What appears to the subscriber to be conceptually a very simple long-distance telephone connection is, in reality, a very complex sequence of circuits and switch connections. This complexity has much to do with the quality of this long circuit, because every complexity in the communications path is an opportunity for quality degradation. The end-to-end circuits can be analog, digital, or a hybrid of the two, as shown in Fig. 7-1. An analog circuit is analog from one end to the other; all its constituent links are analog. Similarly, a digital circuit is digital from end to end. In a hybrid circuit, some of the links are analog and some are digital. Today, and probably for a long time to come, by far the majority of the links connecting subscribers to their end offices are analog, because they are there primarily to serve analog telephones. Since much of the rest of the network is digital, the hybrid circuit today is the rule rather than the exception.

What can we say about the accuracy or quality of such links? The situation with pure analog and digital links is clear. An all-analog circuit suffers more degradation the more links there are in the chain, since the

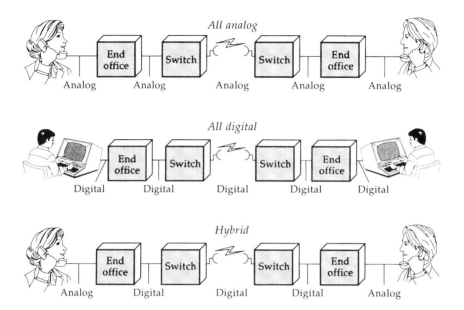

Figure 7-1   Circuits in the public switched networks.

characteristics of all the individual links cascade. In contrast, the all-digital circuit has high accuracy no matter how many circuits are linked. The communications carriers choose modulation/coding systems for the digital links that guarantee error rates low enough to allow excellent voice service. Since these circuits are used for multiple applications, some of the various techniques for maximizing the rate that we discussed earlier—particularly feedback techniques for varying the data rate or correcting erasures—are not permitted within the network, although users are free to use any or all of these techniques on an end-to-end basis.

A hybrid circuit is somewhere in between. In the most typical case where the subscriber "tail" circuits are analog, as in Fig. 7-1, and the rest are digital, the circuit quality is ultimately determined by the quality of the tail circuits. Wherever the characteristics of these are well controlled, the circuit quality is high; wherever they are not, the quality suffers. Since most of the circuit degradation is contributed by the local analog connections, a long-distance circuit is not very different in quality from a local circuit. Subscribers used to express surprise when a voice coming from thousands of miles away sounded as if it were "next door." The reason is the high-quality digital connection between end offices.

The hybrid circuit also introduces the peculiarity of a double digitization. A digital link in a hybrid network has to be able to accommodate any kind of signal. This means that the technique used by the carrier for digitizing a signal cannot depend on the nature of the signal. For this reason, a digital link within the network converts a 3-kHz analog signal into a 64-kbps digital signal using a technique that is equally effective on voice, facsimile, or computer signals. This means that when you use such a hybrid circuit to send data at a rate of, say, 9.6 kbps, then these digital waveforms from your modem are converted into a 64-kbps stream in the digital transmission and back to the original 9.6-kbps stream in the analog circuit at the other end of the link. (The digitization technique is called pulse-code modulation (PCM) and is discussed in chapter 8.) This conversion of a 9.6-kbps waveform into a 64-kbps waveform may seem wasteful, but it is an essential consequence of a hybrid network serving many functions.

Improving circuit quality is one of the reasons for the increased digitization by the communications carriers. Another is the steadily increasing user demand for data transmission at high rates not easily obtained from the uncertain quality of an analog system. Other, less obvious, factors related to flexibility are becoming increasingly important. Users have been attracted to what are called *enhanced services* associated with both voice and data service: call waiting, call forwarding, conference calling, and other similar convenience features. It takes much less time to make a long-distance connection than it used to, and this, too, is a direct benefit of digitization. The ability to carve virtual private networks out of the public network is still another advantage.

But the most important reason for digitization is cost. Is not this like putting the proverbial cart before the horse? Usually a new technology is introduced to obtain new services, with the expectation that the revenues derived from the services will exceed the cost. The remarkable thing in this case is that the economic benefits of digitization would be of great significance in their own right without any of the above-mentioned service benefits.

7.2.2   A User View of Public Communications Circuits

The previous perspective represents the point of view of the communications provider. When we look at telecommunications from the user's point of view, the perspective is somewhat different. A user is concerned with end-to-end service, the performance of the circuit and how much it costs, and does not usually care what the telephone company does in between. The vast majority of subscribers see an analog telephone *voice-frequency* channel with a bandwidth of about 3 kHz. When you make a call, you have the use of a 3-kHz channel from end to end, whether it is to someone in the next block or halfway around the world. It does not matter whether the telephone companies convert your voice to digits to carry it over part of its internal network. As far as you can tell, you have an analog circuit from end to end.

Of course, this voice channel can also be used for other purposes. When you want to use your personal computer to access the Internet, for example, the most common vehicle for this access is this same ordinary voice channel. You convert this analog channel to digital yourself when you install a modem, and your Internet service provider accommodates you by providing a modem at his or her end of the line that communicates with yours. But there are data-rate constraints imposed by the limited bandwidth of the voice circuit. The maximum rate depends on the quality of the telephone line and the sophistication of your modem. The quality of the circuit varies. When you simply dial up a connection using your normal telephone service, the quality is determined by the characteristics of the two tail circuits and the variable long-distance circuit that happens to be given to you by the switched network. The more of the system that is digitized, the better will be the average quality of your service.

Most subscribers have *switched* service allowing them the flexibility of calling anywhere in the world. There are, however, times when it is economical for a subscriber to pay the additional price of a *dedicated* circuit to one particular location. Such a circuit is guaranteed to be yours 24 hours a day, seven days a week. For your application, it may be worth the cost to have the circuit all to yourself, eliminating the risk of a busy circuit. Sometimes, it is even more important that a dedicated circuit offers the ability to select the line quality that will assure that you operate at the highest rate that your modem provides.

Such a dedicated circuit can also be digital. In this case, you are buying not bandwidth per se, but rather a certain data rate with a guaranteed maximum error rate. The telephone company supplies all the modem equipments necessary to bring digital service to your door. You need not worry about choosing the best modem for your application; that's all done for you by the carrier using an appropriate bandwidth-limited technique. You simply require an interface device that meets the telephone-company standards.

Buying a dedicated digital circuit may be too expensive for the ordinary subscriber. But suppose you are an Internet service provider; your subscribers connect to your computer with analog lines, but you require much higher rates to access the Internet if your subscribers are to enjoy adequate service. You therefore buy a digital circuit from your telephone company that can support a rate of 1.544 Mbps (T_1), or some multiple thereof.

7.2.3   Circuit Switching

Two years after he invented the telephone, Alexander Graham Bell had another great insight, perhaps as important as the invention itself. Bell's original inspiration for the telephone was the notion of a telegraph that talked. After the telephone was introduced, most of Bell's contemporaries continued to think of the telephone in this way. But Bell's thinking had moved on. For the most part, the telegraph system did not send messages from one person to another but from one telegraph office to another. Getting the message to and from the offices was by transportation—you did it yourself or used a messenger boy. Unlike most of his contemporaries, Bell recognized that, unlike the telegraph, the telephone was so easy to use that its proper role was to connect users together directly. In his vision, everyone would have a telephone in his or her home and business that could connect to every other telephone no matter where it was located. It was the beginning of what later came to be called universal service.

Given this vision, how should the connections be made between homes and businesses? The most straightforward way would be to run a telephone circuit between every pair of telephones in the country. Clearly this was not the way to do it even when, as in Bell's day, the number of instruments was small. Any given subscriber would have occasion to talk to only a very small fraction of the other subscribers. Therefore, most of those lines would never be used, and even those that were used would be idle most of the time. But Bell had another idea. Fundamental to his concept was the notion of a *central office* in which telephone signals would be switched from one user to another. Of course, the first switches were plug boards by means of which a telephone operator would manually connect one circuit to another to set up a phone call—a process now known as *circuit switching*. While this manual circuit switching was later replaced by automatic circuit switching using switches of increasing technical sophistication, the basic idea behind it all goes back to Bell.

The principle behind such switched service is resource sharing. Rather than dedicate facilities to individual subscribers who may use them only a small fraction of the time, it is more economical to build a network that shares facilities among many subscribers and thereby minimizes idle time. However, a price is to be paid for this efficiency in terms of network availability. The ordinary subscriber is not usually aware of this limitation but might notice it at a time of unusually heavy usage such as Mother's Day, when it might take several attempts before a call goes through. The switched network has some maximum call-carrying capability, based upon the number of calls that each switch can handle at once and the number of circuits interconnecting the switches. If the number of calls attempted exceeds this capacity, some of the attempts will not be successful.

The telephone system has enough capacity to handle normal daytime business traffic volume but is underused on nights and weekends. This is why the carriers encourage the use of their otherwise idle plants by offering lower long-distance rates at those times. But on the relatively rare occasions of unusually heavy demand, such as Mother's Day and during floods and earthquakes, the traffic may exceed the normal business day traffic, resulting in a deterioration of service. If the networks were sized for these atypical circumstances, they would be underused most of the year, and the rates would reflect that. It's much like a city expressway designed to cope with normal rush-hour traffic becoming immobilized by the occasional emergency that creates peak traffic demands. While we are all prone to grumble when these occur, few of us would be willing to pay the price of a highway system that could cope with such emergencies gracefully.

7.2.4 Switched Data Service

Like voice service, data service may also be switched, with the advantage of resource sharing and the disadvantage of degraded service when the demand exceeds the supply. But there are some inherent differences in the nature of the switched services needed for voice and computer data. Our telephone switching systems are optimized for voice communications. It takes a few seconds to make the connection after dialing the number. Once the connection is made, the circuit is 100% yours until one of the parties hangs up, however long that might be. Only then do you relinquish the circuit. The carriers typically design their network capacities using four minutes as the average duration of a business call.

On the other hand, if you are at your computer and want to exchange data with another computer interactively, you dial up the remote computer, and then the two computers alternately send data to each other. The session might last for hours rather than minutes, but, within that session, data might be transmitted only sporadically, a few seconds at a time, with large gaps in between. For example, you might send a brief message to the remote computer that might respond quickly with a burst of data sufficient to fill your monitor screen. You might not respond for minutes or longer. This type of transaction calls for a system that will provide rapid communication when either computer has data to send. At all other times, the resources of the network might just as well be used by someone else, provided that your connection can be restored on a moment's notice.

A circuit-switched system could do this if it were able to set up and take down a circuit in a fraction of a second, far more rapidly than is now possible. Otherwise, the time to restore the connection could be a significant fraction of the entire transaction time, a situation that a subscriber would deem unacceptable. For these reasons, another form of switching called *packet switching* was devised with characteristics optimized for interactive data transfer. The data in a transaction are divided into short segments called packets. In contrast to a circuit-switched network in which the integrity of the 3-kHz circuit is always preserved even though high-rate digital trunks may carry these circuits within the system, in a packet-switched network the high-rate trunk carries the packets from all users using the full bandwidth. This allows the packets to be sent over the path at very high speed in the order in which they are received at the switch. Packets may have to wait their turn by an amount of time that depends upon the instantaneous traffic load, but that is no problem unless there are unusually heavy traffic loads. This system gives the user an illusion of full-time connectivity, yet reserves network capacity only for the time taken to actually transmit the data.

The concept of packet switching dates from the 1960s, close to 90 years after Bell's first notions of circuit switching. The first packet-switched network, the *ARPANET*, built under the auspices of the Defense Department's Advanced Projects Research Agency (ARPA), went into operation in 1973. Its use was restricted to Defense Department personnel and their contractors. It was not too long before other similar networks were built, and by the late 1970s, the concepts of internetting were developed, allowing subscribers of the various networks to communicate with one another. It was this interconnected set of networks that became known as the Internet. All the Internet's constituent networks were under government auspices until 1988 when commercial networks were allowed to join. And it was this extension to the private sector that has been responsible for the Internet's extraordinary growth since that time.

Packet-switched service is primarily for interactive data transmission and similar applications. A circuit-switched system will work just as well or even better for massive bulk data transfers between computers. For digital voice, the time that each packet must wait at the switch can present a fundamental problem, since each packet is delayed a slightly different amount of time. If uncorrected, this would have a disastrous effect on speech quality. Therefore, to make packet switching work for voice, these differential delays from one packet to the next must be compensated for, so that they are not evident to listeners.

7.2.5   Digits at Your Front Door?

If the public networks were destined to be forever devoted primarily to voice service, then the hybrid situation of a digital network with analog tails would be quite adequate. But the communications world is anything but static. There is an inexorable demand for more bandwidth for more and varied data services. The spurt in the popularity of the World Wide Web in the 1990s is due largely to the fact that the Web is graphics based, and transmitting graphical images clearly requires more bandwidth than does text if the response time is to be adequate. In addition, there is no reason why the Internet cannot transmit video as well if the user channels can accommodate the still wider bandwidths required.

While the achievement of data rates of 28.8 kbps over ordinary telephone lines represents a remarkable tour de force, it is clear that it is not possible to extend these rates too much higher as long as telephone lines remain as they are. (In this regard, it should be noted that the so-called 56-kbps modems that have come on the market provide this high rate *from* the network *to* the user with a lower rate in the other direction. They do this by using the two-way capacity of the circuit in one direction part of the time.) It is not that the bandwidth of a pair of copper wires is inherently limited to the 3-kHz range. If the wires are short—say, less than a mile—and if the loading coils are removed—loading coils restrict the bandwidth to reduce the noise and extend the range—then the usable bandwidth can be significantly larger, and rates high enough to support digital television can be achieved. However, such measures are short term. In the long run, a fundamental change in the nature of the public communications that we use for all our needs will be needed.

If the goal is to support video, these rates have to be at least in the megabit per second range—and even these rates would not be sufficient were it not for the great strides made in video compression that we shall discuss in the next chapter. There are many who predict that in the end much higher rates (perhaps as high as a gigabit per second) will be needed for sets of other applications, such as medical monitoring and education, and that to achieve these very high rates, today's local area communications have to be eventually supplanted by optical fiber transmission. Such high-capacity networks would incorporate switches using a scheme called *asynchronous transfer mode* (ATM), a form of packet switching with parameters making it suitable for the continuous data streams produced by voice and video transmissions as well as for bursty computer data, the application for which packet switching was originally invented.

Enough research and development was done in the late 1980s and early 1990s to assure that the technology necessary for the upgrade will be in hand. Nevertheless, the great expense of this upgrade will prevent it from happening overnight. In the meantime, many favor the widespread adoption of an intermediate approach known as the Integrated Services Digital Network (ISDN), which gains some of the advantages of the very high rate system at a much lower cost. They argue that ISDN can offer, in a more modest way, many of the innovations that the high-speed networks promise, and at a small fraction of the cost—because there is no need for optical transmission and the current generation of circuit and packet switches is quite adequate. It provides a vehicle for attacking the chicken-and-egg problem of building information services even while cultivating demand for their use, much of which can be done without the full-blown superhighway.

The concept of the ISDN has been around since the early 1980s, along with predictions that it would be widely implemented in the 1990s. Its name is a well-chosen one that indicates some of its advantages over the analog state of affairs that has existed for decades. It is *digital* from end to end. In addition, it *integrates* various kinds of services through a single digital connection that does the whole job in place of separate analog phone lines for each computer, telephone and fax machine. Finally—and this is probably the most important in the near term—it provides considerably higher data speeds than ordinarily obtainable over the analog network. It is this latter feature that makes the ISDN a halting first step on the way to the ATM-based *Broadband ISDN* (B-ISDN).

For example, one of the standard offerings under ISDN is 144-kbps service. This will give a user two circuits at 64 kbps per circuit, each of which can be used for either voice or data, plus 16 kbps for low-speed data. The network will then provide switched or dedicated connections using whatever technology is appropriate. It might, for example, send interactive data to a packet-switched network and voice to a circuit-switched network. How the carriers deliver the service is not important. What is important to the customer is that the communications carriers guarantee to meet a standard set of specifications at an affordable price.

The pace of ISDN implementation has, in fact, been much slower than anticipated because of its steep price. The fact of the matter is that neither digitization nor integration provides a spectacular enough advance over today's digital networks with analog tails to warrant much additional cost to the subscriber for the *same* services. It is only when one gets to *new* services that can take advantage of the higher data rate that the subscriber becomes really interested. As an example, the popularity of the World Wide Web with its emphasis on graphics accelerated the use of ISDN connectivity in the mid 1990s among business subscribers, but not among home subscribers where its high price remained a deterrent even to the most avid Web surfers.

End-to-end digital service is something that is coming in one form or another. But the expense of providing such service is so high that it will be a long time before it is universal. This means that the hybrid network with circuits that look analog to the user will be with us for a long time to come whether they be narrowband circuits from the telephone companies or wideband circuits from the cable television companies. Either type circuit confronts us with a bandwidth-limited channel, and much of the remainder of this chapter is devoted to the techniques for transmitting data over such channels at reasonably high rates.

When you connect your computer to the Internet through the telephone system, your signals travel through a part of the circuit-switched network to reach your Internet service provider's access point, a short- or long-distance connection depending on where you live. From there they go through various packet-switched networks that comprise the Internet.

On the other hand, when you send a fax from one place to another, the digital signals from your fax modem travel through the circuit-switched network over the same paths as voice signals. In either case, the route your signals take is almost always through a partly digital, partly analog path, and the data rate achievable by your modem will depend on the nature of this path. For this reason, all modern telephone-line modems have multiple rate capabilities to accommodate to the variability of the circuit you happen to get when your modem makes its call.

7.3 Modulation for Bandwidth-Limited Channels— Quadrature-Amplitude Modulation

In discussing the power-limited channel in the previous chapter, we made the point that amplitude modulation was not appropriate, because in a channel where the power is limited, the maximum available power should be used all the time. In those situations, we were left with frequency or phase modulation as the only sensible schemes available for use. In the bandwidth-limited case, we are faced with the opposite situation. The bandwidth limitation means that a modulation system such as FSK that uses frequency lavishly is not appropriate if maximizing the rate is our objective. But now in an environment of high signal-to-noise ratio, amplitude modulation is eminently sensible. Phase modulation is appropriate in either case.

In the bandwidth-limited channel, the basic strategy is to transmit pulses over the channel as fast as the bandwidth will allow, modulate these pulses with as many amplitudes and phases as possible, and then introduce constraints from pulse to pulse to achieve the redundancy that will permit demodulation errors to be cleaned up. For example, one way of achieving the common 14.4-kbps rate is to transmit pulses at the rate of 2400 per second, with each pulse carrying 7 bits designating one of 128 amplitude-phase combinations, coupled to a code of rate 6/7.

The modulation scheme in which one point in a constellation of points in amplitude and phase is selected is called *quadrature-amplitude modulation* (QAM). The best way to show the amplitude and phase combinations is in a plot such as Fig.7-2 in which every point is represented by a particular amplitude and phase or, equivalently, by a complex number, the *x* component of which is the real part and the *y* component is the

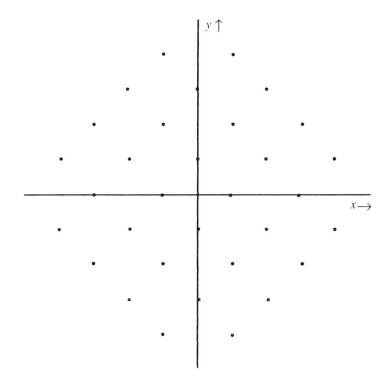

Figure 7-2   A thirty-two-point QAM signal constellation.

imaginary part. The figure shows thirty-two such points in a diamond-shaped array. To transmit a signal corresponding to a particular point, the x-component multiplies a cosine carrier and the y-component multiplies a sine carrier. At the receiver the two carriers are demodulated separately and the amplitudes recombined vectorially to obtain the received point. Of course, noise will cause the received point to differ from the transmitted point to a greater or lesser extent, or, said in another way, each point in the constellation is smeared out by the noise. And if noise brings a received point closer to some point in the signal constellation than to the transmitted point, then the demodulator makes a symbol error. Clearly, one objective of signal design is to distribute the desired number of amplitude-phase combinations as far as possible from one another to minimize the error probability. The constellation in Fig. 7-2 is moderate in size for the sake of simplicity and clarity. As we shall see, modern modems use much larger constellations. Clearly, the larger the number

of signals, the closer their spacing and the greater chance of a misidentification.

This process is quite analogous to the process we described for BPSK
in chapter 6. In that case we were able to compute the probability of error
by making the assumption that the noise was Gaussian. We noted above
that there are many non-Gaussian noise sources that have to be coped
with in the telephone channel in addition to the normal receiver noise.
However, the most important source of noise is none of these, rather it is
the interference caused by successive signals on one another called *intersymbol interference*.

7.3.1   Intersymbol Interference and Equalization

It is easy to see the source of intersymbol interference. Assume an idealized band-pass channel with a rectangular frequency response. This ideal
filter is a reasonable first approximation for a typical telephone line, the
passband characteristics of which are shown in Fig. 7-3. To get the most
out of the channel, we want to use a signal with a spectrum filling up the

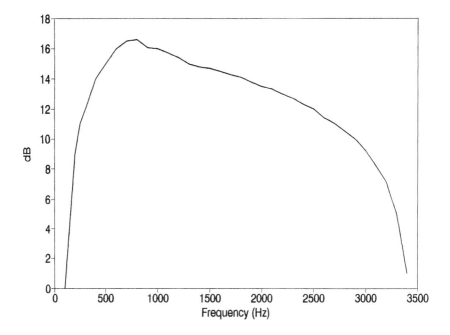

Figure 7-3   Typical telephone-line passband.

bandwidth. But a signal with a frequency response with such steep edges has a time waveform with a sin x/x shape with tails that fall off relatively slowly and that are bound to interfere with adjacent signals. Of course, the signals can be spaced far enough apart in time to avoid the intersymbol interference, but that defeats the idea of efficient use of the channel. The way around this problem is to use the Nyquist signals that we introduced in chapter 6, that is, signals that are forced to be 0 at the sampling times of adjacent signals. The sin x/x waveform is the simplest form of Nyquist pulse, provided that the pulse signaling rate is matched to the zero crossings of the sin x/x function.

There are well-known techniques for designing such pulses, and if we always used the same telephone line, we could measure its frequency response and design the signals. Even then we would have the problem of coping with time variations of this response that inevitably occur for various reasons. In the more useful case of switched service, we have to deal with a diversity of telephone lines each with its own characteristics as well as with the problem of time variation. The way in which we approach the problem is by *equalizing* the telephone line, that is, by building a filter that compensates for the telephone-line characteristics. At the lower rates a fixed equalization based upon the average characteristics of telephone lines is adequate. But for the higher rates, the equalization must be tailored to the individual line by a measurement process at the demodulator—the process known as *adaptive equalization*.

The way equalization works is not too difficult to understand. Assume the idealized telephone line with a rectangular passband of width W. If the transmitted pulses are rectangular, then the received signals have zero crossings every $1/T$ s, corresponding to the zero crossings of the filter's impulse response. Therefore, if the transmitted pulses occur every T s, we meet the criterion of Nyquist pulses having zero crossings at the sampling times of adjacent pulses. All that is required is to measure the precise bandwidth of the rectangular channel and send the signals at the appropriate rate to match the zero crossings of the channel impulse response.

Of course, life is never that simple. Besides, it would be terribly inconvenient to have to vary the pulse rate at both transmitter and receiver to match the bandwidth of the channel precisely. It is highly preferable to maintain a fixed rate in the correct ballpark and then modify the telephone-line characteristics to match the pulse. We do this with a filter at the receiver shown in Fig. 7-4. Its form is that of a tapped delay line with constants multiplying the outputs of the taps. The delay elements are pre-

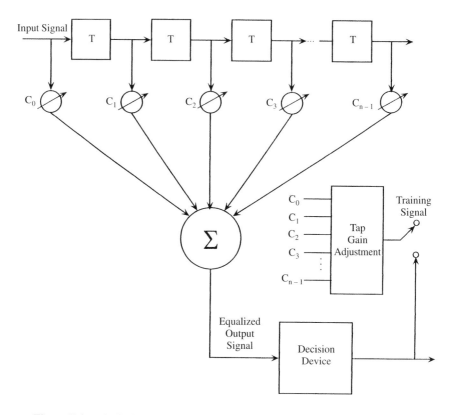

Figure 7-4   Block diagram of an adaptive equalizer.

cisely the separation T of the transmitted pulses. The multipliers at the taps are adjusted to set the output to 0 at all times except at the correct sampling time for each pulse.

A fixed equalizer will have its tap multipliers set for the "average" telephone line. An adaptive equalizer will adjust the taps initially to the particular line being used. To do this, the transmitter sends out a "training sequence" known to the receiver before the data transmission begins. With the switch in the top position in Fig. 7-4, the receiver adjusts the tap gain to maximize the receiver's performance. Once the taps are set, the receiver signals the transmitter to begin sending data. Then the receiver switches the input to the tap-gain adjustment circuit from the top to the bottom position and continues to fine-tune the tap settings using the demodulated signals as a reference in place of the training sequence.

7.3.2   Trellis Coding

The purpose of this equalization process is to reduce the intersymbol interference so that the total noise from intersymbol interference and all other sources is low enough to permit the demodulator to locate the correct point in the constellation almost all the time. Of course, the larger the constellation, the smaller the separation of individual points, and the greater the probability of error. For example, achieving rates as high as 14.4 and 28.8 kbps demands constellations with up to one thousand points. In such large constellations, adjacent points in the plane are very close to one another, and it does not take very much noise of any kind to cause a misidentification. It is quite analogous to the power-limited case when we push the channel by transmitting so fast that the noise makes a misidentification highly likely. We showed earlier that the way out in the power-limited case was to base decisions not on a single-channel waveform but on a sequence of waveforms defined by a code matched to the waveforms.

We do an analogous thing in the bandwidth-limited case, that is, apply coding matched to the waveforms such that decisions are based on a sequence of channel waveforms. But we only have to observe a signal constellation to recognize that the coding has to be different. For one thing, the Hamming distance is no longer an appropriate metric to describe the distance between points in the constellation. Recall that the Hamming distance between two binary sequences is the number of digits in which the two sequences differ. This measure of distance makes sense in a binary symmetric channel because it is proportional to the logarithm of the probability that noise converts the one sequence to the other. A better metric for points in the constellation is the *Euclidean* distance between them. Consider, for example, the four-point constellation shown in Fig. 7-5, where the points are distributed uniformly around the unit circle at 45, 135, 225, and 315 degrees. It is easy to see that each point is a distance of $\sqrt{2}$ from its nearest neighbors.

Figure 7-6 shows an eight-point constellation. These points are also uniformly distributed along the unit circle. But since there are more of them, the distance between nearest neighbors is now smaller with the value $\sqrt{(2 - \sqrt{2})}$. In both figures we label the points of the constellation by decimal digits. When it comes to implementation, binary numbers have to be assigned to the decimal digits. In both figures we have used the standard binary representation of digital numbers. But it does not have to

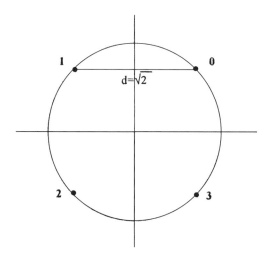

Figure 7-5   A four-point signal constellation.

be that way. As we shall see, when such constellations are matched to codes, the particular bit assignment is done in such a way as to simplify the encoding operation.

The way we code for a channel of this kind is to use a constellation with more points than necessary and then assign messages to sequences of points, as we do in binary coding. For example, if we want to transmit at a rate corresponding to 2 bits per channel symbol, instead of using a constellation of four points as in Fig. 7-5, we use the constellation of eight points shown in Fig. 7-6. That is, we transmit 3 bits/symbol instead of 2 bits/symbol. With such a constellation, there are 8^n possible sequences of length n. But we only use 4^n of these sequences as determined by a so-called *trellis* code. As you might expect from its name, a trellis code has many of the attributes of a convolutional code. It uses a sliding window rather than a jumping window as in a block code. It is characterized by a constraint length k and by a coding rate r. There are even ways of implementing such a code with a shift register. And, as you also might expect, the Viterbi algorithm is the most efficient way of searching a trellis to decode each symbol, providing the highest level of performance with soft-decision demodulation.

Figure 7-7 shows a trellis code illustrating the above case. It has four states corresponding to the last information symbol (two information bits). Four branches originate at each state signifying the choice of the next information symbol, and each of these branches is labeled by one of

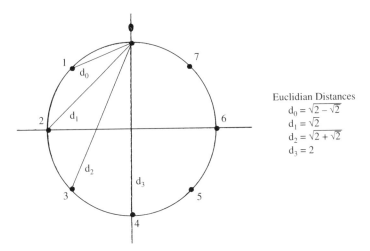

Euclidian Distances
$$d_0 = \sqrt{2 - \sqrt{2}}$$
$$d_1 = \sqrt{2}$$
$$d_2 = \sqrt{2 + \sqrt{2}}$$
$$d_3 = 2$$

Figure 7-6   An eight-point signal constellation.

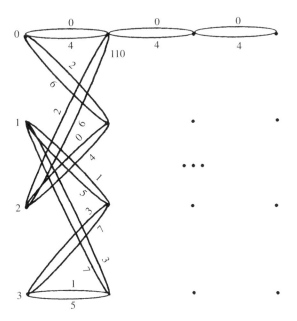

Figure 7-7   A four-state trellis.

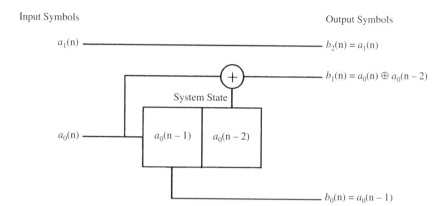

Figure 7-8   A trellis encoder.

the eight possible transmitted symbols from the constellation of Fig. 7-6. Figure 7-8 is a block diagram showing a way of implementing this code with a shift register. The input bits a_1 and a_0 together with the previous two values of a_0 determine the next transmitted character. These previous values of a_0 define the current state of the system. Note that only the successive a_0 bits and not the a_1 bits pass through the shift register. The output symbol is determined by the three bits b_2, b_1, b_0. Table 7-1 shows the bit patterns for this coder for the input states 0 and 1. The first two columns designate the current state, and columns 2 and 3 designate the next state. The rightmost three columns designate the output 8-ary symbol associated with the state transition. For example, when the system is in state 1 (01), an input symbol 1 (01) leads to the next state 2 (10) with the transmission of 8-ary symbol 5 (101).

Table 7-1   State Transitions for the Trellis Encoder of Fig. 7-8

$a_0(n-2)$	$a_0(n-1)$	$a_0(n)$	$a_1(n)$	$b_2(n)$	$b_1(n)$	$b_0(n)$
0	0	0	0	0	0	0
0	0	0	1	1	0	0
0	0	1	0	0	1	0
0	0	1	1	1	1	0
0	1	0	0	0	0	1
0	1	0	1	1	0	1
0	1	1	0	0	1	1
0	1	1	1	1	1	1

The fact that only one of the input bits passes through the shift register and that the system state is defined by the shift register leads to the peculiar appearance of the trellis in Fig. 7-7 in which pairs of paths lead from one state to the next. Despite its peculiar appearance, the code represented by this particular trellis is a good one with a minimum Euclidean distance of 2. You can see this by looking at the top of the trellis. The topmost path is labeled by three 0 symbols in cascade. Just below it are three paths, each of which has two 0 symbols and a single 4 symbol, which you can see from Fig. 7-6 is a distance of 2 away from the 0 point in the constellation. Figure 7-9 compares the performance of the uncoded four-state case with the trellis coded eight-state case shown in Fig. 7-2. The performance advantage in the vicinity of 3 dB is impressive.

Of course when we get to the higher rates achievable with modern modems, we are involved with much larger signal constellations. For example, in one of the modes available under the V.34 international standard, 3200 symbols per second are transmitted with each symbol carrying nine information bits to achieve a data rate of 28,800 bps. It uses 768 points in a constellation, that has a total of 960 points. To select a particular point in the constellation, a single redundant bit is appended to the nine

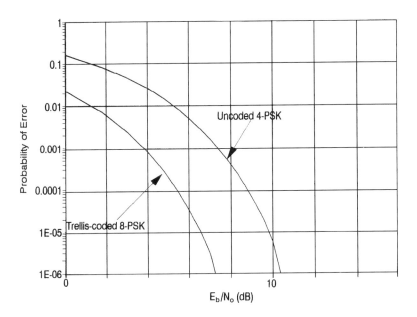

Figure 7-9 Performance advantage of trellis coding.

information bits. This bit is derived from an encoder with a constraint length of 3, 4, or 5, resulting in a trellis with either 8, 16, or 32 states.

This constraint length flexibility is only one of the many variables offered by the V.34 standard. In addition, the standard incorporates a variety of symbol rates and constellation sizes, allowing the selection of many data rates, each in several different ways using different combinations of the parameters. As noted above, this flexibility is necessary because of the variability of the telephone lines with which the modems built to the standard have to work. When a link is established, there is a protocol by which the two modems test the line to establish the optimum setting of the parameters. Then if the conditions should change either for the worse or the better, the protocol allows the modems to shift the data rate down or up as the case may be.

8

DIGITIZING AUDIO AND VIDEO

8.0 Trade-offs in Sending Analog Information Digitally

The reason for communicating or recording analog sources of information digitally rather than using the more natural analog processes is to obtain the benefits of the controlled accuracy that only digital techniques can offer. The digital process, modeled in Fig. 8-1, is quite simple and straightforward. The analog signal is first converted to a stream of digits in a device called an *analog-to-digital* (A/D) *converter.* These digits are transported over the communications channel in much the same way as digits obtained from a computer file. Then, at the destination, the analog signal is recovered by passing the digits through a *digital-to-analog* (D/A) *converter.*

The diagram also models the information flow from source to destination. The source generates information at a certain rate, and the signal reaching the destination carries information at a rate that cannot exceed that of the source. In a perfectly accurate system, no information is lost in the process; all the information in the source is transferred to the digital stream, and the digits are received at the destination with perfect accuracy. But achieving performance close to perfection can be expensive. It stands to reason that the higher the data rate from the A/D conversion, the more faithfully the digital stream represents the source, but the more expensive it is to communicate with high accuracy. Thus, in any practical system, the information transfer from source to destination must be diminished either by reducing the digitization rate or the communications accuracy. Which is preferable depends upon the situation. But any system that communicates or records analog information in digital form requires a trade-off between the two processes.

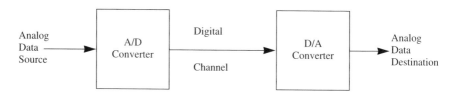

Figure 8-1   Digitization of analog waveforms.

8.1   Digitization Approaches

There are two fundamental approaches to the problem of digitizing analog signals. The most straightforward of these is called *pulse code modulation* (PCM). It has at its root the preservation of as much of the information content of the source as possible. It ignores any special characteristics of the source, taking as its basic premise the fact that a waveform is a waveform, characterized, in accordance with Fourier analysis, by a set of frequency components. Pulse code modulation provides the standard way of digitizing a signal when the objective is high fidelity or something reasonably close, and, as we saw in chapter 7, this is precisely the technique used by the carriers in digitizing links within their networks. Central to this approach is another fundamental and elegant mathematical concept called the *sampling theorem*. This theorem provides the theoretical basis for the digitization process, just as Shannon's coding theorem provides the theoretical basis for communication.

But PCM carries with it the inefficiency inherent in ignoring the nature of the source. The inefficiency manifests itself in the fact that the digitization rate usually far exceeds the source information rate. It seems reasonable that if one is forced to reduce the digitization rate significantly below that required for high-fidelity reproduction, some knowledge of the nature of the waveform source might be of considerable benefit. After all, a facsimile waveform and a speech waveform might have the same overall bandwidth but might also have significant differences that unique digitization processes could use to their advantage. This is the premise underlying the second digitization approach.

But even when this second approach is taken to reduce the digitization rate, it invariably follows an initial digitization by the first approach. Thus all digitization processes whether or not they ultimately make use of any inherent knowledge of the nature of the source begin with a PCM process.

8.2   Digitizing a Waveform by Pulse Code Modulation

Figure 8-2 shows the major elements of the standard digitization process. It begins with *sampling*. A train of narrow pulses occurring at periodic intervals samples the waveform by capturing its amplitude at those particular instants of time. The sampling process therefore converts the waveform from a continuous analog signal (point *a*) to a series of narrow pulses with the amplitudes of the waveform at those points in time (point *b*). Even though they occur at discrete points in time, these amplitudes are as analog as the waveform that they represent. They are converted to digits by a process called *quantization*. This process measures the amplitude of each sample and then converts the amplitude value into a number with as many digits as is consistent with the precision of the measurement. These digits are transmitted through the communications channel or stored on the compact disc or digital audio tape.

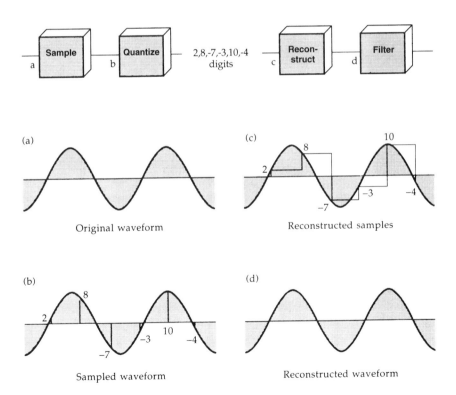

Figure 8-2   The digitization process.

The signal reconstruction or D/A conversion process is just the reverse. First, the samples are recovered from the digits. If we assume that no errors are made in the digital processes, then the digits entering the sample recovery processing are *identical* to those leaving the quantizer. The resulting sequence of samples is almost the same as the sequence of samples entering the quantizer, differing only as a result of any inaccuracies in the quantization process. Converting these samples back to waveforms, we first obtain a crude "staircase" approximation to the original (point *c*). Finally, to recover the original waveform (point *d*), we remove the rough edges from the staircase by using a filtering operation, which is clarified in the following. For the moment, think of the steep sides of the staircase waveform as being caused by the presence of high-frequency components that the filter will remove.

The accuracy with which the analog waveforms are represented by digits depends upon both the sampling rate and the quantization granularity: the more often the samples are taken and the more digits used to represent each sample, the more accurately the received samples will match the original. If the quantization process is so precise that the difference between the quantized samples and the original analog samples is too small to be observable, then the only source of inaccuracy is the sampling process itself. The closer together the samples, the closer the staircase approximation is to the source waveform. But must the samples be so close to each other that the staircase matches the waveform almost exactly, or is a slower sampling rate adequate?

The answer to this question is of practical importance. Take the example of digital voice transmission. The total data rate needed to represent the audio signal is given by the product of the sampling rate and the quantization rate. Typically, the signal is sampled at an 8-kHz rate (one sample every 0.125 ms), and each of the samples is quantized into 256 levels, equivalent to 8 bits for each sample. The required channel data rate then is 8000 samples/s $\times$ 8 bits/sample, or 64 kbps. If we had to sample at twice that rate to obtain sufficient speech quality, we would require 128 kbps. In the first case, the channel would have to support a transmission rate of 64 kbps, and in the second case, 128 kbps. Doubling the rate over a channel can be expensive whether it is achieved by doubling the capacity of the channel or by doubling the efficiency of transmission through the use of information-theory techniques. Therefore, we must understand just what the parameters of the A/D conversion have to be to understand the costs of digital transmission and, of course, recording as well.

8.3   The Sampling Theorem

The *sampling theorem* was formulated by Shannon based on work begun in the 1920s primarily by Harry Nyquist, an older colleague at the Bell Laboratories. While this is the most well known, it is only one of Nyquist's many contributions to communication theory that paved the way for Shannon's work some two decades later. It is interesting to note that Nyquist did this pioneering work long before anyone could have dreamed how significant digital technology was going to become in the latter part of the twentieth century.

The sampling theorem addresses the problem of how rapidly samples of waveforms must be taken to retain the information in the waveforms. The result is simple and elegant. It says that if the signal contains a band of frequencies, then as long as the sampling rate is higher than *twice* the highest frequency in the band, the original waveform can be reconstructed from the samples without loss of information. To state it another way, suppose that the signal contains a band of frequency components from 0 to some maximum (the bandwidth). Then sampling the signal at a rate of twice the bandwidth or greater will permit reconstruction of the original signal with *perfect* accuracy.

But why twice the bandwidth? Why not 1.5 times or three times or ten times? The number 2 seems like sheer magic. In Fig. 8-2 the samples are taken at a rate of five times the sine wave frequency, and it is not obvious that the crude staircase shown there can reproduce the waveform exactly. Fortunately, application of Fourier analysis to the problem goes a long way toward explaining the situation and toward making the nonintuitive more intuitive.

8.3.1   Understanding Sampling

As we just saw, the sampling operation is a simple multiplication. A sequence of equally spaced sampling pulses $s(t)$ multiplies a time function $x(t)$ to produce the product function $y(t) = x(t)s(t)$ that captures the values of the function at the sampling times. The easiest way to understand the effect of sampling is to move from the time to the frequency domain, because it is the spectrum $Y(f)$ of the time function $y(t)$ that gives us this understanding. The question, then, is: How is this spectrum related to the spectra, $X(f)$ and $S(f)$ of the input time functions?

As it turns out, $Y(f)$ is obtained by convolving the two spectra, $X(f)$ and $S(f)$, that is, by sliding the two spectra past each other and summing up the results. We have seen the convolution operation before. In chapter 6, it appeared in the description of the filtering process. There we stated that when a signal $x(t)$ is passed through a filter with impulse response $h(t)$, the output $y(t)$ is given by the convolution of the two time functions, and the spectrum $Y(f)$ is the product of the spectrum $X(f)$ of the input and the frequency response $H(f)$ of the filter, or, in symbols,

$$y(t)\int_0^t x(t')h(t - t')dt' = x(t) * h(t),$$

$$Y(f) = X(f)\,H(f), \tag{8-1}$$

where we have used the asterisk symbol as shorthand notation for the convolution operation.

Mathematically speaking, sampling is the dual of filtering. Whereas in filtering the frequency functions are multiplied, in sampling it is the time functions that are multiplied. Because of the symmetrical relationships between frequency and time in the Fourier equations, it follows that in sampling the frequency functions should be related by the convolution operation, or, in symbols,

$$y(t) = x(t)\,s(t),$$

$$Y(f) = X(f) * S(f). \tag{8-2}$$

These equations apply to any functions that have Fourier transforms, not only sampled functions. For example, if $x(t)$ and $s(t)$ are sine waves at two frequencies, their product $y(t)$ represents one amplitude modulated by the other. We saw in chapter 3 that the modulated signal contains the sum and difference of the two frequencies, a result that followed very simply from the application of a trigonometric identity. It is useful to do this again using the Fourier transform just to get a feeling for what the convolution does. Suppose that $s(t)$ is the carrier sinusoid and $x(t)$ is the modulating sinusoid as follows:

$$s(t) = \cos 2\pi f_c t,$$

$$x(t) = \cos 2\pi f_m t, \tag{8-3}$$

Since both of these functions are sinusoids, they are represented in the frequency domain by delta (or impulse) functions at the two frequencies, as follows:

$$X(f) = \delta\,(f + f_m) + \delta\,(f - f_m),$$

$$S(f) = \delta\,(f + f_c) + \delta\,(f - f_c). \tag{8-4}$$

Note that these spectra include the negative as well as the positive delta functions, needed to keep the mathematics straight.

The convolution operation is as follows:

$$X(f) * S(f) = \int_{-\infty}^{\infty} X(f')S(f - f')df' =$$

$$\int_{-\infty}^{\infty} [\delta\,(f' + f_m) + \delta\,(f' - f_m)]\,[\delta\,(f - f' + f_c) + \delta\,(f - f' - f_c)]df'. \tag{8-5}$$

The integral looks a lot more complicated than it really is. When you multiply out the two bracketed functions in the integrand, you obtain four terms. In the first term,

$$\delta\,(f' + f_m)\,\delta\,(f - f' + f_c),$$

the first factor is nonzero only when $f' = -f_m$, and the second factor is nonzero only when $f = f' - f_c$. Therefore, f has to equal $-(f_c + f_m)$ for the product of the two factors to be nonzero. When all the terms are evaluated in this way, the result is the sum of two pairs of impulse functions, one pair at the sum and difference frequencies of the carrier and modulating frequencies and the other pair at their negative values. This confirms the fact that the product of the two sinusoids has the form of the sum of sinusoids at the sum and difference frequencies.

We can interpret this graphically as in Fig. 8-3, which shows the time and frequency domain pictures of the waveforms. The top picture (a) is of a 500-Hz sine wave, represented in the frequency domain as an impulse. In (b) we multiply (modulate) the 500-Hz sine wave by a 100-Hz sine wave, creating the sum and difference frequencies shown as impulses at 400 and 600 Hz in the frequency domain. Figures 8-3(c) and 8-3(d) show what happens when the carrier is a train of sampling pulses. In (c) the 500-Hz sine wave carrier of (a) is replaced by the sampling pulses occurring at a 500-Hz rate. As shown in chapter 4, this results in a spectrum containing a series of lines at 500 Hz and its multiples. Figure 8-3(d) then shows that each of these lines is split into two 100 Hz above and below the line when the 100-Hz sine wave is sampled.

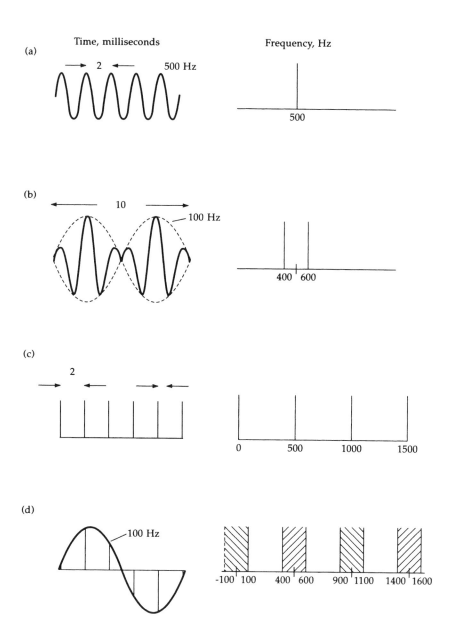

Figure 8-3 Sampling an audio waveform.

8.3.2   Proving the Sampling Theorem

To prove the sampling theorem, we will take the model of Fig. 8-3, vary the sampling rate, and then observe the way the spectra of the signals behave. We do this with the aid of Fig. 8-4, showing a number of sketches like those in Fig. 8-3(d), each with a different sampling frequency. Figure 8-4(a) is the same as Fig. 8-3(d), with a sampling frequency of 500 Hz. In Fig. 8-4(b), the sampling rate is reduced to 250 Hz, or a sample every 4 ms. The frequency picture is qualitatively the same. But since the harmonics of the sampling pulses are closer together, the lower sideband of each harmonic is now closer to the upper sideband of the harmonic below. Figure 8-4(c) shows the interesting case that occurs when the sampling pulses are 5 ms apart, corresponding to a sampling frequency of 200 Hz. Now the lower sideband of each harmonic falls directly on top of the upper sideband of the next lower harmonic. Finally, Fig. 8-4(d) shows what happens when the samples are still farther apart. With samples occurring every 6 ms (167-Hz sampling), the sidebands have crossed over one another.

The case shown in Fig. 8-4(c) is the limiting case stated in the sampling theorem, since here the sampling rate is exactly twice the frequency of the audio signal being sampled. This threshold rate is called the *Nyquist rate*. According to the theorem, it and the cases above it should result in perfect recovery of the audio from the samples, while the case below it, with the low sampling rate, should not. Let's see why.

We saw in Fig. 8-2 that the reconstruction process requires a filtering operation. I stated that the purpose of the filter was to eliminate the jaggedness in the waveform resulting from the sampling and reconstructing processes. Of course, removing the jaggedness is a qualitative way of saying filter out the high-frequency components. We can now see what this means quantitatively. In the diagrams in Fig. 8-4, the sampled signals have frequency components extending to infinity. But since the reconstructed waveform must be a single 100-Hz tone, we must eliminate all the frequency components above 100 Hz, and the obvious way to do this is with a lowpass filter that passes the 100-Hz line and eliminates all the lines above it. Even the slightest departure from this ideal results in the reconstructed function differing from the original.

Figure 8-5 expands the frequency-domain pictures in Fig. 8-4 to show this filtering problem more clearly. When the samples occur every 2 ms as in Fig. 8-5(a), the cutoff frequency of the lowpass filter must lie

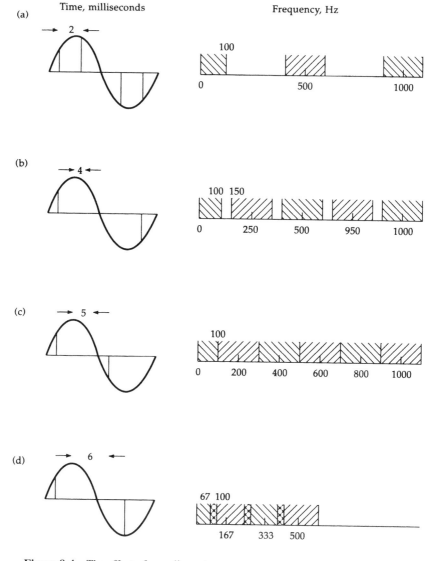

Figure 8-4   The effect of sampling rate.

between 100 and 400 Hz to pass the 100-Hz component and exclude all the higher components. When the samples occur every 4 ms as in Fig. 8-5(b), the filtering job is a little harder, since the filter now must discriminate between the desired 100-Hz line and the undesired 150-Hz line. In Fig. 8-5(c), when the sampling frequency is exactly twice the audio fre-

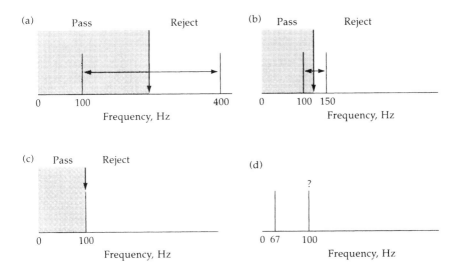

Figure 8-5 Filtering the sampled sine wave.

quency, the filtering job looks easier than in the previous case, but that is just an illusion as we observe what happens in Fig. 8-5(d) where the lower sideband of the 167-Hz component falls below the desired 100-Hz component. There is no way of capturing the 100-Hz component by itself with a lowpass filter. The result is the sum of a 100- and 67-Hz sine wave, an obvious distortion of the original audio signal.

Of course, in any real-world case, the signal being sampled is not simply a sine wave as in the previous example but rather a signal with some arbitrary spectrum. But the sine-wave result is still applicable with the appropriate interpretation. In accordance with Fourier's theorem, we express the arbitrary signal as a sum of sines and cosines. Then when the signal is sampled, each of these frequency components is modulated about the spectral harmonics of the sampling pulses as in Figs. 8-4 and 8-5. Since each frequency component behaves in this way, then so does their sum, giving us the result that the spectrum of the signal being sampled amplitude modulates each of the harmonics of the sampling frequency. It follows from this that the picture of Fig. 8-5 carries right over to the general signal if the sine wave in the figure is interpreted as the *highest* frequency in the signal being sampled or the bandwidth W when the signal is a baseband signal. From this line of reasoning, we can readily conclude that it is only possible to recover the signal by a filtering operation if the sampling frequency f_s exceeds twice the signal bandwidth, or, in symbols,

$$f_s \geq 2W, \tag{8-6}$$

which is just the Sampling theorem. As previously noted, this threshold sampling rate is called the Nyquist rate. At this limiting point a theoretically perfect filter could separate the two spectra. But if the sampling rate is below the Nyquist rate as in Fig. 8-5(d), then you can see that the right end of the spectrum and the left end of its first replica overlap. There is no way that a filter can separate them, and a distorted result is inevitable.

8.4   Practical Sampling Rates

Aliasing is the picturesque word used to describe what happens when the spectra overlap as the result of sampling below the Nyquist rate. Realistically speaking, however, the Nyquist rate is one of those mathematical limits that can be approached but not reached in practice. Since aliasing represents a gross distortion of the signal, it is to be avoided at all costs. Therefore, the sampling frequency must always *exceed* the Nyquist rate. But the Nyquist rate depends on the sampled signal having a well-defined bandwidth, and signals hardly ever come that way naturally. More often than not, the signal spectrum trails off in frequency, rather than falling off sharply. When this happens, two approaches may be taken to avoid the sin of aliasing: (1) sample at a high enough rate so that the signal energy at half the sampling frequency is imperceptible, or (2) prefilter the signal before sampling it to artificially reduce its bandwidth, thereby permitting sampling at a lower frequency.

In the first approach, all of the signal is captured with a high sampling frequency. In the second, the highest frequencies are lost, but the economy of a lower sampling rate is gained. This choice represents a compromise between bandwidth (and, hence, fidelity) and digitization rate. The wider the bandwidth, the higher the fidelity of the signal, but the more bits required to represent the signal. In digital recording, the more bits used to represent the audio, the shorter the playing time on a disc of a given size. If the choice is to limit the bit rate by limiting the sampling rate, it is always necessary to limit the bandwidth by prefiltering rather than by sampling at a rate below the Nyquist rate and thereby causing aliasing.

The filtering operation itself is also idealized. It is not possible to build a *perfect* filter shown in Fig. 8-6(a) that passes *all* the frequencies below a cutoff frequency and *none* above the cutoff. In practice, filters have a small slope-off region, as shown in Fig. 8-6(b). This means that the sampling rate must be enough higher than the Nyquist rate to allow the practical filter to discriminate between the desired and undesired frequency components. The figure shows that, to avoid even the smallest amount of aliasing, a practical filter must use a slightly higher sampling frequency than would be needed with a perfect filter.

An example illustrates the practical issues. The standard used by telephone companies for digital transmission of voice is either 56 or 64 kbps, derived from a sampling frequency of 8 kHz. This means that the bandwidth of the speech signals could be, at most, 4 kHz if the filters were perfect. Practically speaking, the actual spectrum is limited to around 3.6 kHz. The human voice has frequency components well above 4 kHz. Therefore, no matter how perfect the filters, the speech signals must be prefiltered before the sampling process to eliminate some of the higher-frequency components. But analog speech transmission over the phone is also limited by the inherent bandwidth of telephone lines to something in the vicinity of 2700 Hz. Therefore, whether the audio is filtered at 3.6 or 4 kHz is less important than the fact that either of these frequencies is

(a)

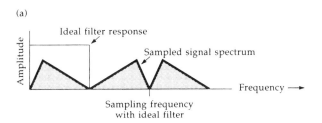

(b)

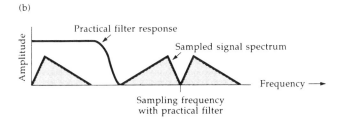

Figure 8-6   Practical filters.

well above the bandwidth cutoff of the telephone line. From this we can see that digital telephone speech is of higher quality than analog, even taking into account the practicalities of filters and sampling rates.

In compact discs, the sampling frequency standard is 44.1 kHz, which allows the use of practical filters to recover the audio samples in a bandwidth of at least 20 kHz. Since 20 kHz is about the highest frequency perceptible to the human ear, this allows enough bandwidth for very high-quality sound reproduction.

8.5   Quantization of the Samples

Having sampled a waveform at a frequency above the Nyquist rate, perfect reproduction is theoretically possible with infinitely precise quantization. Let's examine the effects of realistic quantization. Figure 8-7 shows a sine wave quantized into different numbers of levels. Each picture can be viewed as a measurement of the sample amplitude with a ruler that has a specific degree of precision. In Fig. 8-6(a) the amplitude definition is very crude. All we are doing is measuring whether the sample is positive or negative. To do this, we need two numbers—we can call them + and – or 1 and 2 or 0 and 1, or anything else. Whatever we call them, what matters is that there are two and only two unambiguous numbers that are used to designate the sample amplitude. This is a *two-level* or, equivalently, *one-bit* or binary quantization. While it is not a very accurate way to represent the signal amplitude, there are cases where it is adequate. If we were to sample a speech signal and then quantize it to one bit, the resulting speech, when reconstituted in analog form, would have an unpleasant hoarse sound, but would be quite intelligible. The effect of crude quantization is similar to that of superimposing noise on top of the voice signal. For this reason, this effect is called *quantization noise*.

Four-level or two-bit quantization is shown in Fig. 8-7(b). Here we have defined four equal-size intervals, two positive and two negative. Since we can call them anything we like, let's use the designations $+1$ and $+2$ for the two positive intervals and -1 and -2 for the two negative intervals. (Recall the discussion of soft-decision demodulation in chapter 6 in which we gave an example of four-level quantization.) We quantize the signal into one of these four intervals by replacing its actual amplitude with the amplitude of the interval into which the signal falls, as

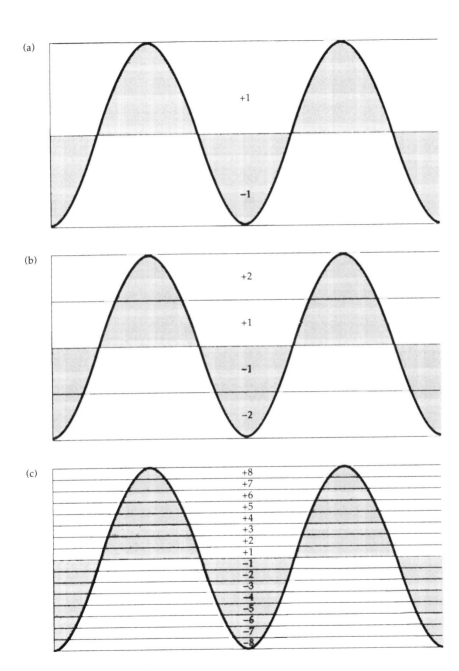

Figure 8-7 Quantization.

shown in the picture. While this representation of the sine wave is a little more accurate than that provided by the single-bit quantization, it is still quite crude. The resulting speech sounds a little less noisy than when quantized to a single bit. We can continue this process as long as we like. Figure 8-7(c) shows four-bit quantization, which quantizes the waveform amplitude into one of sixteen levels, a much better approximation, but still somewhat noisy.

How much is enough? That depends on how accurate we want the process to be. Quantization to any precision introduces some level of distortion or noise; the only question is how much. With analog signals, we must control every process with a high degree of precision to preserve the integrity of waveforms. With digital signals, we determine ahead of time how accurate we want the representation to be, we sample it often enough to preserve the amount of bandwidth that we want, and we quantize it to enough levels to give us the desired level of approximation.

In all the examples shown in Fig. 8-7, the intervals used to measure the signal amplitudes are all the same size. When this is the case, the quantization is said to be *linear*. The intervals do not have to be the same size. In fact, the standard 8-bit quantization scheme used for the 64-Kbps PCM speech uses a nonlinear scheme known as *μ-law* quantization. (The slightly different European standard is called *A-law*.) This quantization technique divides the amplitude of each sample into 256 levels spaced so as to assign smaller intervals to the signals with lower amplitudes than to those with higher amplitudes. For example, the interval assigned to the highest level signals is 128 times as large as that assigned to the lowest level signals. The reason for this is the fact that normal speech contains a preponderance of low amplitudes that have to be represented accurately for high-quality reproduction. On the other hand, compact discs use 16-bit or 65,536-level linear quantization. The reason for this particular number has to do with another concept called *dynamic range*.

8.6   Dynamic Range

Frequency range designates the extent of the signal bandwidth. Dynamic range refers to the range of sound loudness or, more generally, signal energy. In a system with narrow dynamic range, there is little difference between soft and loud sounds. In contrast, a system with wide dynamic range allows you to hear all sound levels from very soft *pianissimo* to very loud *fortissimo* without distortion.

The dynamic range needed depends upon the context. A telephone conversation requires enough fidelity to understand what is being said and to recognize the talker, regardless of how much emotion he or she may be displaying. Requirements for music reproduction are much stricter. A recording should approximate the sound heard in the concert hall. When a symphony orchestra performs, the dynamic range is enormous, extending from very soft passages in which perhaps a single instrument is being played pianissimo to gigantic fortissimos involving one hundred or more players. Clearly, a high-fidelity recording demands considerably more dynamic range than does voice telecommunications.

Because the dynamic range of audio is so large, it is convenient to measure it with a logarithmic unit, the *decibel*. The loudest fortissimos produced by a symphony orchestra are some 10 billion times louder than its quietest pianissimos, a dynamic range of well over 100 dB. That means that a recording needs a very wide dynamic range to represent the music of a symphony orchestra with high fidelity. The old analog vinyl records have a dynamic range of 60–70 dB, far less than the range of much of the music that they store. In the recording process, dynamic compression must be introduced to keep the signal from overloading the capability of the recording medium. You may be familiar with the result. A passage of music with dynamic range so wide that it makes your spine tingle in the concert hall, ends up sounding tame in your living room. You want to turn up your volume control to approximate the concert hall effect, only to be frustrated by a combination of record scratch and amplifier distortion at the higher sound levels.

A compact disc or digital tape stores signals with a dynamic range of about 90 dB corresponding to a power ratio of one billion. We can see where this value of 90 dB comes from by considering the implications of the 16-bit or 65,536-level quantization that is used. There are 32,768 each positive and negative zones into which the audio signals are quantized, or, in other words, the largest signal amplitude is about 32,000 times the smallest signal amplitude, or, equivalently, the power at the upper end of the range is more than one billion times that at the lower end. Decibels represent signal strength *ratios*, not absolute values of power. The amplifier in a hi-fi set has a dynamic range that represents the ratio of the highest to the lowest signal that it can handle. The lowest signal is determined by the noise level in the system. This includes any noise that might be introduced by the amplifier itself, together with noise that comes from the music source, the record scratch or tape hiss, or noise of any origin in the FM radio receiver. Since most modern amplifiers are virtually free of audible noise, the music source is effectively the lowest signal limit. The largest signal depends upon the characteristics of the amplifier itself. When the volume control is turned way up, the distortion of the resulting sound becomes audible. Amplifiers are rated by their maximum undistorted power output level. Therefore, the dynamic range achievable in the amplifier is the ratio of this maximum power level to the noise level of the source. If the system is noisy, the dynamic range is decreased for a given amplifier power level.

A digital music source such as a compact disc or digital audio tape, in contrast to an analog record or tape source, introduces no noise at all. This fact, together with the additional dynamic range, make digital music sources much superior to analog sources, impelling many listeners to upgrade the dynamic range of their home audio equipment. I am sure that my own reaction upon hearing a compact disc recording for the first time on a good audio system was shared by many others. The absolute silence in the background was startling; I could hear quiet sounds that had always been at least partially masked by noise in analog recordings. And the contrasting fortissimo passages were breathtaking. The total experience was closer to the concert hall than I had believed possible.

8.7   Reducing the Digitization Rate

Pulse code modulation is a straightforward technique designed to represent the analog signal faithfully, independent of the nature of the source and without too much regard for the resulting data rate. The channel then must pass that rate with suitably high accuracy. In chapter 2 we saw that it was possible to reduce the transmitted digit rate to something closer to the information rate of the messages that the digits represent. These are general techniques that have nothing to do with the nature of the source, analog or digital, from which the digits were derived.

For example, the so-called "memory doublers" sold by software companies do just this. They examine all the bits stored on the computer hard disk, eliminate whatever redundancy they can, and store the compressed data back on the disk. The data is decompressed to its original form whenever you want to use it. Similarly, vendors of large programs such as today's large, highly sophisticated word processors will compress their programs before recording them on floppy disks to reduce the number of floppies that have to be supplied. Then when you install the program, a decompression algorithm is set into action. Clearly, no information can be lost in these compression operations.

The processing performed in these doublers is similar, in principle, to the Huffman coding algorithm that was described in chapter 2. But you will recall that Huffman coding depended on a knowledge of the relative probabilities of the various messages to be sent. In an operation such as memory compression and in other similar operations, you do not know ahead of time what these probabilities are. What these algorithms do is to measure the probabilities during the operation. The measurements might be inaccurate at the start, but they soon converge to effective measurements.

Context-independent reversible compression algorithms such as these are very useful under some circumstances such as memory compression. Their results are relatively modest, however. Consequently, for analog sources such as speech and video, the majority of effort has gone into context-dependent operations. Some of these schemes do obvious things such as digitizing the source at a lower rate, either by reducing its bandwidth or by using coarser quantization in the attempt to fool the eye and ear. Other schemes are far more sophisticated, depending on the detailed knowledge of characteristics of the information source and the way we perceive them. The first such source that we consider is speech.

8.8   Compressing Digital Speech— The Telephone Network Environment

Before going into some of the compression techniques used with speech, it is important to address the environment for digital speech, as it has evolved. Most speech communication is carried out over the telephone networks. As we saw in chapter 7, these networks have evolved from their completely analog origins to their current hybrid state on the way to an all-digital future at some indeterminate time. When the networks were all-analog, there was only one pressing reason for digital speech—security, that is, protection against eavesdropping. This is because there is no satisfactory analog encryption technique.

In the world of the mid-1990s, most of the telephone network's backbone uses digital transmission for the variety of reasons that we discussed in chapter 7. The connection to the subscriber, however, remains analog as before. However, improvements in the modem state of the art, which have increased the standard data rate from 2.4 kbps to 14.4 and 28.8 kbps in just a few years, have made the job of speech compression less demanding. Radio systems are moving to digital more rapidly. For example, cellular radio that started out as analog will likely migrate to all-digital more rapidly than the wire-line telephone networks.

As long as the telephone connections to the subscriber are analog, speech will remain analog except for special applications such as security. When these connections become digital, speech will be digital from end to end, and the digitization technique will be PCM, as for example, with ISDN.

8.8.1   The Information Content of Speech

Consider the problem of transmitting digital speech. The standard digitization rate for good-quality speech is 64 kbps. If that rate could be reduced by compressing the source bandwidth in some way, then at least some money could be saved. In some cases, it might be the only way to render digital transmission feasible at all.

It is interesting to examine the relationship between the bit rate yielded by PCM and the actual information content of the signal. For example, how much information is transferred when a person talks? Let's do a simple computation. The usual speaking rate is a few words per second—let's say five. Assume also that a word is, on the average, five characters long, giving us twenty-five characters per second. If we use eight bits for a character, the resulting information rate is 400 bps, a tiny fraction of the 64,000 bps that we usually use to send speech. Why the large difference?

Our calculation gave us the amount of information in the spoken words, that is, the information that would be transferred if the speaker's words were converted to electronic mail at the speaking rate. Nothing at all is conveyed about the fact that a person is speaking the words, the characteristics of the speaker's voice, or of the emotion with which he or she speaks his words. The speaker might be bored, excited, or trying to end the conversation. In each case, the sound pattern would be different. Thus some of the difference between the two information rates must be related to the amount of information contained in the human voice characteristics. There have even been attempts to capitalize upon the uniqueness of the human voice by using recordings of the speech spectrum as an identification mechanism analogous to the fingerprint. However, it is easier to mimic the human voice than fingerprints, and the courts have been reluctant to admit this kind of evidence.

The large disparity between the information in the text and the information in the voice speaking the text is related to the amount of choice in sending voice signals, resulting from the wide range of voice characteristics. If we could compress the speech in some way so that it is represented by a smaller number of bits per second, we would effectively reduce this choice. But at the same time, reducing the number of bits or, equivalently, the choice is very likely to diminish the ability of the listener to recognize the speaker and might degrade the quality of the transmitted speech in other ways.

The economic trade-off in data-rate compression is similar to the other trade-offs that we have already discussed. By using compression, we reduce the cost of communicating the data, but this is partially offset by the cost of the compression itself. Compression makes economic sense if it costs less than the savings gained by the reduced data rate. The other cost of compression, the reduced quality of the transmission, is harder to measure in dollars and cents. Like everything else, it must be "good enough" for the application.

8.8.2   Speech Compression Techniques

The simplest techniques—filtering the signal to reduce its bandwidth and sampling rate, quantizing the samples more coarsely, or some combination of the two—are satisfactory up to a point. We have already noted that the 4-kHz bandwidth used for digitization at 56 or 64 kbps cuts off the highest-frequency components of some of the consonants. Therefore, the 64-kbps digital speech standard is not what an audio expert would call high fidelity. Nevertheless, its quality is still quite good and more than acceptable in most circumstances, which is why it was chosen as the standard. But when we try to reduce the rate much below this value, even by as little as a factor of 2, simply by reducing the bandwidth or the quantization precision, the quality begins to degrade rapidly. We need more sophisticated approaches that use our knowledge of the properties of speech.

One technique that is sometimes used to gain a factor of 2 in data rate takes advantage of the fact that telephone conversations are two-way—

one person usually (but not always) listens while the other person is talking. Therefore, although some people talk a great deal more than they listen, when averaged over (say) ten or more speakers, you can expect that people will talk and listen about half the time. A telecommunications company typically bundles a large number of telephone signals together in a wideband trunk between two locations. A technique called *digital speech interpolation* is sometimes used to sense when talkers are inactive and fill in these gaps with pieces of other conversations. In this way, the overall data rate can be cut in half. Theoretically, even more compression can be gained by taking advantage of the silences between words and phrases as well. But the penalty paid for this added economy is that the low-energy beginning and end of a syllable may be clipped off; the more compression that is attempted, the more likely it is that this clipping occurs.

Digital speech interpolation achieves compression from the statistics of speech conversations rather than from properties of the speech signals themselves. Another whole class of techniques does use the properties of the speech signals. The only characteristics of the source that straightforward PCM depends upon are its bandwidth and its dynamic range. But there must be other characteristics of the source that depend upon its nature. The fact that the waveform is speech and not something else must give it some features that might help in compressing it below the rate achievable with PCM.

A key feature of PCM is that successive samples are obtained completely independently. One important class of compression techniques takes advantage of the fact that *most* of the time, successive speech samples have amplitudes that are not too different. Because of this, we can save digits by encoding successive samples relative to each other. For example, if one sample has amplitude 13 and the next sample has amplitude 15, fewer bits are needed to send a 2 (the difference between the two sample amplitudes) than to send the amplitude itself. Of course, there will be occasions when the speech amplitude changes by a large amount between successive samples. Whenever this happens, the reduced number of bits is not sufficient to represent the speech as accurately as with the full complement of bits, and there will be some degradation in quality. But the ear can tolerate this kind of degradation if it does not occur too often. Using this class of technique, it is relatively easy to reduce the speech rate from 64 to 32 kbps with little degradation in quality.

There are many varieties of speech compressors in this category. The one that has become the standard beginning in the 1980s is called *adap-*

tive differential pulse code modulation. That name is such a mouthful that its abbreviation ADPCM is a virtual necessity. Because of its good quality, the communications carriers sometimes use 32-kbps ADPCM to represent speech on their digital trunks, sometimes in conjunction with digital speech interpolation. The cost of the compression devices is quite modest, mostly because they use large-scale integrated-circuit technology. Since the quality of speech compressed to a rate of 32 kbps remains better than that of ordinary analog telephone-quality speech, the small degradation in quality is acceptable. However, it is important to note that since compression schemes of this kind depend on the peculiarities of speech, they cannot be used if the lines carry data traffic such as fax or E-mail. Any carrier that uses these compression techniques in its network has to separate out the data traffic and route it over uncompressed trunks.

How much can this class of techniques reduce the data rate? The lower the rate, the greater the likelihood that successive samples will be too far apart in amplitude to fit into the limited number of bits allotted to changes. As it turns out, the limit is about 16 kbps, while still maintaining acceptable levels of degradation. It is significant that this class of compressor is now compatible with the higher-rate modems that work in a satisfactory way in much of today's telephone network. To go much below this limit requires radically different approaches that make use of our knowledge of the human speech production mechanism.

These compression systems are called *vocoders*, an abbreviation for voice coders. They contain special-purpose computers that extract certain features of the speech based upon models of the vocal cords and vocal tract and then synthesize the speech using these features. They do this at rates as low as 2400 bps. The resulting speech at these low rates is intelligible, but of relatively low quality. Users sometimes complain that the speech sounds artificial. "Like Donald Duck" is the usual comment. In addition, when these vocoders were first built using the digital technology available at the time, they were large and expensive. Indeed they had few redeeming features aside from the fact that they constituted the *only* way of achieving security over ordinary telephone circuits. The earliest vocoders were developed during World War II. General Eisenhower is said to have found their quality to be so objectionable that he refused to use them. As the technology advanced, vocoders were used more widely. By the mid-1960s, a vocoder had been installed on the presidential aircraft. It was used by President Johnson's aides whenever security or privacy was warranted, but not by the president himself. His aides were so fearful of his reaction to the quality of the vocoder that they declined to tell him of its installation on the aircraft. They were forced, therefore, to take the calculated risk that the president would commit some indiscretion over the air that could be potentially embarrassing. As a case in point, the story is told that once when the plane was returning to Washington on a route near the Canadian border, the president radioed the White House to state his seating preferences for a state dinner to be held that evening in honor of the Canadian Prime Minister. When told that his preferences would violate accepted protocol, the president is alleged to have referred to protocol and the Prime Minister in his characteristically earthy way. We do not know whether the Canadians heard the comments or were offended by the seating arrangements. Any strain in the relations between the two countries resulting from the incident has remained a dark secret.

There has been progress since those days in both speech research and computer technology. Modern vocoders sound quite respectable, if not high fidelity. They are about the size of a telephone console and cost in the $1000 range. But, as I indicated above, they are slowly being replaced by waveform decoders even on the ubiquitous dial-up analog line as the modem art improves.

8.9   Digital Video

Digital video transmission is another area in which compression of some kind is virtually mandatory. Even the venerable standard analog television, in place since the 1940s, depends upon a form of compression known as *interlaced scanning* to allow it to be broadcast in a standard 6-MHz channel. The straightforward way of scanning a picture is called *progressive.* As the name implies, a progressive scan covers the entire picture rapidly, and the resulting signal is then broadcast. This process is then repeated at some rate, say, 30 frames/s. With interlacing, the picture is scanned in noncontiguous stripes, analogous to the stripes in the American flag, that cover half the picture. Imagine one scan covering the red stripes. Then the next scan fills in the gaps by covering the white stripes. This technique works because we continue to see an image flashed before our eyes for a small fraction of a second after the image is removed. This visual phenomenon, called *persistence of vision*, causes our eyes to fuse the two interlaced scans into a single image provided that scanning rate is greater than about 25 Hz. It is the same phenomenon that lets us perceive continuous motion from a rapid sequence of still frames in a motion picture. This process cuts the bandwidth approximately in half to around 4 MHz, allowing the signals to be easily accommodated by the 6-MHz channel. Background or slowly moving objects in the picture are unaffected by the interlacing process. However, rapidly moving objects do suffer reduced definition, and flicker occurs at the edges of objects such as text, which makes interlaced scanning undesirable for computer monitors.

Of course, all this is transmitted with analog signals. A straightforward conversion of these signals to digital would require a data rate of tens of megabits per second, too high to fit into a standard 6-MHz channel. For example, standard definition television has about 500 lines per frame. Since the picture is 1 $\frac{1}{3}$ times as wide as it is high, digital television would contain about 670 $\times$ 500 or about 335,000 picture elements (pixels) in all. Transmitting at 15 frames/s (30 frames/s with interlacing), the transmission rate is about 5 million pixels/s. Even a relatively crude 6-bit quantization results in a data rate of 30 Mbps. So why digitize video at all?

Paradoxically, the most important motivator of digital television was the advent of high-definition television (HDTV); HDTV, with approximately twice the definition of standard television in each dimension, requires at least four times the bandwidth of standard video. It follows that if digitized standard television is beyond the capability of a 6-MHz channel, then digitized HDTV is even more beyond this capability, and one would expect it to be beyond consideration. In fact, the first high-definition television system to be developed, the Muse system, was analog. It originated in Japan and went into operation in 1989, where it has been a technical but not an economic success, largely because its bandwidth requirements are so large that a special satellite-based delivery system is required. To be a commercial success, HDTV has to be broadcast in existing channels, demanding compression of such an extent that only digital television can provide.

The other important application is the compact disc. The argument here is different than with broadcast television. The CD is already digital, developed to reproduce high-fidelity audio, and therefore can store digitized video as well as digitized audio. But since video bandwidths are so much greater than audio, compression is essential if the CD is to hold more than negligible amounts of video.

8.10   The High-Definition Television Story

The quality that we perceive in any picture depends not only on its inherent resolution but also on how much it is magnified. For example, motion pictures use 35-mm and often 70-mm film to give them the very high resolution that permits us to enjoy them on enormous screens even when we sit near the front of the theater where the apparent magnification is the greatest. The resolution of standard television is much poorer, comparable to that of the 16-mm film that was once standard for home movies, but far better than the 8-mm film that was the home standard when the television format was first adopted. But this reduced definition as compared to the movies is less significant than one might think as long as most of us are content to watch television programs on small screens—a typical home television set uses a screen 12 in. in height, called a 20-in. screen after the length of its diagonal. We typically sit some 6 to 12 ft. from the screen, a comfortable distance in our living or family rooms. A viewer would have to sit closer than 6 ft. from a screen of this size to notice any granularity in the television picture.

The single factor that makes the current standard potentially unsatisfactory is the advent of the large screen display. As long as the viewing public is content with relatively small screens, the broadcast television granularity standard is as adequate today as it was in the early days of television when much larger screens were not technically feasible for home viewers. But the technology of large-screen displays has advanced over the intervening years, and it is these larger screens that show up the limitations of the present standard. For example, the picture on a 3-ft.-high screen would begin to look granular to a viewer sitting within 18 ft. of the picture, three times farther than when a 1-ft.-high screen is used. And as the screen gets larger, the problem increases proportionally. A 4-ft.-high screen, not unusual for projecting home movies, would send the viewer back 24 ft., perhaps out of the room, to avoid the granularity. These facts of life constitute a fundamental limitation on the quality of today's large-screen systems. An improvement in definition by two to three times in both the horizontal and vertical dimensions could bring the quality of these large-screen displays up to that of the motion picture theater at a reasonable viewing distance. On the other hand, viewers who continued to use small screens would hardly notice the difference.

The shape of the screen is also important. Today's television screens are wider than they are high by the ratio of 4:3. This ratio was chosen in the early days of television broadcasting following the lead of the motion pictures of the World War II era. Later the cinematographers began to experiment with ways of creating the illusion of a three-dimensional image without resorting to the cumbersome stereoscopic technique in which two images are projected and the viewers are forced to wear polarized glasses to restrict each eye to see only one of the images. They found that a wide screen gave a viewer seated front and center something of the experience of being inside a three-dimensional image. So when you miss a new film in theaters and wait for the video release a few months later, you may suffer much more than the delay. Especially for films in which broad expanses of scenery are an important part of the action, the viewing sensation is far different in the theater from what it is on the home screen.

Indeed, much of the motivation for HDTV is to reduce this difference to make the sensation of home viewing more like that of the theater. It means developing large display screens that are economical enough for the mass market. Then it requires the higher definition format needed for the larger screens along with a higher ratio of width to height than currently used. While this larger ratio (16/9, or 1.78, vs. 4/3) is still a bit less than that used in the movies (1.85 or 2.25), it is large enough to capture some of the wide-screen effects.

One of the problems that faces the introduction of any new broadcast system goes by the name of *compatibility*. The market is now saturated with television sets meeting the current standards. If a station begins broadcasting its programs in the high-definition format, what will be the affect on all the television sets now installed in people's homes?

High-definition television is not the first new technology to pose compatibility problems. When color television was first introduced, there were millions of black and white receivers in homes, and the Federal Communications Commission (FCC) demanded that these old sets be able to receive the color transmissions in black and white. However, color television did not pose the bandwidth problem of HDTV. While some additional bandwidth was needed to carry the additional color information, the prescribed 6-MHz channels that were carrying the older black and white television were sufficiently wide to carry the color signals.

Stereo audio recordings were introduced at about the same time as color broadcasting. The millions of existing monaural phonographs created a similar compatibility problem. And, as in the television situation, the technique for impressing stereo signals on records was one that permitted the existing monaural phonographs to extract monaural sound from the new stereo records. The television standard required the approval of the FCC, which was adamant on the subject of compatibility. There is no such regulation in the recording industry. But since radio broadcasting is so important to the recording industry, it was essential that the stereo broadcasting format meet the FCC compatibility demands, and the format chosen permitted the large number of existing monaural FM receivers to receive the FM stereo broadcasts.

To select the best scheme among the many contenders, the FCC established a formal technical evaluation. At the start, the conventional wisdom held that the leading contender for the U.S. standard was the Japanese Muse System. But by the time the evaluation was nearing a conclusion in the spring of 1993, all the analog contenders, including one that was a variant of the Muse system, had dropped out. Decisions by the FCC on the issues of compatibility and channel allocations made this inevitable.

The demands of HDTV are so substantial that there is no relatively simple solution for compatibility as was found for color television or FM stereo. Convinced of this fact, the FCC stipulated in 1990 that rather than demanding compatibility in the conventional sense on a single channel, a station broadcasting a program in the HDTV format would be required to broadcast the same program in the older format simultaneously, using separate channels for each broadcast. This approach makes the assumption that the older format will wither away in time as the older television sets wear out, and the bandwidth reserved for serving them can gradually be turned over to the newer format.

Initially, the FCC left open the question of how much bandwidth would be allowed for the HDTV channel. Later it ruled that the existing channel structure would have to be maintained and that a single 6-MHz channel was all that would be allowed. This decision made compression mandatory, and, since the only really practical way of doing compression was digital, this tipped the scale away from analog and toward digital approaches. Of course, video compression is just as useful in compressing the bandwidth of standard television signals as it is of HDTV. It follows that the same compression schemes that will enable HDTV signals to fit into a 6-MHz channel will permit several standard signals to be squeezed into the same channel, and, understandably, this turned out to be the strongest motivation factor among broadcasters of all kinds to move toward digital transmission. The competition concluded with a "grand alliance" of the residual competitors combining the best features of each into a hybrid design incorporating sufficient compression to fit the resultant signal into a 6-MHz channel.

8.1.1   Video on Compact Discs

Optical disc technology appeared in the 1970s for the recording of video in analog form before the digital CD hit the market. Its principal application was home movies. Recorded on both sides of a 12-in. platter, the *LaserDisc* could hold about 2 hours of video programming with a sound track. Despite this remarkable piece of technology, the LaserDisc made hardly a ripple. Because no sooner did it appear, then along came the video cassette recorder that offered a way not only to play prerecorded material but also to record television programs off the air and to make home video recordings. Even though the LaserDiscs had a small video quality advantage over magnetic tape, it faded into a temporary oblivion.

Following the success of the CD in bringing digital audio to the market, the LaserDisc made its second appearance, this time with a digital sound track accompanying the still-analog video. With this modified format, the LaserDisc offers sound quality distinctly superior to that available on the video cassette. It is a natural medium for high-quality presentations of operas and symphony videos where the sound quality must be first-rate. LaserDisc players permit the sound track to be played on audio equipment independent of the television receiver, and this new flexibility has increased the marketability of the optical technology. But the LaserDisc is still analog, and all the arguments for the digitization of broadcast video apply as well to video recorded on these video discs. Of course, the obstacle to this digitization is the same as the obstacle to recording video on the compact disc: the capacity of the disc.

The arguments for recording video on CDs using compression techniques become especially cogent with the computer version of the CD known as the CD-ROM. While the CD stores digital audio only in one particular very high-fidelity format, and a CD player's one function is to extract the stored audio digits and convert them into audio signals, the CD-ROM can store any kind of information in digital form: computer programs, text, graphics, and video as well as audio.

This large capacity of the CD-ROM made the multimedia computer possible in the aftermath of its introduction. Thus a computer can obtain information from CD-ROMs or from the Internet or other on-line networks. Regardless of the source, compression is essential if more than token amounts of video are to be included. The same thing is true of the *compact disc interactive* or CD-I, a stand-alone version of the CD-ROM that works with a small interface box to a television set rather than with a computer.

8.1.2   Video Compression

The techniques used to compress video take advantage of (1) the spatial redundancy in the picture, that is, the fact that within each transmitted frame there is redundant information and (2) temporal redundancy, that is, that in going from frame to frame much of the picture either does not change at all, changes only slightly, or changes in a predictable way. All compression schemes use a variety of techniques to take advantage of both forms of redundancy.

The first step in the digitization process is to divide the picture into a rectangular array of pixels. However, the processing operations necessary for compression are not performed in the time domain as these pixels are scanned, but rather on their two-dimensional transform in the frequency domain. The transformation is performed with a variation of the Fourier transform called the *discrete cosine transform* (DCT). The picture is first divided into an array of pixels at discrete locations to provide the data upon which the DCT works. The fact that this array is discrete rather than continuous is one of the ways in which the DCT differs from the Fourier transform as we described it in chapter 4. A second difference is that it uses only cosines and not sines (or, equivalently, it is real valued).

As the picture is scanned, the DCT maps an 8 by 8 pixel area of a frame into an 8 by 8 array of points in a two-dimensional array of Fourier coefficients. If quantization were not an issue, this process would be perfectly reversible with no loss. That is to say, passing the DCT coefficients through an inverse DCT would yield the original pixel information. But when the Fourier coefficients are quantized, the situation can be different, and the output of an inverse DCT will, in general, differ from the input information. In fact, it is not the pixels from each scan that are passed through the DCT but rather the difference between this spatial information and the reconstructed version of the previous scan. Since much of the picture is background and does not change at all, the transform of the difference will contain large numbers of 0s. This means that the sequence of bits from the DCT leads to runs of 0s of variable length, just the kind of data that is ideal for compression by Huffman coding.

While this process of encoding the difference between successive scans does an excellent job of compressing the information from the background, more sophisticated processing is needed for compressing those portions of the picture that are in motion. To compress this information, the encoder predicts the position of moving objects in a given frame from their positions in previous frames. Then it encodes the difference between the actual location and the predicted location. Techniques of this kind can save between 50 and 80% in bit rate. Understandably, there is room for considerable variation in this motion processing, depending on the amount of motion and its rapidity. A football game, for example, will require more bits for accurate reproduction than will a news anchor reading from a TelePrompTer™. But even in a football game, the rapid motion is not continuous, and the use of buffering can help smooth out the sporadic need for a high digitization rate. Different broadcast situations demand different approaches to this inherently variable-rate processing. Under some circumstances, a single digitization rate has to be chosen, the particular rate being a compromise between quality and compression. In situations in which a single broadcast channel is used for several television signals, statistical multiplexing can be used to advantage.

Two international compression standards have been established, called respectively MPEG-1 and MPEG-2 (the abbreviation MPEG stands for Motion Picture Experts Group). MPEG-1, developed for the CD-ROM, is applicable to low-definition television with a 360 × 240 array of pixels, transmitted at a rate of 30 frames/s with no interlacing, resulting in a data rate about 2.6 million pixels/s, one-half that of standard-definition television. It is compressed to a bit rate in the range from 1 to 3 Mbps, allowing the storage of from about 10 to 30 min of video on the CD.

MPEG-2 was developed for television broadcasting, both standard and high definition. In addition to the MPEG-1 capabilities, it includes the ability to handle interlaced as well as progressive scanning. Its compressed data rate is in the range of 3 to 15 Mbps for standard-definition television and in the 15 to 20 Mbps range for high-definition television.

There is a whole other class of video in which motion is so severely restricted that one would expect to be able to compress into rates well below the MPEG-1 range. An example is video teleconferencing—after all, how rapid can the motion be when conferees are sitting around a table? Such so-called *nearly full-motion* video conferencing has been available to businesses since the early 1980s at rates from T1 (1.544 Mbps) down. The high compression takes advantage of the fact that in a conferencing situation, in contrast to a motion picture, there is very little change from frame to frame. Should a conferee become overly emotional and start gesticulating rapidly, his transmitted image might be blurred a bit, but that could even be an advantage. At the extreme is the video telephone in which the transmitted picture is of a single person moving only slightly. Another standard called MPEG-4 is under development for this class of low-rate, restricted-motion systems.

8.1.3   But You Cannot Cut Corners with High-Fidelity Music

All the video compression schemes include compressed sound along with the video. However, this is not so with recorded high-fidelity audio. In this category efficiency must give way to quality on all counts. The very essence of the use of digits is the fact that the digits appearing at the home playback machine are identical to those generated at the source. Therefore, compression is out of the question; the original digits must be recorded. Or in the language of communications systems, the *capacity* of the recording medium must be large enough to accommodate the number of digits needed to represent the audio with high fidelity.

9

DIGITAL RECORDING—
THE COMPACT DISC

9.0   The Meteoric Rise of the Compact Disc

One of the most significant aspects of the development of the digital computer has been the rapid advance in the capacity and speed of storage media. Among the important early developments was the digital tape recorder, and it did not take long for these same recorders to become standard equipment for studio recording of audio. But digital recorders were much too expensive for consumer application, and, until relatively recently, the media that brought audio to consumers remained analog. Then along came the compact disc, and, faster than anyone dreamed, consumer audio became digital. The development work on the compact disc began in the 1970s at about the same time as the first personal computers were being designed and built, and it was the same microprocessor technology that made both systems economically feasible. The compact disc was such a success that it was only a matter of time before it was applied to general-purpose computer storage. And both applications have benefited from the extension of the CD to storing video as well as audio.

9.1   A Brief History of Audio Recording

The remarkable improvements that have resulted from digital audio are simply the latest in a long sequence of advances in audio reproduction. It all began in 1877 when Thomas Edison recorded the nursery rhyme "Mary Had a Little Lamb" on a helical track embossed on a layer of tin foil covering a rotating cylinder. We cannot fully appreciate the benefits of digital audio without the perspective of this recording history.

This history is a tale of steady advance in the achievement of its two objectives: producing a track in a recording medium as close as possible to a replica of the acoustic signal, and playing back the recorded signal as faithfully as possible with minimum extraneous noise. So rapidly did the technology advance in the early years, and so popular did the new invention become, that by the 1890s, recordings were being made regularly, and *phonographs* (Edison's term) or *gramophones* (as they became known in Europe) became production items. By the beginning of this century, Edison's cylinder had given way to the familiar disk as the recording medium, and by 1910, virtually all the singers of the first rank were making them. We still treasure those primitive recordings made by the great singers of the era, artists such as Enrico Caruso, the Italian tenor who reigned supreme at the Metropolitan Opera during the first two decades of this century.

The phonograph was invented long before the development of electronic amplification techniques, and so the original recording and playback processes were severely constrained by the limitations of the entirely mechanical process. Vocalists were forced to sing as loudly as possible into a large acoustical recording horn that concentrated the singer's acoustic vibrations into a small volume, and this mechanically amplified sound provided the energy to cut the groove on the cylinder or record. Aside from the fact that the singers often had to strain their voices to generate enough energy, the horn introduced large distortions of the frequency components of the music. The fact that it was sensitive only to sound sources directly in front of it constituted even more serious a limitation. For this reason, those early mechanical recordings were limited to ensembles of artists small enough to be grouped directly in front of the horn, virtually excluding any but the smallest orchestral ensembles.

Playback was also mechanical. A needle riding in the groove of the record picked up the mechanical vibrations corresponding to the recorded audio. The needle also picked up unwanted scratching noises from the surface of the record. These recorded sounds were amplified to an audible level by another horn. Revolutionary though mechanical audio recording may have been in its time, its quality was nevertheless exceedingly poor by any standard. It is a pity that the great artists of the day lived before the time when recording could leave the later generations an adequate picture of their artistry.

A revolutionary change occurred in 1925, when the recording and playback processes became electromechanical. For only when the techniques of electronic amplification became available could the recording process be freed from the limitations of the acoustic horn. The new recording device became the microphone, and the acoustic vibrations, once converted to electrical form, could now be amplified before being converted back to mechanical form for the cutting of the record grooves. Aside from the improved fidelity of the new techniques, the elimination of the horn meant that, for the first time, the size of the orchestra was no longer a limitation. Although the new process was still primitive by today's standards, its fidelity was a revelation in its day.

The next major milestone occurred in 1948 when the 78-RPM record was replaced by the vinyl long-playing or LP record. The most revolutionary change was a large increase in the storage capacity of the disk. A 12-in. 78-RPM record could store only about 5 min of audio on a side, necessitating a multiple-record album for a medium-length symphony less than one-half hour in duration. Recording of long works—for example, a full-length opera lasting 2 to 3 hours—was quite impractical. The combination of the slower rotation speed and the much narrower "microgrooves" gave the LP its "long-playing" capability, up to one-half hour per side of a 12-in. record. The LP also had improved reproduction quality, due to the development of new materials and techniques that permitted a much wider frequency response and much quieter surfaces.

Ten years later, stereo LP recordings made monaural recording obsolete. Everyone is familiar with the result. Almost every work of any length ever written has been recorded in stereo, some many times by many artists, and with increasingly high quality. In the days before stereo, any audio equipment that made even a pretense at faithful reproduction was called *high fidelity* or hi-fi for short. Once stereophonic recording became common, the audio equipment that reproduced it became known as *stereo*, relegating the term high fidelity to monaural systems.

Then came the incursion of digital technology into audio reproduction. The first step in the evolution from all-analog to all-digital recording was a hybrid stage in which the original audio from the microphone was recorded on digital magnetic tape. This conversion to digital at the start of the process provided a controlled-accuracy source from which the records could be cut. Since the disks were still analog, the recorded digits had to be converted back to analog before they could be cut. Some years later, the compact disc began competing with the LP as the vehicle for supplying the audio program material to the end users in digital form. I am sure that the developers of the compact disc believed that the new medium would ultimately supplant the LP. But I also conjecture that they along with everyone else were surprised at the speed at which this took place.

The compact disc is a remarkable engineering tour de force, a credit to those who worked so diligently and successfully upon it. While we know that Thomas Edison invented the phonograph, we do not know the name of any one individual who developed the compact disc system. It is rare these days when a single individual can be named as the father of a particular piece of technology. More often it is a large company, or, in this case, two such companies, Philips of The Netherlands and Sony of Japan, that deserve the credit.

9.2 Telecommunications and Recording: The Information Theory Connection

Engineers are strongly motivated to develop technology that will find widespread application. However, they often underestimate the complexity of their technology and, accordingly, are frustrated when their inventions do not find practical application. So it was with communications engineers. As we noted in chapter 5, there was very little practical application of Shannon's theory in the early years despite all the highly inventive research work. As time went on, there was more application in telecommunication systems. But it took the recording industry to provide the most widespread application.

How did this come about? First, in the years between the invention and the application, the revolution in digital technology converted coders and decoders from large and expensive devices into cheap, marketable products. Second, the engineers at Sony and Philips had the insight and flexibility to adapt the techniques and technology of digital communications to the mass market of the recording industry.

Table 9-1 shows the connection between communications and recording more explicitly. The compact disc is a medium for delayed communication of the digitized audio from source to destination. And the storage medium, like the communications medium, is subjected to noise processes. In the compact disc, noise arises during disc manufacture,

Table 9-1   The Telecommunications/Recording Connection

	Telecommunications	*Recording*
Channel	Transmission medium	Compact disc
Information source	Digitized audio waveform	Digitized audio wave-form
Communications objective	Balance of high rate, high accuracy, acceptable cost	Balance of high storage density, high accuracy, acceptable cost
Noise	Transmission impairments	Storage defects
Channel capacity	Maximum transmission rate with perfect accuracy	Maximum storage density with perfect accuracy

recording, and playback and limits the equivalent storage capacity. The benchmark against which we measure the overall performance of a system is how economically we are able to approach the equivalent *capacity* of the recording/playback channel—the maximum amount of audio that can be stored and retrieved without error. More precisely, the objective is to obtain an appropriate balance between high recording capacity or storage density, suitably high accuracy, and economic feasibility.

The ultimate judge of audio accuracy is the human ear. The ear is relatively tolerant—the frequency of errors acceptable in an audio system is higher than the error frequency acceptable in most data transmission situations. However, that changes the problem only in degree, not in kind, since the ultimate virtue of the digital system is its ability to obtain some desired level of accuracy, whatever that might be for the problem at hand.

High recording capacity is also a very important issue. The fact that the LP record stored about six times as much music as its predecessor had a revolutionary impact upon the recording industry. The standard CD is 12 cm, or about 4 $^3/_4$ in., in diameter and has a maximum playing time of 74 min. An LP record is 12 in. in diameter and has a maximum playing time of slightly less than 30 min on each side. Thus, the CD holds about 25% more material on one side than does a two-sided LP. But even this modest difference can mean a great deal. There is a perhaps apocryphal story that credits the late Herbert von Karajan, then the eminent conductor of the Berlin Philharmonic, with advising Philips Corporation that a compact disc should have sufficient capacity to hold *his* recording of Beethoven's Ninth. In contrast, Karajan's older LP recording requires three sides.

The CD's relatively small size is an important feature. It means that a CD player can be made small enough to be portable, or to be mounted conveniently on an automobile dashboard. It also means that less shelf space is required to store the discs themselves. But to get all that playing time on a small disc is no mean feat, and it requires the use of modern techniques based upon information theory.

9.3   Compact Disc Storage—Capacity Considerations

A disc of a given diameter has a fixed amount of area available for use in storing audio. The smaller the area required to represent 1 bit of information, the more bits can be squeezed onto the disc. The bit pattern is represented on the disc as a spiral of pits and associated land areas. For playback, the digits are retrieved from the disc using a very sharply focused beam of light. The smaller the light-spot size, the smaller the pits can be and remain resolvable, up to some limit that depends upon the essential granularity of the disc material. Once that limit is reached, it does no good to decrease the light-spot size still further, just as increasing the signal-to-noise ratio in a communications channel does no good once the capabilities of the bandwidth have been exhausted. The equivalent to bandwidth in a communications channel is the number of resolvable spots on the CD's surface. The capacity of the CD as a channel is the maximum number of bits that can be stored and retrieved without error using practical laser technology.

The problem in CD recording and playback is to find a technique that achieves a packing density of bits on the disc that is a reasonable fraction of the channel capacity, with sufficiently accurate retrieval. This means using the equivalent of modulation and coding techniques to achieve performance close to that predicted by Shannon's theorem. These equivalent techniques for CD technology mean using very small pit and land areas, although necessarily larger than the minimum resolvable areas, with an error rate low enough for error-correction techniques to overcome.

9.3.1   The CD Storage Mechanism

The mechanism for storing digits on compact discs is remarkably simple. A sequence of pits is etched in a long, spiral track that covers much of the

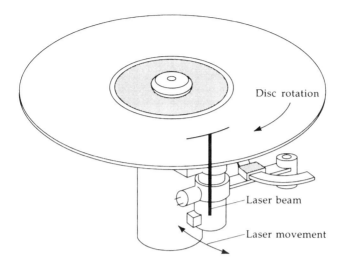

Figure 9-1   A compact disc rotating above a laser pickup (from Richard Bruno, "Making Compact Discs Interactive," *IEEE Spectrum,* 1987, © 1987 IEEE).

disc area. The etching is done chemically following a process in which a laser beam draws out the intricate pattern to be etched. The disc is played by scanning another laser beam along the track. Figure 9-1 shows a sketch of a disc rotating on its turntable while being illuminated from below by the playback laser beam. Figure 9-2 shows a cross section of the disc being illuminated by this laser beam. Note in Fig. 9-2 that the underside of the pits and lands is coated with a material that reflects the fine laser readout beam. The entire structure of pits and lands is only about a

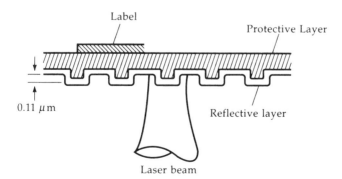

Figure 9-2   Pits and lands on a compact disc (courtesy of Sony Electronics Inc.).

micrometer (40 millionths of an inch) thick. This very fragile structure is encased in a protective material slightly over a millimeter thick that provides mechanical rigidity. This material must be transparent on the bottom to permit the playback light beam to penetrate to the pits and surrounding land areas where the information is stored.

The playback process must provide a way for the light beam to distinguish between a pit and a land. Figure 9-3 shows this mechanism with an expanded view of the pit–land cross section. Note that the light reflected from the land areas travels farther than that reflected from the pit areas by twice the pit depth. This additional distance is about half the wavelength of the light, causing the light reflected from pits and lands to be out of phase. The result is that whenever the beam partially illuminates a land and pit area, as illustrated in Fig. 9-3, the reflected light intensity will be less than when a land area alone is illuminated, because of the partial cancellation of the light reflected from the pit and land areas. In practice, the signals never cancel out exactly, but even partial cancellation permits the optical receiver to detect when the light beam crosses a pit–land boundary from the changed intensity of the reflected light.

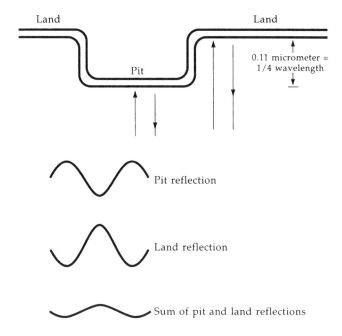

Figure 9-3   Reflections from pits and lands cancel each other.

Specifically, whenever the light beam crosses from land to pit, the signal level drops as a result of the increased cancellation; conversely, whenever the beam crosses from pit to land, the signal level increases as this cancellation disappears.

This phenomenon provides a convenient mechanism for storing bits. A 1 is stored at every transition between a pit and a land. The digits between these transitions are all 0s. Figure 9-4 shows a typical pattern of 0s and 1s. The optical system detects the presence of 1s by detecting the pit–land boundaries from the changes in signal level. It detects 0s by measuring the distances between the intensity changes. This technique allows the bits to be packed together closely; in fact, by a distance well under a beam width.

This scheme depends critically upon representing the digits in such a way that there are no 1s in succession. This is done with a form of code. The audio is converted to digital with 16-bit samples, and each of these PCM samples is divided into two 8-bit segments, or bytes. These segments are the fundamental elements that are manipulated before being stored on the disc. Since any given sample amplitude can be anything at all, these 8-bit segments can contain any of the total of 256 possible combinations of 0s and 1s, many of which have contiguous 1s. The code expands each 8-bit number into a 14-bit number. It turns out that 256 of the total of 16,134 14-bit numbers (about 1.6%) have at least two 0s between every pair of 1s, and these are the numbers selected for the expansion. The name given to this scheme, *eight-to-fourteen modulation*, is quite descriptive if not terribly imaginative.

An example will illustrate the process. The code transforms the 8-bit segment 01101111 into the 14-bit number 00100001000010. The original

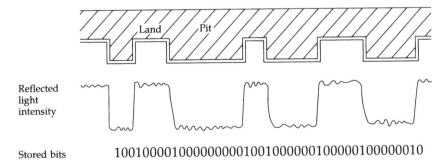

Reflected light intensity

Stored bits   10010000100000000010010000001000001000000010

Figure 9-4 How the compact disc stores bits.

8-bit number contains six 1s, two in a row and four in a row, while the 14-bit number contains only three 1s each surrounded by 0s. The three 1s require three transitions or 1 $^1/_2$ pits.

What is the advantage of this scheme? For a given laser beam diameter, there is a minimum-pit size, regardless of how the bits are represented. With this scheme, this minimum-size pit stores three bits, since at least two 0s follow every 1. With a direct recording scheme, this same pit would be able to store only one bit. This gives us an improvement by a factor of 3. When we take into account the increase in the number of bits from 8 to 14, the net improvement that results is a factor of 1.7. Other things being equal, this factor translates into the difference between a disc that can store 74 min of music and one that can store only 44 min, or, in another dimension, the difference between a 12-cm and 16-cm disc diameter for the same capacity.

9.3.2   Noise Mechanisms on the CD

To return now to our analogy of recording and playback as communication processes, let's examine the issue of signal-to-noise ratio. In a communications system, the signal energy must be made large enough to overcome the thermal noise in the receiver. This turns out not to be a problem in a CD system, regardless of the beam and pit dimensions, so we can forget about this source of noise. But how about other sources of noise, especially those associated with the disc?

One noise source results from imperfections in the pit fabrication process. If the pit edge is fuzzy, or if there are spurious pit edges between normal ones resulting from imperfect etching during the manufacture of the disc, the signals representing 1s and 0s will become less distinguishable. The smaller the pit size, the more important these anomalies become, or, equivalently, the less the signal-to-noise ratio becomes. Because these pit imperfections are random, the effect is very similar to that of thermal noise in communication systems.

Pit anomalies represent only one noise mechanism on compact discs. More significant are imperfections on the disc surface itself, which can make large sections of the disc either unusable or at least very unreliable. This results in lengthy bursts of errors similar in some respects to the large error bursts that often occur on telephone lines.

Still another source of noise is surface contamination of the disc: for example, scratches and finger marks caused by careless handling. Fortunately, surface contamination is of little concern if minimal care is taken. The reason is that the light beam used to retrieve the data from the disc is focused to a very fine point on the pits themselves. The beam is out of focus at the surface of the disc, so any surface imperfections are smeared out by the light beam. In fact, the degree of care required is far less than that required in the handling of vinyl analog records.

In the same way that communications channel noise becomes more of a problem as the data rate increases, all three CD noise sources become more important as the pit size decreases (or as the recording density increases). The techniques used to combat this CD recording/playback noise are similar to those used in communications systems—error correction and detection.

The single most annoying source of noise in an analog recording is not present in the compact disc, because the CD playback mechanism is optical rather than mechanical. In contrast to the analog record, nothing physical touches the CD during playback. Thus as long as the surface is not physically abused in handling, there is nothing in the compact disc equivalent to the noise that we call "record scratch," nor is there the corresponding record wear that ultimately degrades the quality of analog recordings. Part of the evolutionary improvement in analog techniques that occurred over the years was the development of playback systems that required increasingly smaller forces exerted on the record by the playback stylus. But no matter how light the tonearm and how low the stylus pressure on the disk, there must be some, and with each playing of the disk, the record surface is eroded ever so slightly and eventually becomes too noisy to use. The radio stations vastly prefer CDs to their old LPs because of their durability, despite the fact that the improved quality of the digital technique is, for the most part, lost in the broadcasting processes.

9.3.3   Controlling CD Noise

We have seen how the efficiency of a communications channel is increased by increasing the modulation rate to the point where errors are made and then applying coding techniques to correct those errors. That is precisely the philosophy that underlies the choice of parameters of the compact disc. The pits are very small (about 10,000/cm or 25,000/in.), resulting in an error rate due to the pit imperfections of between 1 in 10,000 and 1 in 100,000. If these pit imperfections, which behave like thermal noise, were the only consideration, it would pay to reduce the spot size still more and correct the increased error rate with still more powerful coding. However, it turns out that the limiting factor is actually the disc imperfections that make large areas of the disc relatively unreliable; and the smaller the pit size, the greater the size of the error bursts that must be corrected.

The coding used to correct CD errors is from the Reed–Solomon family described in chapter 6. In the coding process, eight check bits are appended to every twenty-four information bits derived from the quantized audio samples of the audio. (The next section shows exactly how these information bits are obtained.) It does this in two coding stages: the first stage is a (28, 24) Reed–Solomon code that appends four check bits to the twenty-four information bits; the second stage is a (32, 28) Reed–Solomon code, producing, effectively, a (32, 24) code. But it is not nearly that simple. The 28-bit input to the second encoder is not the direct output of the first encoder. Rather, the 28 bits are the outputs of the first decoder from previous frames, each bit from a different frame. The effect is to apply the coding to bits derived from different parts of the audio. In this way consecutive samples of audio are distributed throughout the disc rather than being stored adjacent to one another. This interleaving of the source digits tends to randomize the channel, making it more like a binary symmetric channel where the code is most effective. This pair of codes with an overhead of 25% reduces the random error rate to about one in a billion, effectively correcting almost all the random errors. Even more significant, the coding can correct large bursts of errors and detect many more without correction. Even those error bursts that survive the decoding process without being either corrected or detected are distributed in time where the effects are much less audible. Discs containing areas of imperfection so large that they cannot be handled adequately by these coding techniques are weeded out in the quality-control processes at the manufacturing plants.

9.3.4   Summary of the CD Recording Process

A summary of the compact disc recording process is shown in Fig. 9-5. First, audio samples are taken at the standard rate of 44,100 samples/s. These samples are quantized to 16 bits to obtain the desired dynamic range. For recording purposes, the basic time element is 135.6 μs, the time it takes to accumulate six audio samples at the sampling rate. In this basic time element, 192 bits of audio are generated: six samples from each of the stereo channels, with 16 bits per sample. The Reed–Solomon coding appends eight check bits to each twenty-four information bits, resulting in a total of 256 bits derived from the 192 information bits. Then comes the eight-to-fourteen modulation that expands the number of bits from 256 to 448. Finally, an additional 140 bits are appended for bookkeeping purposes, giving us a grand total of 588 bits to be recorded on the disc as the basic recording unit.

This scheme expands the original 192 bits of audio by a factor of about 3 into 588 channel bits. By doing this, we achieve high-density, accurate recording and playback according to the principles of information theory. A total of about 20 billion of these channel bits can be stored on the disc, corresponding to about 74 min. of audio.

9.4   CD Playback

The playback process must undo all the operations shown in Fig. 9-5 in reverse order. The optical readout system in the CD player retrieves the modulated bits stored on the disc. The optical mechanism must track the recorded pits on the spiral track with sufficient accuracy to keep this retrieval from being a source of errors. The selection of the minimum pit size is governed by both the size of the light spot and the accuracy with which the spot tracks the pits on the spiral. These bits are demodulated by reversing the eight-to-fourteen modulation and then are decoded and deinterleaved with two Reed–Solomon decoders. The resulting digits are ready to be converted back to audio and then played through an amplifier and speaker.

But first, some more error processing is needed. The Reed–Solomon decoding will correct some errors and will detect others that it cannot correct. What should be done about the latter? Suppose that a particular sample contains an error somewhere that cannot be corrected. If there is a large difference between the incorrect sample and the adjacent correct samples, conversion of the incorrect sample to audio could produce a very annoying "pop." Rather than reproduce the audio from a sample that is known to be in error, it is preferable to ignore the received sample altogether and set the value of that sample at a value between the preceding and following samples known to be correct. Generally, the human ear is

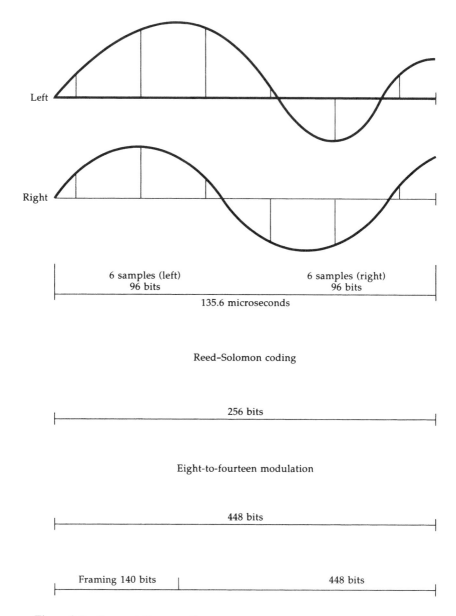

Left

Right

6 samples (left)
96 bits

6 samples (right)
96 bits

135.6 microseconds

Reed–Solomon coding

256 bits

Eight-to-fourteen modulation

448 bits

Framing 140 bits

448 bits

Figure 9-5 Compact disc recording processes.

not able to detect these interpolations provided that they occur relatively infrequently.

9.5   The Success of the CD

The success of the CD was helped by one factor that is not given as much credit as it should be: standardization. The LP record did not replace the 78 as the analog recording standard immediately. At the same time that Columbia Records developed the 33 $^1/_3$ RPM LP, RCA developed the small 45 RPM disks. While the LP ultimately won out, the two schemes existed side by side for a number of years, with the LP used primarily for the classics and other longer works, and the 45s for the popular music of the day. The same thing happened with video cassette recording. Two incompatible schemes, VHS and Beta, were developed and competed side by side for many years.

In contrast, only one CD system was ever marketed. This has meant that the manufacturers of the players were able to concentrate on mass producing a single class of products. This more than anything else led to the rapid decline in the prices of the players, bringing them within the range of almost everyone in our society.

We should not lose sight of the fact that, despite its spectacular quality, the CD is still a recording. As good as it is, the CD is still only an approximation of the concert hall. I jump at the opportunity to hear music in a live performance, even when performed by musicians less skilled than the many outstanding recording artists. For no matter how excellent the recorded performance, no matter how high the quality of the reproduction, every time I listen to the recording I am hearing exactly the same thing. The live performance, in contrast, may be technically less polished but, in compensation, may offer a fresh insight into the music. This is especially so with jazz, where the ingenuity and spontaneity of its performers are more important than the inventiveness of its composers, and with the music of the Baroque composers who left considerable leeway to the performing artists. Even in music where the composer has specified instructions to the performers in elaborate detail, there is ample latitude for the latter to exercise his or her own esthetic judgment. To approximate the spontaneity of the concert hall, even at the risk of deviation from technical polish, some artists (Leonard Bernstein was a notable example in his last years) insist that their recordings be made from live performances rather than the more typical studio recording sessions. Even aside from the spontaneity of a live performance, the sheer sound of live music in the concert hall plays a key role in the esthetic experience derived from the performance, and even the best audio system does not always capture the concert-hall vividness. I remember the first time I heard a live performance of the Brahms Requiem many years ago. In the second movement, a drum sounds repeated notes of progressively increasing intensity, followed immediately by the words "For all flesh is as grass, and all the glory of man as the flower of grass," sung by the chorus in a sustained fortissimo. I have never forgotten the impact of that low-pitched drum crescendo. No LP version even approximates the effect. Compact disc versions with their wide dynamic range are much more realistic, but even when played through a high-quality amplifier and speakers, they do not have quite the bite of the concert-hall sound.

More and more often though, sound passages like this are the exception rather than the rule, and as the quality of recordings has improved over the years, with the fidelity of the playback equipment keeping pace, the living room has become an increasingly acceptable substitute for the sound quality, if not the spontaneity, of the concert hall.

9.6   Erasable Compact Discs

Techniques have been developed that allow the data recorded on discs to be erased, thus converting the CD from a read-only memory to a read–write memory. To do this, the storage mechanism must be different from the standard mechanical process in which pits are etched permanently into the material. The read–write process, like the read-only process, uses a finely focused laser beam, but there the similarity ends. The read–write disc contains a magnetic layer in which the direction of magnetization is modified by the heat generated by the laser beam. Some materials are very difficult to magnetize at room temperature but become much easier to magnetize when the temperature is raised. Therefore, when a low magnetic field is applied at room temperature, the magnetization of the material is unaffected *except* in the very small spot illuminated by the laser in which the temperature has been elevated. In that spot, the magnetization is reversed—a 0 becomes a 1 or a 1 becomes a 0, depending upon the direction of the magnetic field.

The digits are also retrieved from the disc by a laser, this time at a power level so low that the temperature of the illuminated spot is unchanged. The light beam distinguishes between a 0 and a 1 by the polarization of the reflected light, making use of a phenomenon known as the *Faraday effect*. When an electromagnetic wave passes through a magnetic field, its polarization is rotated by an amount proportional to the strength of the field. Thus when a magnetized spot on the disc is illuminated by light from the readout laser, it reflects the light but rotates its polarization clockwise for one direction of magnetization and counterclockwise for the other. A polarizing element in front of the light detector tells the receiver what the polarization of the reflected light is, enabling it to distinguish between a recorded 0 or 1.

These erasable discs have been used to some extent in the computer market as compact, high-capacity substitutes for magnetic disks. As of the mid 1990s, they have not appeared in the entertainment market. It may be that this application will have to wait for the next-generation discs that we discuss later in the chapter.

9.7   Digital Audio Tape

Magnetic tape is used as a storage medium in many contexts, both analog and digital. As an inherently sequential-access medium, it is uniquely suited to audio recording, and both analog and digital audio tapes are widely used for this purpose. It has long been an alternative to the vinyl record as a medium for storing analog audio, with the added ability to record signals as well as play them back. In contrast, digital audio tape for home use is a relatively recent development.

Digital magnetic tape has been with us since the 1950s. One of its earliest and most important applications was in the computer area, primarily as secondary storage. In another important application, it has long been the medium of choice for the initial recording of audio material—the so-called master tape. This master tape then becomes the source for the cutting of discs, analog or digital. But the digital tape recorders used for both computer storage and studio audio recording are large and expensive. For home entertainment purposes, a small cassette device that could be mass-produced at prices comparable to those of analog cassette recorders or CD players is desired. Such a device could be used to make copies of material stored on compact discs, much as an analog cassette tape recorder is used to record LPS. A digital recording made from a radio broadcast would be no better than a high-quality analog recording, since the inherent broadcast quality is generally poorer than that of even analog recording devices. But there is no reason that a digital magnetic tape recorder could not make very high-quality copies of CDs. The digital magnetic tape as a read–write storage medium has the potential to be a very valuable part of a home entertainment center.

The *digital audio tape* medium, with DAT as the inevitable acronym, was developed for this application. It uses credit-card-size cassettes in a small machine. However, a very long time elapsed between the development of these devices and their introduction into the U.S. market. The reason for this has nothing to do with their quality or cost, but rather with the fact that the recording industry, fearful of wholesale CD copying that could potentially impact CD sales, was successful in keeping them off the market until an agreement was reached on the capabilities of the machines. The movie industry had similar reservations about video tape. It would kill the movies, they said. However, not only are movies as strong and profitable as ever but business is booming in movie cassettes designed for the home market. It is very difficult to predict the effect of new technology on the marketplace.

As long as we are dealing with analog media, there is an inevitable degradation of quality in the process of copying audio or video from one medium to another. But digital recording is different. If one can extract the digits from a compact disc and then record these very same digits on tape, there is no degradation at all. Even if there are a few errors in the received data, the degradation in a copy is negligible. This accuracy of digital recording is what makes the DAT problem unique. The recording industry initially attempted to insert digital codes on the CDs that, when detected by a special circuit on the tape recorder, would prevent the discs from being copied onto the digital tape. All these attempts were unsuccessful. Even had someone developed such a technique, it would not have been long before some resourceful young engineers would have developed and sold, legally or not, antidotes to such circuits. Artificially withholding new technology may work for a while, but inevitably it will be defeated. Ultimately, an agreement was reached between the equipment makers and the recording artists. Both supported a bill that modified the intellectual property laws that has permitted digital audio tape recording to come to the market.

9.8   The Digital Versatile Disc—The Next-Generation CD

We noted in chapter 8 that the development of video compression technology has permitted substantial amounts of video to be recorded on compact discs. But it should also be recalled that this recorded video has about half the definition of standard broadcast video. For reasons such as this, it has long been clear to the industry that a higher-capacity compact disc was necessary for large-scale digital video recording.

Many consumer electronic companies began to develop higher-capacity discs with various characteristics. Ultimately, they agreed to cooperate in developing a single approach that has become known as the *digital versatile disc* (DVD). As with the CD, the DVD has several forms, one for entertainment, one for computer storage, and one analogous to the erasable compact disc. The DVD readers are planned to be able to read the older CDs as well.

The DVD with a 12-cm diameter is the same size as the CD, and it uses essentially the same technology as does the CD but advanced in several dimensions to achieve an order of magnitude more capacity. Fundamental to the increased capacity is a reduction in the pit dimensions by a factor of about 2 from those of the CD. This approximately doubles the number of bits that can be stored along the track, and it also permits the approximate doubling of the length of the track by permitting the spiral to be more tightly wound. These two effects increase the number of recorded bits per square centimeter by a factor of close to 5. In order to deal with these smaller dimensions, the laser wavelength has been decreased from 780 to 635 – 650 nm.

The information bit recording density is further increased by a factor of about 7 by changes in the recording format. But there is more. A compact disc contains a single substrate 120-mm thick on which the pits are etched. The DVD contains two such substrates, each one-half as thick mounted with the pitted layers of each substrate facing each other. The simplest way of extracting information from such a disc is to read one side and then physically turn the disc over to read the other side, as we used to be accustomed to doing with a vinyl record. This doubles the capacity once again to fourteen times that of the CD or about 9.4 GB (gigabytes) in all. A more sophisticated reader can extract the information from both substrates from one side at a small loss of efficiency. Yet this permits another almost doubling of capacity to 17 GB by adding another pair of layers to the disc read from the other side.

These capacities in the one-sided or two-sided versions permit the DVD to carry full-length motion pictures compressed in the MPEG-2 variable rate format discussed in chapter 8. It therefore becomes an all-digital replacement for the LaserDisc with the quality and versatility implied by digital technology. In its ROM versions, the increased capacity gives it a large increase of versatility as a computer peripheral.

There will also be an erasable version of the DVD, and this system is likely to use a phenomenon different from the magneto-optical effect used in the erasable CD. In this scheme, a very thin layer of a polycrystalline material is momentarily heated by a laser beam in the recording process changing it from the crystalline to the amorphous state. This change is detected by a low-power readout laser. Such a disc does not require additional equipment such as a polarization detector and hence can, in principle, be read by the same reader used with read-only DVDs.

It will probably take a long time for such a device to compete with a VCR. Recall from chapter 8 that the MPEG-2 processing at the transmitting end is much more complex and expensive than at the receiving end. That means that it will not be practical for the erasable DVD to record uncompressed video at will, although it will be able to record videos that have already been compressed. The copyright situation for such a device is analogous to that of the digital audio tape recorder discussed earlier.

In its many forms, the DVD shows promise of doing for video what the CD has done for audio.

BIBLIOGRAPHY

Books

The following are some useful reference books. Some of these are of an advanced nature and are included for those readers who wish to explore the topics in this book in more technical detail.

Biglieri, Ezio et al. *Introduction to Trellis-Coded Modulation, with Applications,* New York: Macmillan, 1991.

Blahut, Richard E. *Digital Transmission of Information,* Reading, Massachusetts: Addison-Wesley Publishing Co., 1990.

Campbell, Jeremy. *Grammatical Man: Information, Entropy, Language, and Life,* New York: Simon and Schuster, 1982.

Clark, G. C., Jr., and J. B. Cain. *Error Correcting Coding for Digital Communications,* New York: Plenum, 1981.

Davenport, W. B., and William L. Root. *An Introduction to the Theory of Random Signals and Noise,* New York: McGraw-Hill Book Co., 1958.

Davenport, W. P. *Probability and Random Processes,* New York: McGraw-Hill Book Co., 1970.

Lebow, Irwin. *The Digital Connection: A Layman's Guide to the Information Age,* New York: W. H. Freeman and Co., 1991.

Lebow, Irwin. *Information Highways and Byways: From the Telegraph to the 21st Century,* Pascataway, New Jersey: IEEE Press, 1995.

Lucky, R. W., J. Saltz, and E. J. Weldon, Jr. *Principles of Data Communication,* New York: McGraw-Hill Book Co., 1968.

Odenwalder, J. P. "Error Control." Chap. 10 in *Data Communications, Networks and Systems,* edited by T. C. Bartee. Indianapolis: H. W. Sams and Co., 1985.

Pickholtz, R. L. "Modems, Multiplexers, and Concentrators." Chap. 3 in *Data Communications, Networks, and Systems,* edited by T. C. Bartee. Indianapolis: H. W. Sams and Co., 1985.

Pierce, John R., and A. Michael Noll. *Signals: The Science of Telecommunications,* New York: Scientific American Library, 1990.

Pohlmann, K. C. *Principles of Digital Audio,* 3d ed., New York: McGraw-Hill Book Co., 1995.

Schwartz, M. *Information, Transmission, Modulation, and Noise,* 3d ed. New York: McGraw-Hill Book Co., 1980.

Shannon, Claude E., and Warren Weaver. *The Mathematical Theory of Communication,* Urbana: University of Illinois Press, 1949.

Spilker, J. J. *Digital Communications by Satellite,* Englewood Cliffs, New Jersey: Prentice-Hall Inc., 1977.

Wicker, Stephen B. *Error Control Systems for Digital Communication and Storage,* Englewood Cliffs, New Jersey: Prentice-Hall Inc., 1995.

Wicker, Stephen B., and Vijay K. Bhargava, eds. *Reed-Solomon Codes and Their Applications,* Piscataway, New Jersey: IEEE Press, 1994.

Wilson, Stephen G. *Digital Modulation and Coding,* Englewood Cliffs, New Jersey: Prentice-Hall Inc., 1996.

Wozencraft, J. M., and I. M. Jacobs. *Principles of Communication Engineering,* New York: John Wiley and Sons, Inc., 1965.

Papers

There is obviously an enormous literature on the topics covered in this book. More advanced books (e.g., Blahut) have extensive references to this literature. The following is a short list of some of the pioneering papers in the field together with a few tutorials.

Forney, G. D., Jr., R. G. Gallagher, G. R. Lang, F. M. Longstaff, and S. U. Quereshi. "Efficient Modulation for Band-Limited Channels." *IEEE Journal Selected Areas Communications* SAC - (1984): 632–47.

Hamming, R. S. "Error Detecting and Correcting Codes." *Bell System Technical Journal* 29 (1950): 147.

Hartley, R. V. L. "The Transmission of Information." *Bell System Technical Journal* 7 (1928): 5535–63.

Huffman, D. A. "A Method for the Construction of Minimum Redundancy Codes." *Proceedings of the IRE* 40 (1952): 1058.

ITU-T Recommendation V.34. "A modem operating at data signalling rates of up to 28.8 bits/s for use on the general switched telephone network and on leased point-to-point 2-wire telephone-type circuits," Geneva (1994).

Lucky, R. W. "Techniques for Adaptive Equalization of Digital Communications." *Bell System Technical Journal* 45 (1966): 255.

Nyquist, H. "Certain Factors Affecting Telegraph Speed." *Bell System Technical Journal* (April 1924): 324.

Nyquist, H. "Certain Topics in Telegraph Transmission Theory." *Transactions of the AIEE* 47 (1928): 617.

Oliver, B. M., J. R. Pierce, and C. E. Shannon. "The Philosophy of PCM," *Proceedings of the IRE* 36 (1948):11324–31.

Pickholtz, R. L., D. L. Schilling, and L. B. Milstein. "Theory of Spread-Spectrum Communications—A Tutorial." *IEEE Transactions on Communications* COM-30 (1982): 855–84.

Reed, I. S., and G. Solomon. "Polynomial Codes over Certain Finite Fields." *Journal of the Society of Industrial Applied Mathematics* 8 (1960): 300–304.

Rice, S. O. "Mathematical Analysis of Random Noise." *Bell System Technical Journal* 23 (1944): 283–332, and 24 (1945): 46–156.

Shannon, C. E. "A Mathematical Theory of Communication." *Bell System Technical Journal* 27 (1948): 379–423 (Part I); 623–56 (Part II).

Ungerboeck, G. "Trellis Coding with Expanded Channel Signal Sets." *IEEE International Symposium on Information Theory, Book of Abstracts.* Ithaca, New York, 1977.

Van Vleck, J. H., and D. Middleton. "A Theoretical Comparison of Visual, Aural, and Meter Reception of Pulsed Signals in the Presence of Noise." *Journal of Applied Physics* 17 (1946): 940–71.

Viterbi, A. J. "Error Bounds for Convolutional Codes and an Asymptotically Optimum Decoding Algorithm." *IEEE Transactions on Information Theory* IT-13 (1967): 260–69.

Wozencraft, J. M. "Sequential Decoding for Reliable Communication," Part 2, *National IRE Convention Record,* 5, (1957): 11.

INDEX

ABOUT THE AUTHOR

Irwin Lebow was educated as a physicist at MIT, but early in his career, he converted to digital information systems. Starting out at MIT Lincoln Laboratory, he was a codesigner of one of the first all-solid-state computers. This experience led to his first book, *Theory and Design of Digital Machines,* coauthored with two colleagues and published by McGraw-Hill in 1962.

From computing he switched to communications, where he was one of the leaders of a pioneering effort in exploiting satellites for the Defense Department. The stressful demands of the military environment demanded the use of digital techniques at a time when digital communications was in its infancy. He led the group that built a series of Lincoln Experimental Terminals incorporating the first practical application of a powerful technique known as sequential decoding. At Lincoln, he rose to become a member of the laboratory's steering committee.

From Lincoln he moved to Washington as the Chief Scientist-Associate Director, Technology of the Defense Communications Agency (now the Defense Information Systems Agency), the senior civilian at the agency. One of his most important tasks at DCA was to bring military communication into the modern digital world. During his tenure at DCA, the agency assumed the management of the ARPANET, the forerunner of the Internet.

From DCA he went to American Satellite Company (later Contel ASC, and still later merged into GTE) as vice president of engineering, where he led both the day-to-day engineering and research and development efforts of the company that pioneered in digital satellite communications in the commercial marketplace. He later joined Systems Research and Applications Corporation. as a vice president, where he was responsible for both military and commercial telecommunications programs. He has been a private communications consultant since 1987. It was then that he was inspired to begin writing again. In 1986 he wrote the chapter "Satellite Communications in Digital Communications," edited by Bartee. He followed this with two books: *The Digital Connection: A Layman's Guide to the Information Age* (W. H. Freeman & Co.) in 1991, and *Information Highways and Byways: From the Telegraph to the Twenty-First Century* (IEEE Press) in 1995. He is now collaborating with his wife, Grace, and Barbara Kane on a very different book: *Difficult Parents/Desperate Children,* to be published by Avon Books in 1998.

Dr. Lebow is a fellow of both the IEEE and the American Physical Society. He has been a member of the Radio Engineering Advisory Committee of the Voice of America and the DCA Scientific Advisory Group.

Last but not least, he is a very proud husband, father, and grandfather.